Visual Display Units

and their application

Visual Display Units

and their application

Edited by Derrick Grover
Chairman, BCS Displays Group

Published by IPC Science and Technology Press
in association with the British Computer Society

Published by IPC Science and Technology Press Limited, IPC House, 32 High Street, Guildford, Surrey, England GU1 3EW.

ISBN 0 902852 65 5

Typeset by Specialised Offset Services Ltd., 90 The Albany, Old Hall Street, Liverpool. Printed in England by Kingprint Ltd, Orchard Road, Richmond, Surrey.

Contents

	page
Foreword *The President of the British Computer Society*	vii
Introduction	1
1 Review and trends *Derrick Grover*	7
REVIEW	7
Introduction	7
Applications	8
For the newcomer	12
Review of technical aspects	14
TRENDS	23
Television-style systems	26
Other types of display	29
Solid-state displays	31
Conclusion	38
Further reading	38
2 The technology of visual display units *Iorwerth Jones*	40
The monitor	40
The data store	43
The character generator	47
The keyboard	52
Communication interface	55
The whole assembly	58
The power supply	61
Summary	61
3 Communications *Peter Burton*	63
Introduction	63
Serial transmission of digital data	64

Network configurations 71
Communication lines and services 76
Communication interface standards 81
Information flow control 83
Outlook 87

4 Intelligence *Ian Richards* 88
Introduction 88
The reasons for intelligent terminal systems 89
The structure of intelligent terminal systems 90
The power of terminal controllers 96
The uses of intelligence 101
The user interface for a typical application 104
The future 106
Further reading 107

5 Software *Brian Larbalestier* 108
Layered software 108
Terminal handling 110
Formatting and field definition aids 120
Multi-tasking software 127
Further study 136

6 Human factors in the design of visual display units *Roy Gladman* 137
Introduction 137
The display unit 137
The keyboard 142
The display work station 150
Summary 151

7 Human factors in the use of visual display units *Tom Stewart* 153
The man–computer partnership 153
Man–computer dialogues 154
Introducing the VDU into the office environment 168
Possible pitfalls 174
Conclusions 175
Acknowledgements 175
Further reading 176

Glossary 177

Index 201

Foreword

Over the past few years Visual Display Units have emerged as an effective and efficient interface between system users and computing systems. In particular they are a close match to the requirements of many on-line systems. The appearance of this volume is, therefore, both timely and in accordance with the policy of the British Computer Society to promote and maintain the competence of computer professionals in the UK by disseminating to the widest possible audience reliable technical information.

This volume has been prepared under the auspices of the BCS Display Group which, since 1967, has provided a forum for the discussion of display matters and the interchange of knowledge. It reflects the very considerable experience which has been accumulated and will, I am sure, convey that experience to its readers.

I hope this volume will achieve the success it deserves.

Cecil Marks
President of the
British Computer Society

Introduction

The idea of this reference book on Visual Display Units was conceived by the British Computer Society Displays Group Committee as a companion to a tutorial seminar for users and potential users of VDUs. The book has been written by authors who were chosen for their expertise in the field either through being known to the Committee or by being nominated by companies active in the field. The authors were expected to deliver at the seminar a lecture, based upon their chapter.

The text is aimed at users who need to become more knowledgeable in the field, especially those who have some experience of computing but who are expecting to enhance their system with VDUs. Some of the chapters will be useful to middle management who need an introduction to aid their decision-making and to familiarise themselves with some of the terms used and the problems to be encountered.

The Committee expected the authors to use different nomenclature and to differ slightly in their opinions on certain topics. Such differences of opinion are realistic and are to be expected in an art which is still relatively young. Accordingly the differences have been left in and the reader will not expect a single answer to some problems.

An extensive glossary has been prepared with words taken mostly from the chapters of the book. Chapter 1 introduces the reader to the VDU with a review of various aspects involved in a VDU system followed by a discussion of the trends that are apparent in the technology. The justification for the use of a VDU display is shown by applications which utilise different properties of the system. A gentle 'guided tour' for the newcomer follows, prior to a discussion of aspects at a deeper level.

The trends cover both the impact of television-style systems and solid state technology. Television systems are potentially inexpensive and are compatible with other visual information systems. Solid state techniques cover light emitters and light controllers. Plasma panels, electroluminescence, liquid crystals and electrophoresis are among the topics.

The technology of VDUs receives a detailed description in Chapter 2. Various problems must be solved to compensate for the distortions of the cathode ray tube and some aids to improve the visibility and safety of the tube are desirable. The data used to write information on the screen is stored in coded form for the purpose of refreshing the phosphor screen and for making up the message for transmission to a computer. The technology of the cursor and control keys is considered together with the keyboard itself. Various forms of character generator are available, some of which are compatible with TV scan systems. There may be a need to queue or buffer data when working into communications lines, especially when lines are being shared and a polling mode is being used. The chapter concludes with a discussion of power supplies, modular construction and packaging methods.

Chapter 3 provides a comprehensive survey of the many aspects of communications between a VDU and a computer, whether over a direct parallel link or via telephone lines using modems. Serial transmission of data is considered in detail, starting with the merits of synchronous and asynchronous transmission. Full and half-duplex systems are compared.

Network configurations are discussed in regard to minimisation of costs. Beginning with point to point connections, polled and multiplexed networks are then introduced. Concentrators help to utilise data lines more efficiently and switched networks increase the number of terminals that can be catered for by a system.

In the U.K., the services provided by the Post Office vary in price according to the capabilities of the lines employed. The choice is dependent on the speed of transmission required and the error rate that is tolerable. The CCITT V24 standard interface is described and protocols of varying complexity are considered.

Before discussing 'intelligence', Chapter 4 considers the meaning of this term, which is often applied to programmable emulators, small stand-alone processing systems as well as VDUs with their own processing capability. Programmable terminals give flexibility in terms of the interface presented to a system and permit different protocols to be administered. Different manufacturers' VDUs can be emulated by these means.

The editing and formatting of data is performed by the intelligent terminal. Security and data validation methods can be chosen for the needs of the application and a reduction of loading in the host computer is realised by delegating many operations to the terminal. The ability to perform stand-by operations when the host fails is an important aid to system integrity.

Chapter 5 considers the software, resident in the host computer, for servicing VDUs. Software modules are described for handling the data and control messages together with protocols. The systems control aspects are then described with the problems of polling and defining data channels. Software at a higher level is used for formatting the messages to be sent to a terminal and to link with the applications program which defines the data to appear on the screen. Different types of terminals on one system create additional problems and Teletype-compatible terminals are discussed. Data must be buffered if the host computer is performing a multi-task function and flexibility in operation is desirable.

The chapter concludes with a discussion of multi-tasking software. The sequence of operations carried out on behalf of a terminal will not necessarily be the same for all terminals but similar parts must use common routines to minimise the storage requirement. The software architecture is discussed.

Human factors in the design of VDUs are the topic of Chapter 6. The specification and size of characters on the screen must be considered in relation to inter-line spacing to optimise the display for the operator. The type of cursor is important, as is the mode of indicating significant data. The keyboard has evolved to the point where electronic methods are used to optimise the keying action to be light but positive. Rollover capability is necessary to minimise error rates and various keyboard designs are mentioned. The dimensions of the work station have been extensively investigated to ensure adequate space and comfort for the operator.

Chapter 7 considers in detail the human factors in the use of VDUs. The man–computer partnership is an important one and the structure of the dialogue must take into account the function it serves in the overall system and the type of job the user is performing. Procedures and operations for different purposes are discussed. When the VDU is introduced to an office environment there are many factors to be noted in respect of the task to be performed, the workspace available and configuration of the system. A checklist is quoted to help the reader design the best installation for his needs and the chapter concludes by considering the possible pitfalls awaiting the unwary.

Brief biographies of the authors follow:

D.J. Grover — Chapter 1 — *Review and trends*
Derrick Grover is an executive in the Computers and Automation group of the National Research Development Corporation. Prior to joining the corporation he was responsible for the research and design of VDU-compatible low-cost

graphics together with work on VDU systems proposals such as LACES. His further experience includes message switching system design, advanced development of computer circuits and systems in the U.S.A. and research into experimental digital techniques for instruments. He graduated from University College London, and is a Member of the Institute of Physics and a Fellow of the British Computer Society. He has been Chairman of the BCS Displays Specialist Group for the past four years and has published a number of papers in the fields of electronics and computer graphics.

I.A. Jones — Chapter 2 — *Technology of VDUs*
Iori Jones served an apprenticeship in electrical engineering at the British Thomson Houston Co., following which he was Chief Test Engineer for audio equipment. He became a Ground Instrumentation Development Engineer at Armstrong-Whitworth. For four years Mr Jones was a member of the R & D division of ICT at Stevenage working on storage and logic developments during the early years of commercial computing.

He joined Cossor Electronics in 1966. Since then he has been closely involved with every development in computer terminals within Cossor and also within the Raytheon Company. He has been Sales Manager, General Sales Manager and is now Marketing Manager for Cossor-developed products in the data area.

P. Burton — Chapter 3 — *Communications*
Peter Burton is Joint Managing Director of the British data communications manufacturer CASE (Computer and Systems Engineering Ltd). A graduate of University College London, he worked for some years as an electronic systems designer for the British Aircraft Corporation, becoming Head of Electronics at their Stevenage establishment. Attracted by the fast-growing computer industry, he joined IBM as a salesman just before System 360 was announced and was later made Branch Manager for the Research and Education market sector. He left IBM in 1970 to found CASE with fellow squash enthusiast Derek Laval.

I. Richards — Chapter 4 — *Intelligence*
Ian Richards has spent the last 12 years in the computer industry, concerned exclusively with communications, real-time systems and terminals.

From 1964 until 1973 with ICL, he was successively a Research Engineer working on data transmission and error correction techniques, a Design Engineer responsible for the detailed design of communications multiplexors, Communications Manager for the LACES Heathrow Project and the leader of a team developing a display-based intelligent terminal system.

In 1973 he left ICL to join Ferranti, where he is Product Manager responsible for intelligent terminals.

B. Larbalestier — Chapter 5 — *Software*
Brian Larbalestier graduated in computer science from Essex University. He was employed by ICI on mathematical computing before joining Logica in 1970. At Logica he has worked on many systems including air traffic control with particular reference to interactive devices; a multiprocessor telemetry system on the networking and telecommunications aspects, various on-line systems requiring database storage and retrieval, and banking applications.

R.J. Gladman — Chapter 6 — *Human factors in the design of VDUs*
Roy Gladman was for many years a Technical Staff Officer in the British Army, specialising in electronics, principally radar, and the use of computers in the field. He joined IBM in 1968 and worked for four years in the Government area on general accounts and later a special project on the problems of information retrieval in the House of Commons. For the last two years he has been responsible for data entry and terminal equipment within the product marketing department of IBM.

T.F.M. Stewart — Chapter 7 — *Human factors in the use of VDUs*
After graduating in mathematics and physics in 1968 and in psychology in 1970, both from the University of Glasgow, Tom Stewart joined the staff of the Department of Human Sciences at Loughborough University. Since then he has been involved in a number of research and consultancy projects in the man–computer area ranging from computer system evaluation and dialogue design to terminal design and hardware evaluation. He has published and lectured in the U.K. and Sweden on a number of man–computer topics.

The Committee

G.W. Jones
Gareth Jones graduated from the University College of North Wales, Bangor, in physics and electrical materials science in 1970. He then worked for International Computers Ltd as a Problems Analyst on design automation. In 1972 he joined the staff of the journal *Computer Aided Design*. He is now editor of the journal and in addition is editor of a new journal on the hardware, software and applications of microprocessors. He has organised two international conferences on the use of computers in engineering and building design.

D.E. Plews

David Plews is Design Manager for displays and peripherals at Ferranti Ltd. He graduated in electrical engineering at Birmingham University before joining Ferranti Ltd, where he worked on various military projects. He became interested in displays when designing cathode ray tube displays for training simulators. He is now responsible for the design and development of both alphanumeric and graphical displays.

D.H. Taffs

David Taffs is a Civil and Structural Engineer by background, having studied at the Middlesex Polytechnic. His experience includes work with British Railways and George Wimpey & Co Ltd before joining Ove Arup & Partners in 1964. He quickly became involved in the application of computers to engineering design and took up his present position as Head of Computing Services in 1971, which involves running a DEC System 10 installation using a variety of terminal devices.

Dr R.M. Williamson

Michael Williamson graduated in chemistry from Cambridge University in 1966. After working for his PhD, he joined the CAD Centre at Cambridge in 1970, where his work has involved many aspects of CAD including graphics, data structuring, large command languages as well as the design of application facilities. He is a member of the Applications Programming Group, where he has been responsible for a Pipe Data Management system and played a major part in the development of a computer drafting project.

We are grateful for the cooperation we have received from the British Computer Society, especially in the organisation of a very successful seminar at which the topics in each chapter were introduced.

Interactive visual media will play an increasingly important role in the future of computing. We hope that this book will enable the reader to participate more fully.

D.J. Grover — Chairman
G.W. Jones — Hon. treasurer
D.E. Plews
D.H. Taffs — Hon. secretary
R.M. Williamson

British Computer Society Displays Group Committee

1 Review and trends

Derrick Grover

REVIEW

Introduction

Visual information is available from a large number of display media which operate in different ways. The display methods are usually chosen in order to meet the specification of an information system with the minimum cost. Thus pure *optical displays* are available which project images of *microfilm* or pages of *microfiche* onto a screen; these techniques are primarily suited to archival data or data which does not have to be updated very often. The selection of information from a fiche can be automated and the control can be by a command from a computer, if necessary over a telephone line. An effective use of this method employs an *ultrafiche viewer*. About 7000 A5 pages can be stored on one ultrafiche and a page on a fiche can be selected in less than 1 second. Access time is up to 5 seconds for further fiche which can be stored in a magazine holding 150 fiche; this permits a one million page store.

Changeable data requires different methods of presentation. In cases where the data can be limited to a few characters then mechanical, electrical and opto-electrical mechanisms are used. A separate mechanism is usually necessary for each character, for example a Nixietube, mechanical shutters or flaps, or the strobing of images on a rotating drum.

The requirement to write large amounts of changeable data quickly was first catered for by the *teletypewriter*. Enhancements of the conventional teletypewriter now permit printing rates of about 30 characters a second and relatively quiet operation using thermal printing techniques. In cases where hard copy is not necessary the mechanics of the teletypewriter are giving way to the electronic methods of the visual display unit for speed, reliability and interactive facilities.

Visual display units, also known as *alphanumeric displays* or *alphascopes*, provide one of the fastest means of interacting with a computer. The particular advantages lie in the ability to present information in a convenient form quickly and silently and to be able to modify or add to the information easily. The display performs the role of an *information transducer* in which information is presented visually in a form to which the user is accustomed while retaining the information in coded form suitable for transmission to, and interrogation of, a computer.

It is important to distinguish between information stored in coded form and purely visual information. The former retains an identity which can be interpreted by a computer system whereas the latter can be interpreted only by an optical character reader, which is either a human being or an expensive piece of equipment. Thus information which is represented on a VDU screen and refreshed from a character store is associated with data in that store and the data describing the information is available for sending back to the computer, where it is readily recognised. In the event that the characters in the data were generated in optical form or in a *video format* (i.e. as a series of discrete points of light in a succession of television lines) and stored only in that format, then the data defining the information would be lost and the display would have to be read visually. In fact it is not only the data which is lost but also the position of the data in the format and the influence of associated control characters, each of which may be of more significance for rapid interpretation than the data itself. The topic will be met again when we briefly look at simple graphic displays which can be implemented in a television format.

An indication of the range of prices for display units is shown in Figure 1.1. Such an illustration is fraught with difficulties since the price is dependent on the quantity ordered and on the options supplied for a system. The continuing change of component costs and inflation have tended to be opposing but unequal influences in which inflation has been winning in the recent past.

Applications

The justification for displays in commercial use was first seen where the value of up-to-date information was greatest. Thus airlines, which needed to be advised of vacancies on an aeroplane at short notice, possibly up to a few minutes before a flight, were justified in buying the capital equipment necessary to achieve this. The sale of one extra ticket could contribute to a significant part of the cost of the system, since once the aeroplane has taken off the value of any vacancy on board becomes zero. As the cost of displays has fallen, their use has become justified in other fields.

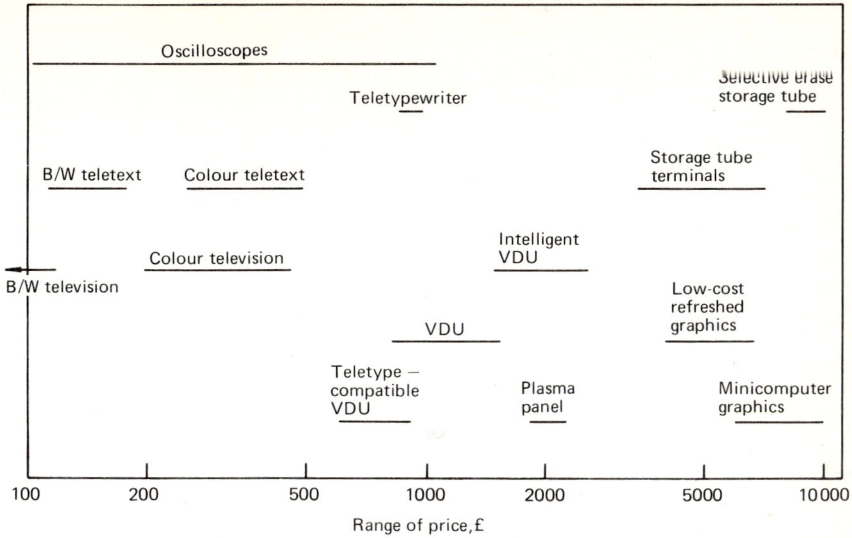

Figure 1.1. Approximate range of prices for different display terminals.

Stock control

The use of a VDU in a stock control system is for the purpose of updating a data base quickly with the minimum of errors. One of the typical procedures would be the checking of delivery notes. Suppliers of products would each have a unique supplier number. The operator 'keys in' this number, and the computer generates on the screen the supplier's name with a list of his products. Spaces alongside the products permit the operator to enter the quantity of the products which have been received. When complete the data entered by the operator is sent back to the computer. Such a system is used by a large multiple store, and it enables management to reconcile the supplier's charge to branches, permits a branch charge to be computed and provides the buyers with information on the products ordered by different branches. One company director concerned with the implementation of VDUs said that his company used them because it was the cheapest way found to process the information required within the time scale allowed to the degree of accuracy demanded.

Information retrieval

Stock market quotations are an example of how VDUs can be used in an information system. The latest stock information is entered into a central processor unit, sorted and filed. The operator can interrogate the central processor unit via a display at a broker's office in order to obtain details such as the number of shares sold, the high and low selling price, history, earnings per share, and similar information.

Hospital computer systems are incorporating VDUs to help with the problem of storing and updating information on patients. The information required for administrative purposes is entered by clerical staff at reception. The use of VDUs by medical staff has been researched at a number of hospitals and various *interactive methods* are being tried in attempts to overcome the need for nurses and doctors to type data in from a keyboard. A *menu* of choices is favoured where the choice is made by depressing a single key associated with that choice. A sequence of menus is necessary and investigations have been conducted into the optimum *tree data structure* required to present the necessary data quickly.

Text editing

A text-editing facility is useful in *debugging* computer programs; a particular use is for assembling the text for legal agreements and standard company letters with the aid of word processing systems.

Updating of information

IPC Business Press Ltd is using VDUs to update information concerning subscribers to journals (Figure 1.2). The information which is relevant is the name and address, the dates on which subscriptions fall due and when and how much money has been paid. Information is received from the subscriber as a letter indicating an error in, or change of, address and it is necessary for the subscriptions clerk to select the appropriate record in order to make the change. The record is identified by a five-letter code taken from the first five letters of the name. Some duplication of this code occurs and accordingly a numeric suffix is generated by the system to give a unique key for that record.

On receiving a notification the clerk types the identifier derived from the name. The VDU then displays the existing address as recorded and then, alongside, the address is repeated for the operator to update as shown in Figure

Figure 1.2. An ICL installation at IPC Business Press Ltd for updating subscription records.

1.3. Below this is shown other information concerned with such details as payments of subscriptions and the period for which the subscription is valid. If the identifier has selected the wrong record because several records are known by that name, then subsequent records can be selected until the further information on the screen such as the full name or address complies with the information on the notification. The data on the left of the screen cannot be altered by the clerk but the information on the right-hand side is variable data which can be over-written by the clerk to insert corrections or change appropriately. The method is efficient because the clerk need change only that which is necessary since all the other information has been presented on the screen. Thus in Figure 1.3 if the correct address were 37 Perrymount Road the operator would position the *cursor* (*see below*) on the '5' in the right-hand copy of the address and type over it with a '7', which also causes the correct code to be substituted in the store. The corrected information can then be sent back

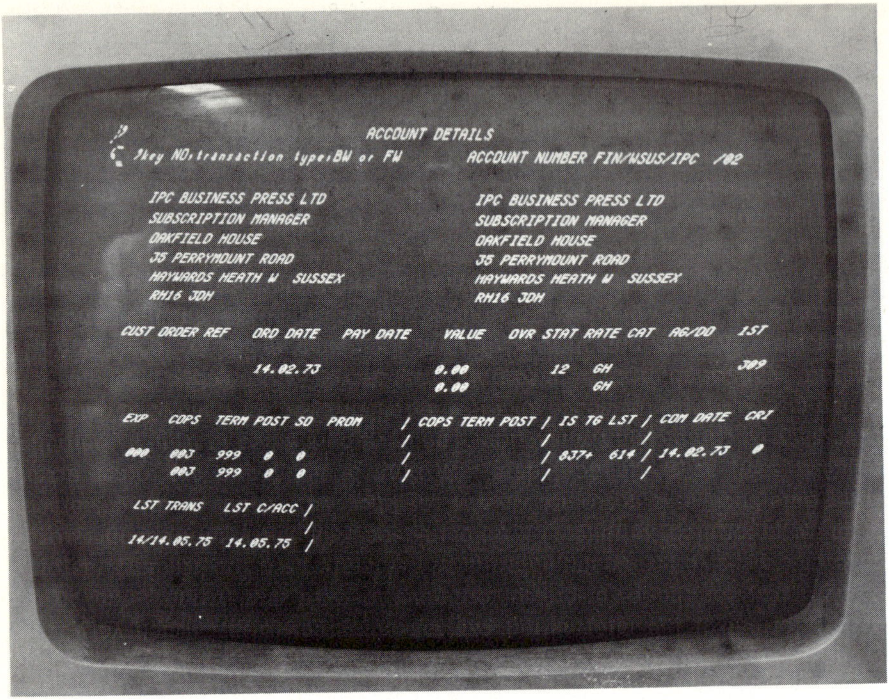

Figure 1.3. A screen format used for updating subscription records.

into the system, which creates a completely new record of the name or address changes and issues a 'delete' instruction regarding the old record. The subscriber files are used for producing labels, for mailing journals and renewals, or preparing invoices.

For the newcomer

For the reader being introduced to the VDU for the first time it is perhaps appropriate to consider the features in the order in which he will notice them. The installation is likely to be at an airport or reservation agency where an operator has access to a display resembling a television set with a typewriter keyboard. On the screen will be seen text consisting of alphabetic characters and numerals, together known as *alphanumerics*. This display will normally contain between 500 and 2000 characters which are formatted to make it easy to understand the information within the constraints of the size of screen. The characters will probably be in a colour such as green, although other colours such as blue and near-white are available. After a short period the observer may notice that the information has suddenly changed, in part or in whole, and that this change occurs as though someone were very rapidly typing characters on the screen. In fact, the writing of the characters may take place at 300–600 characters per second if the system is working over a telephone line, or almost instantaneously if it is interfaced directly to a computer.

On the screen will be seen a *marker* such as a flashing symbol, or alternatively there may be lines over and under a character as a means of identification of a position on the screen. This means of identification is known as a *cursor*, and it controls the position in the data format at which new operations will occur. Thus if the operator were to begin typing in new data, this data would commence from the cursor position and the cursor would advance one character at a time as new characters were entered. Alternatively, information from a computer, if it was not specifically addressed to another point, would commence at the cursor position and continue rather like text typed on paper with a typewriter.

The format of the information can take different forms, which vary from straight text for the lower-priced terminals to *fixed and variable data* in the case of expensive terminals. *Fixed data fields* are used for headings, as on a form (or preprinted stationery), with blank spaces alongside for the operator to enter data such as a customer's name together with details of the customer's request, such as destination, date and time of flight and any other details necessary to complete a transaction. The fixed data is fed in from a computer, which also allocates the space for the variable or operator-controlled data. The operator cannot change the fixed data since there is a protective mechanism in the display. For this reason fixed data is sometimes called *protected data*. In front of the display will be seen a keyboard, which will have alphanumeric keys corresponding to the keys on a typewriter as well as additional keys for control purposes. These controls allow the operator to move the cursor position to the right, left, and up or down, and there are further controls which permit erasure of a character, or alternatively the generation of a space in existing text in order to insert further characters. Other editing features are usually provided. The system thus permits the operator to edit the text on the display in an easy manner and check that all is correct before the new information is sent into a computer system. There may be keys which control other functions such as sending data to the computer or having the text on the screen printed out on paper by a hard copy printer — sometimes these are positioned alongside the display. Displays catering for more sophisticated systems may have a *function keyboard*. The depression of a function key sends a particular code to the computer, which will interpret it as being a command or request of a certain kind. The function keyboard, which usually consists of 16 keys in a 4 × 4 array, often incorporates an *overlay* consisting of a sheet of Perspex with labelled holes with correspond to the keys. The function of the key is thus determined for that mode of operation. The use of another overlay ascribing a different function to a key could be used in a different mode of operation.

Display terminals incorporate varying degrees of electronic and processing capability depending on the requirements of the system; thus they vary from very simple terminals, which are a replacement for a teletypewriter, to *intelligent terminals* incorporating a *microcomputer* for editing and communication functions, together with further facilities peculiar to the operation being catered for. The terminal might be either a local or a remote terminal. The *local terminal* will be situated close to a computer or a control unit which provides the storage for the text being shown on the screen and which continually feeds this information to the display. Alternatively, it may be a *remote terminal* situated on its own at the end of a telephone line, in which case storage will be incorporated within the terminal for feeding information to the display screen. The information being stored is in coded form. The *codes* for each character are presented in turn to a character generator which interprets the information to drive the display mechanism. If the display is a *cathode ray tube*, an electron beam is controlled so that it draws the appropriate symbol on the *phosphor* coating. The communication between this terminal and a computer will be over a telephone line by means of a stream of electronic pulses; the rate of transmission is usually in the range 10–600 characters per second, but may be as high as 1200 characters per second over special lines.

Review of technical aspects

Technology

The *cathode ray tube* (CRT) alphanumeric display has some resemblance to a television set. The similarities are in fact becoming greater since the technology is permitting alphanumerics to be generated on a television format more cheaply than hitherto. In common with the television set, the information on the screen has to be 'refreshed' many times per second. A *phosphor coating* on the inside of the screen is energised rapidly by an electron beam. The phosphor glows momentarily after being energised for a period which is dependent on the type of phosphor used. Long-persistence phosphors were used initially; these have an afterglow of many milliseconds so that they do not need re-energising very frequently. They are more liable to burn under certain conditions and consequently they are known as *soft phosphors*. A *refresh rate* of 15 times per second might be tolerated although the flicker on the screen would be noticeable. The so-called *hard phosphors* are brighter but have a much shorter afterglow and need to be re-energised more frequently. The rate at which flicker is noticeable varies with the person, the lighting conditions and the part of the retina of the eye which is perceiving the image, flicker being more noticeable out of the corner of the eye. A refresh rate of 50 times per second or greater is considered sufficient to overcome this problem.

The need to refresh the screen implies that the data must be presented to the mechanism controlling the energising electron beam at the refresh rate. This is achieved using a store (known as the *refresh store*) which usually holds the data in a serial form and presents each character code in turn. The need to refresh data continuously in serial form is compatible with *re-circulating stores* such as *discs*, *delay lines* and *MOS registers*. MOS registers are taking over from other forms of serial store since they have become more economic and they have advantages such as being largely independent of environmental conditions including temperature and vibration. The rate of movement of the information in an MOS register can be controlled within large limits whereas the transmission of information in a *serial store*, such as a delay line, was determined by physical parameters. Previously the data rate of the store set the standard for the immediate system but more flexibility is now possible.

As already mentioned, the *cursor* is there to enable the operator to determine the position on the screen of the information being acted upon. The position of the cursor is in fact defined by association with a position in store. The cursor is used for several operations which are described in the next chapter.

Character generation

A variety of techniques have been used for character generation; prior to the incorporation of television techniques into the display, each character was generated separately by a sequence of lines or dots chosen from a matrix of possibilities. A popular technique has been the use of a *monoscope*, which is a device with a store of characters painted on to a screen within a special-performance CRT. The *charactron* tube is a similar device in which the characters are portrayed on a screen by punching out the screen in the shape of the character. Various line-drawing techniques have also been used. The advent of *television techniques* has meant that the beam is scanning across a line of characters to the depth of about one-tenth of the line and accordingly it has become necessary to be able to generate the tops of all the characters in the line through one scan and then the second portion in the second line and so forth.

The character generation technique most compatible with this mode of operation is the matrix of dots so that each row of dots can be accessed in turn. An integrated circuit performing this function is now manufactured at a low price and accordingly it is the most competitive commercially.

The facilities within a display are those which can be incorporated readily at low cost. Thus editing facilities such as insertion or deletion of a character can be achieved by simply inserting or deleting a register the length of a character code at the appropriate time. Erasure of a series of characters, for example, to the end of a line can easily be achieved by ignoring all characters occurring from the position of the cursor until a carriage return code has been recognised.

Communications

Communication with a display over a telephone line is expensive; it is therefore desirable to reduce the amount of data that is transmitted. A significant improvement can be achieved by transmitting only data that is changed rather than a complete screen of data. The ability for the computer to *address* the display store is therefore important, and updating of data is achieved by overwriting the data in sequence from the position addressed. Such a position will be addressed by the line number and the character number within the line. *Data reduction* in communications from the display to the computer can be achieved in several ways. The simplest is for the computer to position the cursor at the end of a message ready for the operator to type a reply; if the start of the message is defined at the commencement of the operator action then only the operator's data need be transmitted. An increasingly popular form of data reduction is to use *fixed* and *variable data formats*. The fixed and variable fields of data are separated by control codes and it is usual to give a visual indication by using a different style of character, perhaps black on white rather than white on black, or by using italics. The fixed, 'protected' *data fields* are not allowed to be penetrated by the cursor; thus the operator cannot invade these fields except by a special combination of keys. An action to advance the cursor would jump it over a protected field in a similar manner to the tab action on a typewriter. The cursor would thus have jumped to a variable field following a fixed heading ready for the operator to enter the corresponding data. The variable data is then identified by its position. Communication back to the computer would ignore the fixed data and transmit only the variable data entered by the operator. This variable data would be separated by command codes so that the meaning of the field of data could be interpreted by its position in the total sequence.

Interactive methods

A character on the screen of a VDU may be identified in several ways. Two ways which are of interest here are by (a) the position in store used to control that character position; (b) the spatial position on the screen.

A recirculating store driving a CRT allocates one store position for each character position on the screen and it is possible to identify a character by its store position. In these circumstances the cursor is activated to appear on the screen as a flashing symbol at, or as lines around, the character which is driven by the store position being interrogated. A counter will be used to identify the position and the cursor will be advanced through the text by increasing the number in the counter. The movement, which can be controlled from either a keyboard or computer, permits a character to be identified both visibly for the operator and in code form for the computer.

The *store position cursor* has advantages over the spatial cursor in that it provides a unique identification of data on the screen. This advantage becomes particularly important if the display incorporates graphic data where lines or characters are very close or are superimposed.

The *spatial cursor* (more usual on *storage tube displays*) is often realised as cross wires on the screen, although a small circle or arrow may be used instead. It is used to identify the x, y coordinates of data on the screen and it is therefore necessary to consult a look-up table at the computer. Since the operator may not position the cursor exactly on the location of the symbol or line of interest it becomes necessary to check that the position is within a certain distance of that being held for the data in the display file. A software overhead is thus involved. In the event that the data on the screen is disciplined to lie on a rigid format, then the screen may in essence be compartmentalised so that pointing to any position within each compartment will identify the data in that compartment, thus reducing the possibility of ambiguity.

Other interaction techniques utilise a switch which generates a code to be recognised by the computer. The *function key* or *button* is a common means of providing this code and it is usual so to position the button as to relate to information either on the screen (*see* Figure 1.4) or information held on an overlay which surrounds a function keyboard. The overlay used with a function keyboard carries labels identifying each key position and a code may be incorporated in the overlay itself which determines the mode in which the system will operate. Thus the function key may take on different meanings for different system modes. A more flexible technique involves aligning the function key or function button with data on the screen. Function buttons are

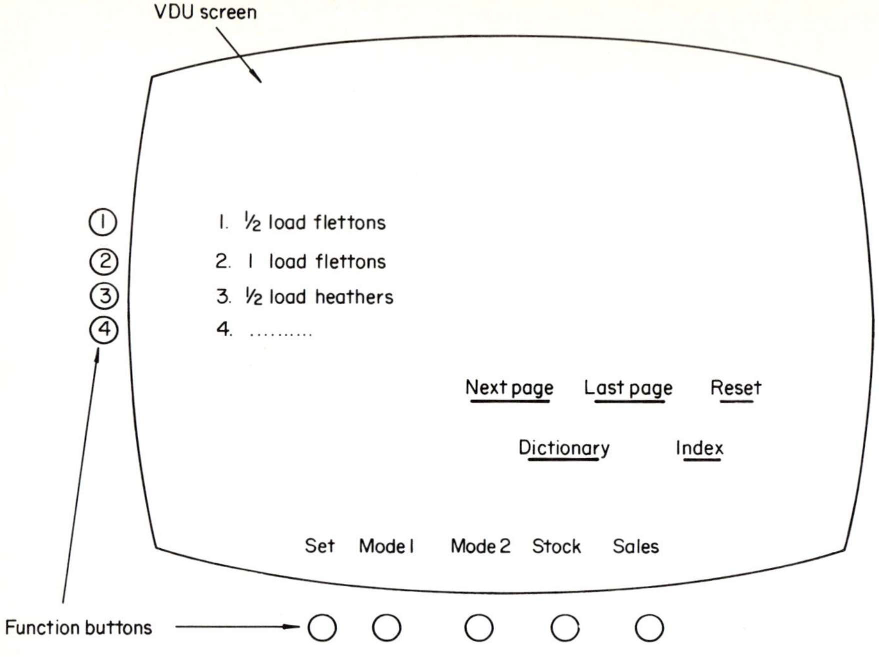

Figure 1.4. Methods of interacting with data on a VDU screen, viz. horizontal and vertical function buttons and the touch wire.

shown in Figure 1.4 which are associated with sentences or commands on the screen format. In order to reduce *parallax* problems the button is numbered to relate to a sentence of the same number. Thus depression of function button (2) would define the item under discussion as being 1 load of flettons. Alternatively, the buttons are placed along the bottom of the screen and a command is displayed immediately above. Thus in this example buttons may be chosen in a suitable sequence to set the mode and request information on stock or sales, etc.

The function buttons have the disadvantage that they are not situated adjacent to the information. The *touch wire* is a device which can be placed directly on the screen and overcomes this disadvantage. It consists of a short length of wire which when pressed causes a code to be generated and sent to the computer system where it will be interpreted as meaning 'next page' or 're-set', etc. It is one of the most ergonomically suitable forms of interaction available and the possible speed of interaction is very fast.

A *light pen* is a light sensor which detects the moment when a line is written on the screen each time the screen is refreshed. The light pen is sometimes used on VDUs to identify a character's position. It defines the information in terms of the store position and it has the same advantages as the store position cursor. It has the additional advantage compared with the cursor of enabling the operator to point directly to the data in question rather than needing the manipulation of cursor keys. It should be noted that a light pen used in conjunction with a television display is acting as a spatial stylus and accordingly the interaction is similar to that of the spatial cursor.

Systems

Communications between a computer and a terminal are subject to various constraints. The first of these occurs if the computer is being used for other purposes as well as servicing the display and it is necessary to determine which is the *master* and which is the *slave* in the transaction. The master determines the time at which a transaction will take place and the slave complies with the time of that transaction. It is usual for the computer to be the master but it is necessary for it to be advised that the display is ready to transfer data. One method is by use of an *interrupt* line which advises the computer of this need. The computer will continue with its existing program until it has reached a position where it can store the results of the program ready to cater for the display activity. A short message is sent to the display advising of readiness to receive data whereupon the display transmits the message from store. In the event that a computer is catering for several displays the problem of contention between displays arises. In this case a *polling* mode is useful. The computer addresses each display in turn with a query asking if a message is to be transmitted. The display either sends a short inactive response, in which case the computer passes on to the next display in the list, or alternatively the display transmits its message which may be a request for action and the computer services this message and sends a reply to the same address before passing on to the next position. Larger systems incorporate *control units* which cater for the problem of polling each display in a cluster. Thus the control unit addresses each display on its circuit and on receiving a positive response leaves that line open until serviced by the computer. Control units vary in their capability and some provide many extra services. The computer is thus saved the labour of finding out which display is active.

Security

Security falls into two main areas. Firstly, checks are made on messages to ensure that errors are not occurring due to interference in the communication line or faults in the equipment. The simplest of these checks is character *parity*, which involves inserting an extra bit into the code so as to give even or odd parity depending on the design of the system. Thus if a character code incorporates an odd number of '1's', then a further '1' would be inserted in the parity position to give even parity. If the code contained an even number of '1's', then a '0' would be inserted in the parity position. A further degree of error checking is achieved by a *block check character*. In this facility the last character in the message is determined according to a formula which sums the bit content of the characters in the message. For systems of greater reliability more than one character can be used to detect combinations of errors which might otherwise escape the system check. It will be seen that if two '1's' in a character code were missing, then the parity check would not detect the error.

The second aspect of security applies to the persons given access to the terminal, either for the utilisation of computer time or for access to restricted data. A conventional method has been to insert a *password* which is recognised by the system. It is desirable that the password should not be illustrated on the screen of the display, and this may imply a non-conventional terminal. The use of a *badge reader* is a common facility which it is less easy to copy, although there are problems if the badge is lost, or in duplicating the badge, which usually consists of a piece of plastic with suitable notches or magnetic stripes encoded in it. Other methods are also available. A Yale-type key is sometimes used to make the terminal operational but this does not advise the system of which person is gaining access. Combinations of these techniques are also possible.

A further aspect of security lies in the *integrity* of the total system. 'Graceful degradation' has been a popular term, and implies that the system is designed so that a single failure does not cause disaster. Fallback facilities have to be available, either by duplication of important parts of the system or by sharing the workload between the surviving members — usually at a slower rate and sometimes without all facilities being available. The design of the mainframe software to cope with system failure, and software errors, is an important consideration. The intelligent terminal may provide fallback facilities.

Software

The software at the host computer has to perform a variety of tasks which depend on the size and type of system and on the data processing requirements. The executive program at the host performs a supervisory function at a basic level. It handles interrupts, the activation and termination of messages, the interfacing of programs, their scheduling and store allocation.

At machine code level, routines are required to assemble the codes into the format necessary for transmission and to sample data received from the line.

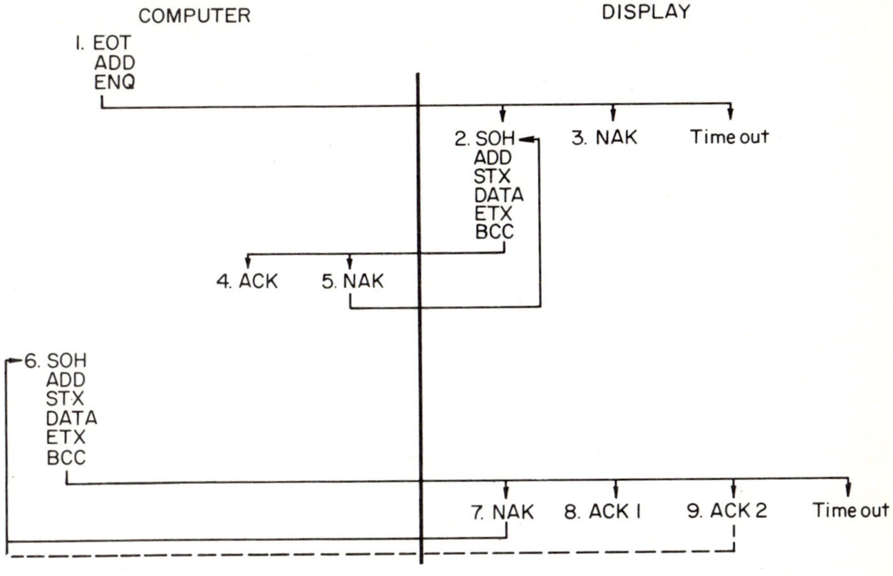

Figure 1.5. Message control procedures for displays polled by a computer over a telephone line. Messages are as follows:

1. *Poll from computer; have you a message?*
2. *Response from display giving its own address, data and block check.*
3. *No message; computer then addresses another display.*
4. *Computer acknowledges correct message after testing block check.*
5. *Block check was incorrect; repeat message.*
6. *Message from computer addressed to display.*
7. *Block check was incorrect; repeat message.*
8. *Display acknowledges correct message.*
9. *Display was unable to receive message because it was not in the receive mode; repeat message later.*

   Time out: No response received from display because of a faulty line or terminal, or because the display is switched off. Computer waits a predetermined time before polling next display.

Once the data has been recognised, further routines are used to recognise information in the message. Thus the control codes must be recognised since they advise when to expect the addresses of the VDU sending the message and when to treat the data as the main text of the message ending with a block check character. The block check character is tested for conformity to the checks performed on the data by software; if there is a difference an error is assumed and a message is sent back requesting another transfer. Such transfers continue until the block and parity checks are valid or until a predetermined number of failures occurs so that a faulty system or inadequate line is assumed. In the case of a telephone link the possibility then occurs of having re-transmission at a lower speed although such a facility is not always available. The *protocol* under software control may take the form shown in Figure 1.5, where it is shown in a simple format. Various subtleties may be added to improve the security of message transfer.

The degree to which the formatting of the messages is under the control of the system designer depends on the level of software implemented. In general the higher the level of language used the more restricted will be the user since he will be constrained to the actions anticipated by the writer of the language. Thus at the highest level the user needs to know little more than the address of fields of fixed and variable data. A lower-level language will permit the user more scope but will require more knowledge on his part.

The organisation of the system to share routines to perform tasks which are common to many terminals can be difficult but necessary since the storage requirement can otherwise be onerous. Chapter 5 considers these matters in more depth.

Data validation software may be important to the user. The types of validation available are numerous. They provide checks of simple facts about the data such as whether there should be numerals only or alphabetic characters only or some defined combination. At a second level checks may be made on the field of data as to its length and whether parts compare with data already held. Impossible or incompatible data can be checked. Thus the age of an employee must be within certain bounds, as must the weight or price of an article. A full list of validation checks can be found from manufacturers' literature.

The intelligent terminal

The intelligent terminal was introduced in the late 1960s to provide more flexibility in the facilities and procedures which could be offered with standard hardware. A particular incentive for the VDU manufacturer to develop an intelligent terminal was the ability such a terminal would have to emulate the different protocols used by different computers, thus increasing the market for his company's display terminal. A microprocessor installed in a terminal is available for the many functions normally performed by wired circuits. The system need not be particularly fast since it is controlling actions performed at the speed of an operator or a telephone line or printer. Certain actions could usefully be given high speed, such as retrieval of information from backing store and data processing needs, and these are sometimes available in more powerful terminals.

The *microprocessor* without store now costs only tens of pounds and accordingly intelligent or programmable terminals are competitive in price. A particular advantage of performing many tasks with a multi-task microprocessor is the reduction in the amount of wiring and connections which would otherwise be required. The standardisation which is possible allows easier design and a more reliable system.

Fallback to a more limited but still useful operation can be provided by the intelligent terminal if the host computer goes down. For example an operator entering data can have the information written onto a backing store (usually cassette tape) which can then be transmitted to the host computer when it is again available.

TRENDS

Displays may be broadly classified as *light emitters* and *light controllers*, as shown in Figure 1.6. The best-known type of light emitter is the CRT, which is used extensively in VDUs and television sets. Other forms of light emitters which use a flat screen are being developed and these are described later. Light emitters are advantageous in low ambient lighting since they do not need external light in order to be visible and indeed light falling on the screen from another source will reduce the contrast. Light emitters such as the *CRT, plasma panels* and systems using *electroluminescence* are sufficiently bright to be viewed in normal ambient lighting. The storage tube sometimes used on graphic displays, and in alphanumeric applications where a very large number of characters are necessary, has a lower intensity and contrast than the conventional CRT but it is sufficiently bright if the ambient lighting is reduced.

Light controllers are used to modulate either incident light or reflected light. They have the advantage over light emitters in that the stronger the ambient lighting the more visible is the display and accordingly they are appropriate for use in bright daylight or sunshine. Some of the display techniques in this category are liquid crystals, electrophoresis, electrochromics and conventional

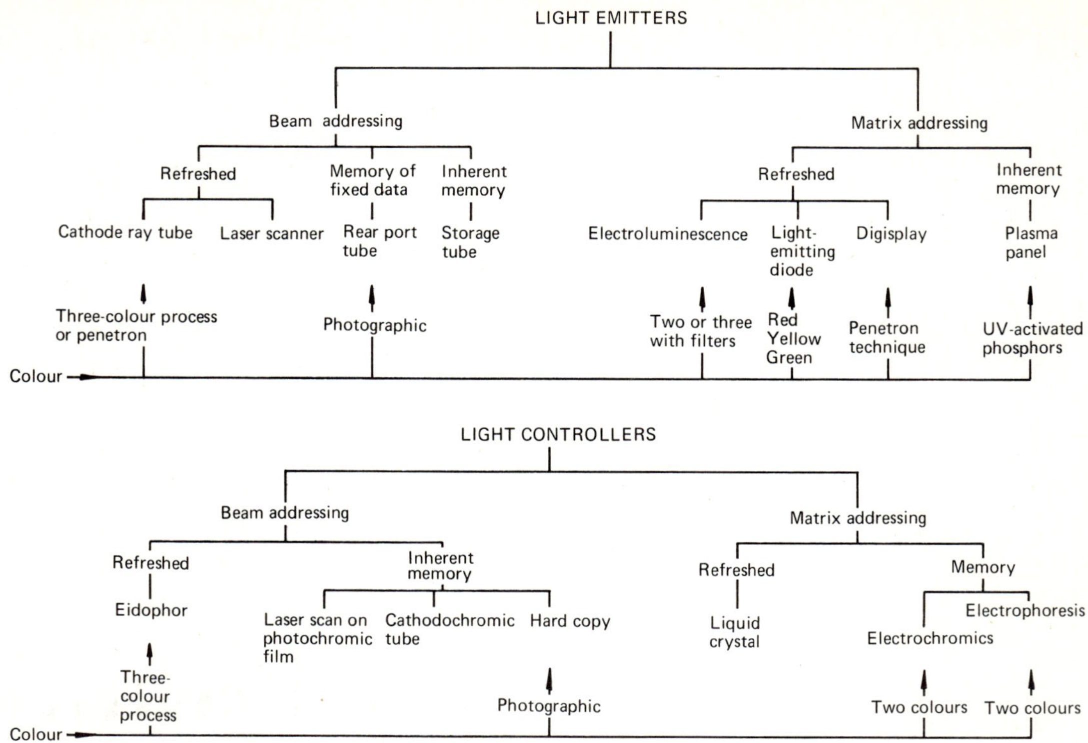

Figure 1.6. Categories of displays with an indication of the possibilities for colour. Copyright © D.J. Grover, 1976.

hard copy. A particular advantage of light controllers is that they require very little power and the drive voltages are compatible with integrated circuit controllers. The *Eidophor* is a form of light controller where a film of oil is distorted by an electron beam so that light reflected from the surface of the oil is modulated by the information on the oil surface. The Eidophor requires high voltages and a very intense light for the purpose of projecting the image onto a large screen.

Colour is available in some of the display techniques, as indicated in Figure 1.6. The CRT has been developed to utilise the three-colour process for television; and if the raster mode of display is used then a television system in colour can be used. If a free-drawing style of operation is required, as is the case for many graphic displays, then it is necessary to use the *Penetron tube*, whereby the colour is determined by the phosphor layer which is activated by the beam. The electron beam is controlled to penetrate to a greater or smaller depth of phosphor and different colours are available, being defined by the two phosphors used and by their combination. Displays using optical techniques can project a slide onto the surface of the screen, as used in the rear port CRT where both optical and electron beam information are superimposed on one screen.

Matrix-addressed light emitters are mostly solid state devices where the colour is dependent on the material being used in the device. Electroluminescence generates a sufficiently broad spectrum around the yellow region so that different filters can be used to isolate up to three distinct colours. Semiconductor *light-emitting diodes* are available in red, yellow and green and some research is being conducted into developing a blue version. Light controllers are not particularly suitable for the generation of coloured pictures. The materials used for *electrophoretic* and *electrochromic* displays, which are described later, can be chosen to give different colours but these colours are limited to two for any particular cell. They are defined by the colours of the electrolyte and the material being deposited, respectively.

If one looks at the overall trends it is clear that the CRT will continue to be used for some time since it has been extensively developed, is fast and suitable for various techniques and has the particular advantage of serial addressing, which minimises the electronics required. Disadvantages are its bulk and the need to provide various EHT voltages. The trend is partly towards the special-purpose system whereby a small CRT is incorporated into a desk console which has various controls and facilities suitable for the particular working environment. One such facility may be the provision of a magnetic store for data entry, a small tube providing the operator with a display of the information being entered in order for him or her to check it before it is stored.

Various terminals incorporating mini- or microcomputers are becoming available as a special-purpose compact unit.

The other clear trend for the CRT is towards the television-compatible information system. The use of standard television components implies low cost and there is the further consideration that the format of the information is compatible with information being retrieved from television cameras. It is also in a suitable form to be transmitted to further monitors such as may be needed for public viewing.

Television-style systems

The use of a television set as an alphanumeric or graphic display has long been anticipated. The television set displaying alphanumerics would be orientated towards a video format composed of a series of dots (from which characters are assembled over perhaps seven successive lines) for which the storage requirement is extensive. The partial solution of the storage problem has been the use of standard codes which interrogate a read-only memory for generating the characters. Conventional stores such as discs and semiconductor memories are, however, achieving sufficient capacity to enable video formats to be stored in their video form. Whereas 14 000 bits of store would be required for ISO/ASCII coding of 2000 characters, over 100 000 bits of store are required for a video format.

Teletext

Broadcast teletext and *wired teletext* are two categories of system postulated. The low-cost VDU of the future will clearly evolve from the teletext terminals which are being developed at the present time. The broadcast teletext system, which was initially designed for the ORACLE and CEEFAX systems for the British television corporations, ITV and BBC respectively, displays a page of textual information on a television screen. The page of information is built up from previously unused sections of the television carrier which holds the normal television programme. Since it is not possible to show pictures during the time that the electron beam is being re-set back to the beginning of the picture, this time is available for the coding of two lines of information. The information transmitted during these line periods consists of ISO/ASCII character code which is entered into a semiconductor store. The store is built up to a full page of information during subsequent refreshing of the screen. The development has awaited the evolution of integrated circuit techniques and low-cost semiconductor storage. The system can be made available in an add-on box which fits into the aerial socket of the television set but it is anticipated that the design will be incorporated into the manufacture of the set and the increase in price is expected to be about the price of a black and white television. The characters are made up from a matrix of 7 × 5 dots which permits 24 rows of information with up to 40 characters in every row.

Figure 1.7 indicates the additional circuits added to a television set consisting of radio and television amplification circuits (1) which supply the video signal to drive the normal operation of the television tube. For receiving teletext the video signal is switched down to block (2), which recognises the codes describing the row and page numbers and thereby formats the received data to assemble the page store shown at (3). The user has a keyboard enabling him to choose the page number required and the system ignores all the page numbers until the chosen one arrives, at which time the data is entered into the store. The page store is circulated in synchronism with the deflection circuits of the television set and the codes which are selected operate the character generator, which feeds an alphanumeric video signal to the circuits driving the television tube. It requires approximately a quarter of a second to transmit a full page of 24 rows so that selection from up to 60 pages may take about 15 seconds to achieve, giving an average selection time of $7\frac{1}{2}$ seconds.

There is interest in the use of a wired teletext system in conjunction with a telephone line. The name of the British Post Office system is *Viewdata*, and interface circuits are designed to read low-speed coding over the telephone line which is fed into the page store of the teletext display. A keyboard is also used in conjunction with the system and it permits the user to interrogate various data banks over a telephone line by entering a suitable sequence of codes. Such a system therefore already simulates the operation of a simple VDU and the next step, to providing a full keyboard capability, is a small one. Functions such as editing and the more sophisticated operations supplied with the VDU would have to be done with the aid of a computer at the other end of the telephone line unless there were enhancements to the teletext system to provide these facilities, but this would imply a higher cost.

Video information systems

Systems permitting mixing or overlaying of information from different sources onto one screen are being manufactured. The type of information permitted is alphanumerics from a computer, text or pictures from a television camera and *microfilm* or *microfiche* data derived from a flying-spot scanner. Such methods are especially useful for information retrieval systems. The data is in a form which is suitable for video transmission to other display monitors, especially,

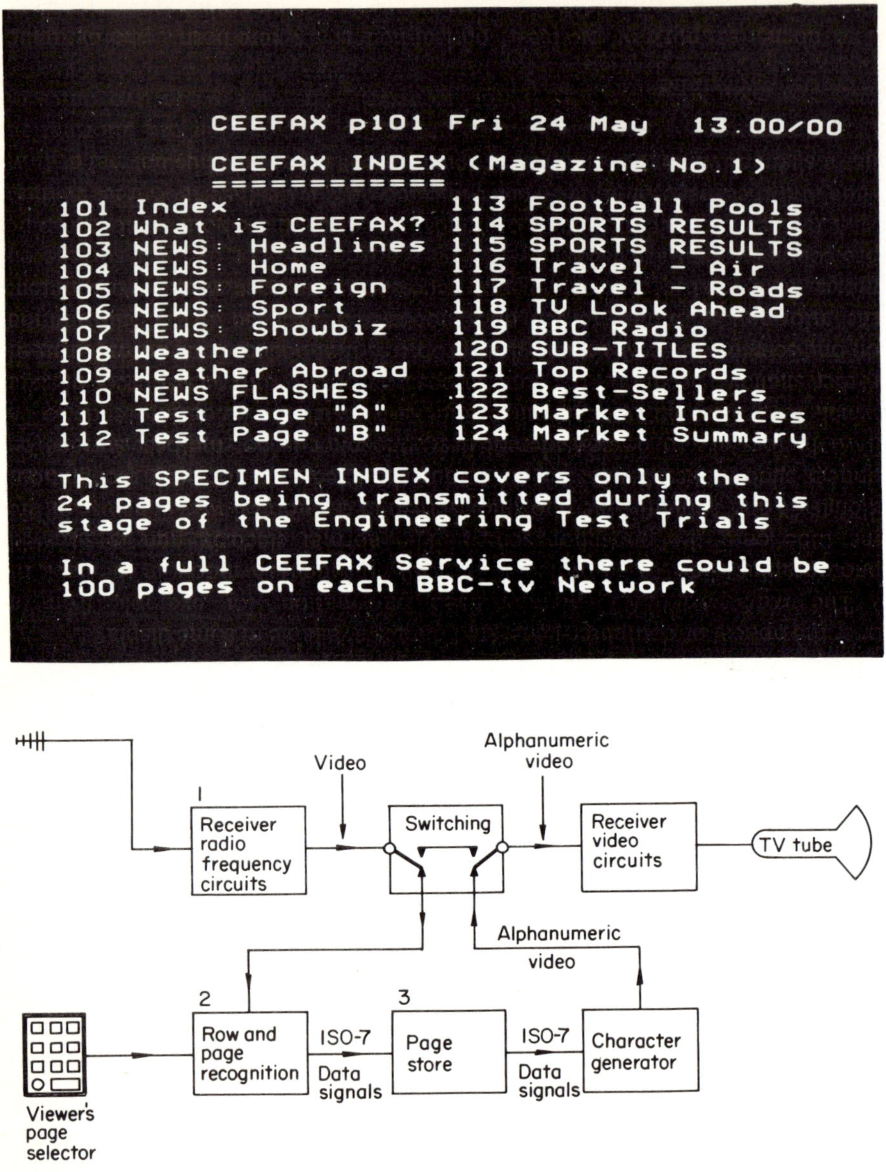

Figure 1.7. The CEEFAX system showing a block diagram of the extra circuits required to provide teletext on a television set. (Courtesy of the BBC.)

for example, where the public or an audience need to be advised of the information.

The converse of this system utilises a terminal with a high-density optical store in the form of *ultrafiche*. The computer simply sends the page and fiche numbers, which is the minimum information required to retrieve the page of interest. Such a system is in operation where 7000 pages are stored on one fiche and the quality of the reproduction is good.

Other types of display

Optically aided displays

It is often necessary to show the format of a form which the operator needs to fill in in the conventional manner. It is desirable to be able to show the headings on this form distinctly so that they are not confused with the data entered by the operator. The use of optical methods to display the form superimposed over the optical or computer-generated data is available in some displays.

The *rear port CRT* permits fixed information, for example from a photographic slide, to be projected optically through a window in the back of the tube onto the phosphor screen. The normal electron gun is situated alongside and activates the phosphor screen in the normal way. The use of the optical slide makes it possible to colour the fixed data for easy recognition. Two factors are to be considered: first, phosphor is not the best surface on which to project an optical image and as a result the colouring tends to be rather shallow. Secondly, the superimposition of two different sources of data on one screen will show up any drift problems that occur. Thus normal drift of the information on the screen does not matter because all the information moves in sympathy but this is not necessarily the case when two different projection systems are used.

A further example of the use of optical means is where both a photographic slide and the image on a CRT are projected onto a third surface. The method has a slight advantage in that the optical image is reproduced better.

Pictorial information

The ability to portray pictorial information is an important one in many applications, especially where an operator is interacting with a system such as a pipeline network, or in any situation where a diagrammatic layout of the information is an aid to understanding. The simplest of the displays which perform these functions uses symbols especially chosen to represent items in the system, such as valves, switches or electrical generators. The symbols usually occupy the same code set as the alphanumerics but a special control code is used which advises the system to switch over to the alternative representation of that code set. There may then be either 64 or 128 possible symbols available. Some of these symbols would be segments of lines which can be joined together to make continuous paths in one of several directions. Accordingly a symbolic representation of a problem can be shown on the screen and the alphanumerics mode used to label paths of the diagram or to give numerical results after performing a calculation. Such systems are constrained in their abilities and where a more free-form line-drawing capability is preferred, then it is necessary to turn to the low-cost graphic displays, the cheapest of which is a storage tube display.

Storage tube displays

The storage tube is incorporated into several types of display terminal. Its first impact was felt in the *graphics* area since it was here that the cost advantage was greatest. Lines or other *graphic information* can be drawn at a relatively low speed which permits lower-cost electronics. The resolution is good and recently a 19-inch (480-millimetre) storage screen which permits over 8000 characters to be displayed has been introduced. The *spatial addressing* on the screen is optionally up to 4096 points per axis. The disadvantages of the storage tube are the limited brightness, which may be insufficient in ambient lighting, together with the need to erase the whole screen when updating information. The problem of updating is helped slightly by *software* routines which allow the operator to delete unwanted data and superimpose the new data. When several such changes have been made the whole screen can then be refreshed to show the correct data only. A partial solution to the problem has been to incorporate a *refreshed line* of alphanumerics at the top of the tube so that the operator can interact with this line in the normal way and edit the data before sending the single line into the computer. The computer may then write that line on the storage part of the tube for advisory purposes while the operator caters for the next line of information.

There are storage tubes which permit selective erasure. They use an electrical *storage mesh* which can be selectively erased by overwriting the appropriate position of the mesh with the same electron beam but under different conditions which cause the stored data to be erased. Selecting data on a spatial store of this kind requires analogue positioning, which is subject to positioning tolerances due to *drift*. Accordingly if two adjacent lines were close together there could be a danger of erasing the second line. Such considerations limit the density of data on the screen if selective erasure is required.

Low-cost refreshed graphics

Low-cost refreshed graphics have become cheaper and are now economically feasible for many applications. Thus an intelligent line-drawing terminal using a refreshed tube which can be updated quickly is available for about £8000. It can be used with a *light pen* which enables the operator to select items of data on the screen and also select from a menu on the screen a command defining the next action to be performed. The quantity of lines that can be drawn without flicker is less than on the storage tube but for interactive operation the line-drawing capabilities are adequate and further information will tend to confuse the operator.

Solid state displays

A replacement for the CRT has been sought for many years. Its large volume has determined the size of equipment and most of the other components have been packed in the spaces remaining at the side of the tube. It also uses high voltages of 12–15 kilovolts. The research has been aimed at producing a flat-screen display which could be driven from the low voltages supplied by integrated transistor circuits. Several devices are marketed although none of them is yet competitive with the CRT for large numbers of characters. The particular advantage of the CRT is that the information can be applied serially over one line and thus share the electronics required for addressing. The flat-screen systems either have individual drive electronics for each character or some multiplexing is possible by using a matrix of individual points which are activated by the sum of two drivers which are addressed in the x and y directions in the plane of the screen. Thus $(m \times n)$ points are addressed by $(m+n)$ drivers. In order for this system to operate it is necessary for the display phenomenon to have a threshold below which it is not activated. The drive circuits are designed so that one by itself is below the threshold but the sum of two drives is above it.

A further consideration is the advantage of inherent memory in the display phenomenon. A display point with inherent memory will, once activated, continue to generate (or control) light until it is turned off. A display technique without memory must be refreshed many times a second to prevent flicker. A display screen composed of a matrix of 500 + 500 points necessitates refreshing 250 000 points at perhaps 30 times per second. The brightness of each point must be sufficient to compensate for its being off while the remainder of the points are refreshed. The result may be a dimmer display (or one with lower contrast) even though the technology is driven to its limit. There are, however, various techniques used to compensate for the problem.

Light emitters

Plasma panels. These consist of a screen incorporating a honeycomb of cells. The cells are usually filled with neon gas to give a multitude of tiny neon lamps. Thin transparent parallel metal strips are plated on the front of the screen and similar strips are plated on the back at right angles so that the intersection of two strips provides two electrodes for the neon cells between them. Plasma panels fall into three categories:

(i) The *DC plasma panel* is the simplest to understand since it simulates the operation of a normal neon tube many times over the area of the screen. Success in achieving an economical design awaited the development of a method of depositing the series resistors associated with each cell to the required tolerance in order to take advantage of the *inherent memory* in a DC cell. *Thick-film resistor technology* has met the required specification and DC plasma panels displaying 32 lines of characters with 40 characters per line have been marketed.

A cell is addressed by activating the two electrodes common to the cell with the *striking voltage*, while a 'maintaining voltage' is applied to all cells via the thick-film resistors. Erasure is carried out by supplying erase pulses to the common electrodes of the cell.

Character writing times are 1 millisecond; dissipation is 60 milliwatts per character. The *maintaining voltage* is 170 volts and a *strike pulse* of 50 volts is required. A 300-character display screen typically measures 150 × 150 × 100 millimetres without power supply.

(ii) The *AC plasma panel* is operated with a high-frequency drive of 50–100 kilohertz. The high-frequency drive voltages which are applied to orthogonal electrodes can energise the cell capacitively so that the gas can be encapsulated in glass and the electrodes applied separately. Good resolution has been obtained giving 60 lines per inch. The panel is given inherent memory by driving with a sustaining square wave upon which is imposed a strike pulse to activate a single cell. Panels of 512 × 512 lines and a character capacity of 4000 have been produced. The resolution of the panel is sufficient for line drawing for graphic displays but the number of drive circuits required for the display makes it costly.

(iii) The *self-scan plasma panel* utilises a technique of preferential *glow transfer* and glow movement to reduce the number of drive circuits required to maintain a display. The *cathode wires* are orthogonally associated with two sets of *anode wires*. Cathode ionisation occurs in one part of the cell where it is not visible to the viewer and is then selectively transferred to a visible portion of the cell. A *three-phase clock* is used to transfer the glow from column to column and refreshing is obtained without the use of column drivers.

The cost of the display makes it competitive with the CRT for less than 500 characters. The advantage of a *flat screen*, separated from the controller (which can be placed under a desk), has caused it to be chosen for some situations where the number of characters is limited. It is illustrated in Figure 1.8.

Developments in the generation of colour by plasma panels utilise phosphors of different colour. These are energised by the ultraviolet light emitted from adjacent gas discharge cells.

Electroluminescent displays. Electroluminescence can be energised using either AC, DC or pulsed drive voltages, pulsed drives being the most efficient and permitting a greater lifetime. The display consists of a phosphor coating over a

Figure 1.8. A plasma display shown with the screen separated from the control unit and keyboard. (Photograph courtesy of Burroughs Machines Ltd.)

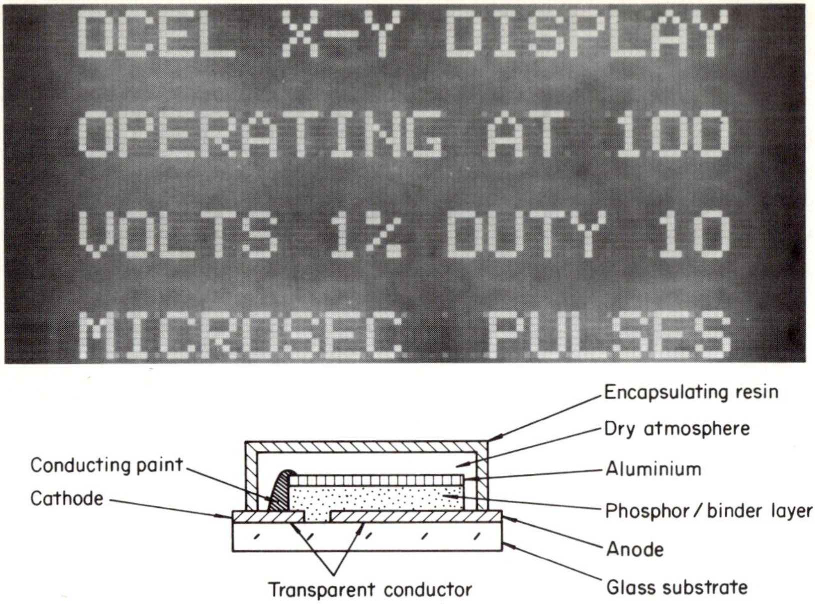

Figure 1.9. A DC-pulsed electroluminescent display showing the construction of the panel. (Courtesy of Phosphor Products Company Ltd.)

flat screen which is energised by an electric field applied at the junction of the phosphor layer and a transparent conducting film. An example of the display is shown in Figure 1.9. During manufacture the material is formed for emission at a certain electric field and application of a higher voltage during use will form that material to a higher voltage. For this reason application of a continuous DC voltage is unsuitable but application of a pulsed voltage in excess of the *forming voltage* gives a higher brightness without re-forming the material. Alphanumeric displays have been made to give up to 25 rows of 50 characters in the form of a 7 × 5 dot matrix. The advantage of the technique is that it is very robust. The display is generated on a *flat panel*, *greyscales* can be shown and the cost per element is low. Different colours can be produced with the use of *filters*. The disadvantages are that there is no internal memory and there is no threshold to permit multiplexing of the drive circuit. These displays are not compatible with integrated circuits since the drive voltage is of the order of 100–130 volts but they nevertheless represent a strong contender to replace the CRT.

Light-emitting films. These utilise an evaporated film of phosphor which is energised by a high-frequency electric field. A drive voltage of 600–700 volts peak to peak is applied at about 1 kilohertz. Multiplexing is possible since the persistence of the films is about 100 times the excitation period and a 1% duty cycle is used. The persistence lasts for 2–3 milliseconds.

Light-emitting diodes. These are essentially a replacement for the indicator filament lamp. They are semiconductor crystals and consequently robust, and can be made very small. They can be obtained in three colours, namely red, yellow and green. They are very bright, are compatible with integrated circuits and have a reputation for reliability. It is possible to combine them with further semiconductor technology to provide memory in the form of a latch-on capability. The disadvantage is that the cost per element is essentially high and proportional to the area of the display. The driving current is significant if many elements are required.

Light controllers

Liquid crystal displays. These are important since they require the least power of any display means. They use optical *anisotropic material* (which means that light is affected differently by the direction in which it passes through the material) which can be electrically controlled in several different ways. The liquid crystal display consists of a sandwich of the liquid between two transparent electrodes as shown in Figure 1.10. The rod-like molecular structure of the liquid can be orientated by an electric field. *Dynamic scattering* is the simplest technique. In the absence of an electric field, the molecules are aligned to allow light to pass through. Application of a voltage to the electrodes causes the molecules to scatter, giving a frosty appearance. The electrodes are shaped so that the scattered molecules follow the desired character form.

The alternative is *field effect methods*, the most promising and best-known of which uses *twisted nematic material*. The molecular structure of the material is orientated in a helical mode by the design of the substrate surfaces. The orientation of the molecules is caused to rotate by 90° in moving from the front to the back of the crystal. The effect is that *polarised light* entering one surface is rotated through 90° and consequently if the liquid crystal cell is placed between *cross-polarisers* the orientation of the polarised light is compatible at the two surfaces and light passes through. The application of an electric field to the crystal changes the molecular ordering so that the polarised light is no longer rotated to be compatible with the filter and light does not pass through. The method uses about one-tenth of the power required for the dynamic

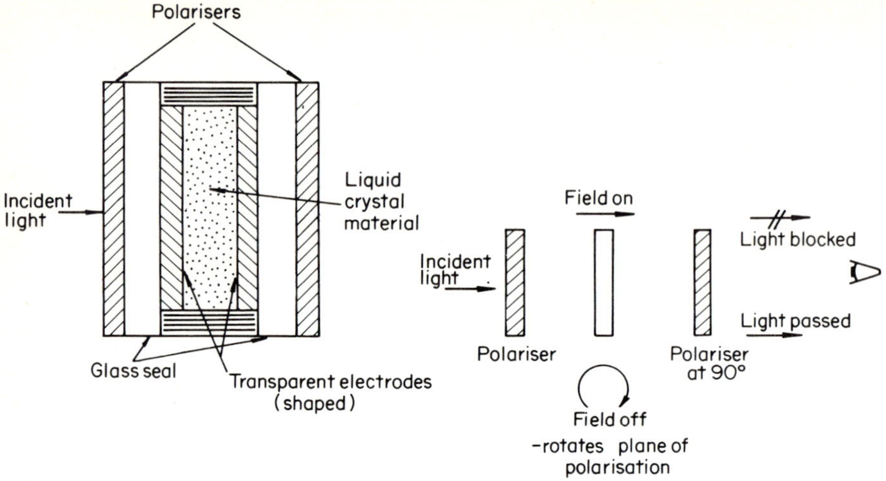

Figure 1.10. A twisted nematic liquid crystal display showing the operation of the polarisers.

scattering method and voltages as low as 2 volts are sufficient for operation. The power requirement of such a liquid crystal is of the order of 1 microamp with a drive voltage ranging from 2 to 50 volts depending on the speed of operation required. It is necessary for the voltage to be alternating, and a frequency range of 25 hertz to 30 kilohertz is appropriate. The decay time when turning off the crystal is comparatively long, ranging from 100 to 500 milliseconds, but the turn-on time, which is dependent on the drive voltage, can be as low as 20 milliseconds.

A large-area liquid crystal display capable of displaying 640 characters has been reported. The characters are generated on a 9 × 7 *dot matrix. Threshold* has been achieved by the use of additives to the liquid crystal material and addressing is by *x* and *y* drivers. The response time is 1–1.5 seconds and the decay time is about 700 milliseconds. The display, which is experimental, has a screen measuring 400 × 500 millimetres.

To summarise, the advantages of liquid crystal displays are: good contrast in bright ambient lighting, very low power, compatibility with *integrated circuits* and in particular with *CMOS*. The cost per element is low and the technology is potentially suitable for large displays. The disadvantages include a limited temperature range, from −10 °C to +60 °C. Also, liquid crystal displays require memory for each element of a character and the switching speed is slow. The question of reliability has received some attention; it is claimed that the early problems with liquid crystal displays were due to bad sealing of the cell. A *lifetime* of 100 000 hours is now to be expected.

Electrophoretic displays. These use electrically charged particles suspended in a coloured liquid contained between two plates which also act as electrodes. The front electrode, at least, must be transparent. The liquid and the particles are in contrasting colours. Application of a potential difference to the plates generates an electric field which causes the particles to migrate to the front electrode or to the back electrode so that either the colour of the particle or the colour of the liquid is seen (*see* Figure 1.11). The system has *inherent memory* since the particles, once positioned, may stay for long periods after the electric field is removed. The front electrode may be segmented in order to generate alphanumerics. The operating voltages vary between 15 and 45 volts and a lifetime of 10^7 operations is expected when operated with switching once per second. The switching speed is in the range of 20 to 100 milliseconds and the operating current required is of the order of 0.01 microamp per square millimetre.

Electrochromic displays. These consist of a cell in which material is electroplated onto the front surface. The material, which is often a dye,

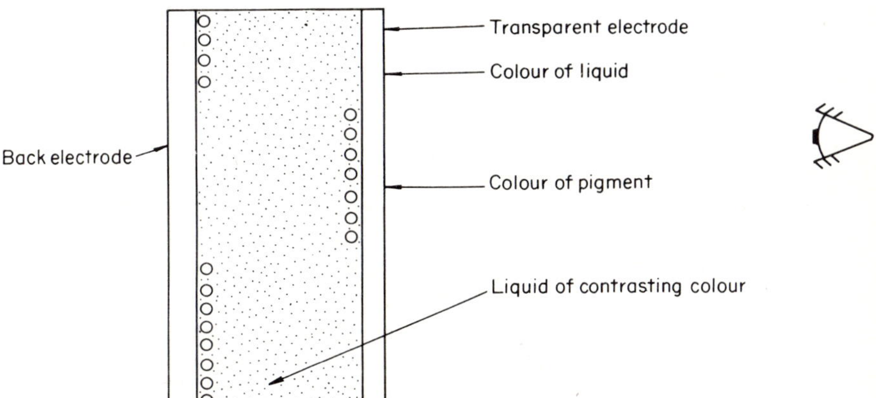

Figure 1.11. A diagram showing the cross-section of an electrophoretic display.

contrasts with the electrolyte filling the cell. The electrodes receiving the plating are shaped to form sections of a character.

Electrochromic devices are slow and have a rise time of 10–100 milliseconds. Operating voltage is in the range of 0.2–2.0 volts and a relatively high current is required. The cell has *inherent memory* with a storage time exceeding a month. Erasure is possible in 10–50 milliseconds and a lifetime of 10^5 write–erase cycles is expected.

Conclusion

Improvements are occurring in all aspects. It is to be expected that the display terminal will tend towards a fraction of its present cost if *large-scale integration* is taken to the limit. A solid state display compatible with the integrated circuits is clearly necessary and given adequate development the display technique is likely to be compatible with integrated manufacture. The most expensive part of the display (with the trends in electronics) will be mechanical parts such as the keyboard. Electronic methods of sensing a finger on a *tablet* are potentially a low-cost substitute for the keyboard.

Communications rates improve steadily as modem technology is further refined. Experiments are being conducted into fibre optic channels, which can be used to transmit data by modulating a light beam. The bandwidth of such a system is considerable so that many thousands of data channels can be transmitted over one optic fibre. An important consideration is the security which is possible since an *optic fibre* cannot be *tapped* without breaking the channel and so warning the user.

Further work on methods of presenting information is desirable, especially with regard to the addition of diagrammatic or pictorial information. The investigations into the possibilities of teletext are a step in this direction.

Further reading

R.P. Backhaus and J. Tippett, Control of operations in British European Airways. *Datafair 73*, Vol. 1, pp 233–240. The British Computer Society.

W.K. English, D.C. Engelbert and M.L. Berman, Display selection techniques for text manipulation. *IEEE Trans. Hum. Factors Electron.*, March 1967, No.5.

W.D. Fuller, *Physician–machine interface in a hospital information system.* Information Systems Organization, Lockheed Missiles & Space Co., Sunnyvale, Calif.

I.E. Gordon and L.K. Anderson, New display technologies — an editorial viewpoint. *Proc. IEEE*, **61** (1973), 807–813.

D.J. Grover, Review Paper. Interaction with visual information. *CAD 74 Conference*, Imperial College, London, Sept. 1974. IPC Science and Technology Press, Guildford.

D.J. Grover, A survey of interactive graphic devices. *Comput. Bull.*, Ser. 2, No. 4, June 1975, pp. 27–28.

D.G. Harris, Tesco and the visual display unit. *Computer Graphics 70*, Vol. 1, Section 1, April 1970. Brunel University.

C. Hilsum, Solid state displays. *Electron. Power*, Displays supplement, Sept. 1973, pp. S3–S12.

I.A. Jones, Display terminal design. *Comput. Bull.*, (1969), 391–395.

J. Kirton and R.W. Sarginson, Some new display techniques — a critical survey. *Opto-electronics*, **6** (1974), 340–367.

M.C. Lane-Serff, The use of visual displays in the insurance industry. *Datafair 73*, Vol. 1, pp. 223–227. The British Computer Society.

I. Ohishi *et al.*, An experimental real-time colour-TV display with a DC gas discharge panel. *Proc. Soc. Inf. Disp.*, **16** (1975),

Proceedings 1st European Electro-Optics Markets and Technology Conference, Geneva, Sept. 1972, Session 9, pp. 324–362.

A. Vecht, N. Werring *et al.*, Direct current electroluminescence in zinc sulphide. *Proc. IEEE*, **61** (1973), 902–907.

2 The technology of visual display units

Iorwerth Jones

Five basic ingredients are necessary in a VDU:

The monitor, or display screen
The data store
The character generator
The keyboard, or operator interface
The communication interface

These will be dealt with separately, in order to build up a picture of the whole which is cogent and realistic. A typical VDU is shown in Figure 2.1.

The monitor

The writing of alphanumeric characters electronically has attracted development since the *cathode ray tube* (CRT) first became available. However, it is only since the mid-1960s that practical and economic devices have been produced. The influence of television made available a variety of display CRTs having high brightness and reasonable resolution. CRT technology is a very highly developed one, made possible by a large demand for domestic television, and the magnetically scanned television tube dominates VDU design. It is likely that this will continue to be so for the immediate future, although other forms of display screen are under intensive development.

The use of the CRT is not without problems, particularly when the highest quality of display is sought. The normal aberrations for which corrections are necessary fall into two main groups — those associated with linearity and those with resolution.

Linearity

Magnetically deflected CRTs have many imperfections, some of which are

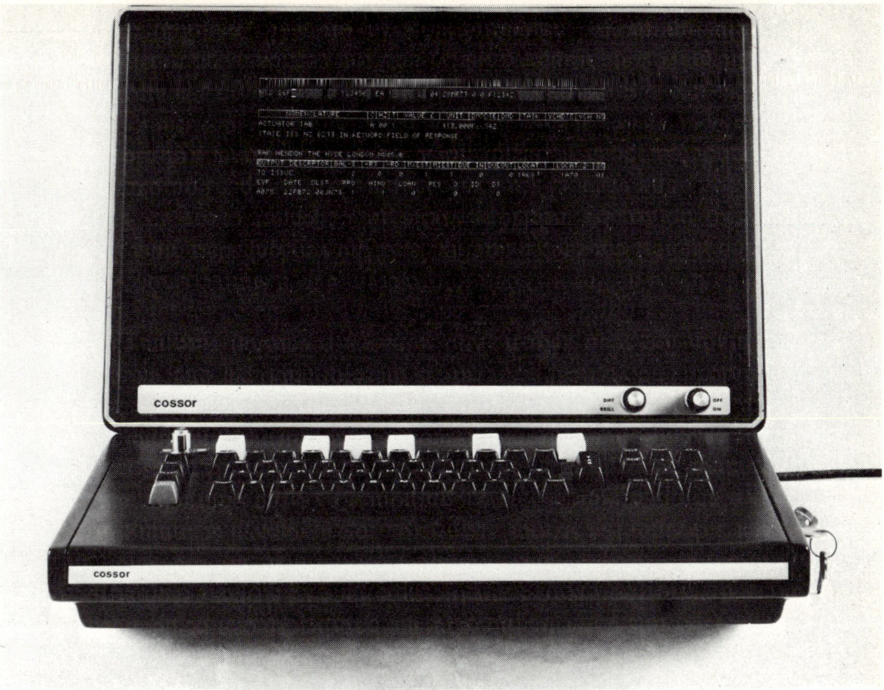

Figure 2.1. General view of a typical professional VDU.

inherent and others which are introduced by the ergonomic factors imposed. Principal amongst the latter are the problems related to the 'flat-faced' display tube. Magnetically scanned beams have near-optical properties, and the optimum focal point is at a constant radius from the centre of the lens system, or gun. There is therefore an inherent tendency for the beam to move out of focus when being scanned away from the centre of the tube face.

Deflection sensitivity also changes, since the distance from gun to tube face is not constant. These errors are exaggerated by the practical limitations of the lens system, formed from coils and magnetic cores.

So, for any practical display, corrections are introduced which minimise the aberrations that would otherwise be visible. *Pincushion* or *barrel* distortions are corrected for by disposing simple bar magnets round the neck of the tube. *Deflection defocusing* is corrected by introducing an electronic waveform into the scanning system which corrects for the natural distortion. *Cigar* distortion, or the tendency for characters to be larger in the centre of the line scan than they are at the edge, is also corrected electronically by modulating the deflection waveform.

In practice, CRTs are adjusted for optimum performance when viewed under a parallax-correcting grid, and the inherent stability of the scanning system is such that the optimum is not difficult to maintain, particularly if the power supply system is stable.

Focusing

The readability of characters is determined to a great extent by the resolution of the CRT system. Most commercial CRTs are somewhat deficient in this respect, and suppliers can provide specially designed, or selected, gun systems to give higher than normal optical performance. It is important to reduce the effect of astigmatism, which can degrade resolution in one co-ordinate when the other is optimised, and corrections for this are usually incorporated.

The *phosphor* of the CRT screen has an important role in the whole process. Early designs usually relied on long or medium persistence to sustain a viewable image at low refresh rates. Some VDUs still use medium persistence, but most units are now designed for short-persistence phosphors and high refresh rates. Practical studies carried out in the 1960s showed that refresh frequencies as high as 50 times per second could, under conditions of high brightness and fringe area vision, give unacceptable visual flicker. This effect can be detected easily on a domestic television screen, where the interlace — giving a refresh rate of 50 times per second when well adjusted — still yields a visible flicker when viewed from the edge of the eye's angle of acceptance. The effect is normally masked by the interest of the programme and by the fact that it is viewed directly.

Two phosphors, one green and the other white, tend to dominate the designs currently available. Green (P31) is a hard, short-persistence phosphor, having excellent brightness and ruggedness; white (P4) is preferred by some users, is almost equally hard and rugged, and, of course, commonly available in standard television CRTs.

The final acceleration potential in most designs is about 12 kilovolts. This voltage gives good brightness and general performance, and virtually complete immunity from secondary radiation of any kind. This is important, since VDU operators tend to sit much closer to VDU screens than do domestic viewers. For the same reason, it is usual to provide protection for the viewer from the effects of CRT failure.

The rim-guard type of CRT is almost always used. The effect of the rim band, which is always under tension, is to hold the elements of the tube face together during failure. Additional protection, adequately provided by a Perspex screen, is usually included against the remote possibility of flying particles. The screen also affords the opportunity of modifying the appearance of the VDU.

Surface reflections from the CRT screen are a recurring issue. Generally, these are more apparent than real; reflections are not in the same plane as the viewed data, and, for a normally seated operator, are virtually invisible. However, comparative assessments by assessors who view everything with clinical detachment can attach considerable importance to them. Surface treatment has been used to reduce reflectivity, and a very light moulded etch is commonly used. A visible reduction of surface shine is always accompanied by a reduction in legibility caused by the diffusion induced. The problem is compounded by the non-flatness of the 'flat-faced' CRT. Truly flat CRT screens are not practical, and moulded face plates with non-reflective qualities have, necessarily, to be as close as possible to the phosphor layer. The solution is therefore expensive and also a compromise.

Neutral-grey filter screens can improve the contrast very noticeably, and yield an apparent gain by reducing reflections from the tube surface (the plane of vision). Their effect is, however, normally dependent on a practical space between the flat face plate and the tube screen, and of course, there is high surface shine on the face plate. The overall performance is acceptable, and operators are universally agreed that the VDUs are comfortable to work with. Other devices, including screens which reduce the viewing angle, have been tried but with little success.

An important effect of the CRT is that it determines the size and shape of a VDU to a very significant degree. Most VDUs are as high, wide and deep as the CRT determines they must be.

The data store

The most economic method of storing data is to use the same technique that was successfully developed for computer storage and transmission — that is, binary coding. The adoption of a standard coding system using combinations of up to eight bits was formalised by the American Standard Code for Information Interchange, or ASCII. This clearly determines the relationship in most Western languages for the codes used to represent the variety of letters implicit in them. For English-speaking nations, the code is comprehensive, providing a small variable section for national differences (£ and $). Other European languages have found it possible to work in the same structure, but many have difficulties with accents, diphthongs and other subtleties.

With some languages there are problems which seem almost insuperable — those in the Middle and Far East are especially difficult — but there is a general tendency towards the adoption of some form of basic ASCII for world-wide use.

ASCII has a total of 128 variants, and, of these, 32 are reserved for control codes. The reason for this is that simple data cannot be received or actioned in a practical system without a considerable number of supervisory codes which request or command action by the receiving system without which the data would often be meaningless. At the simplest level, control codes are used to command essential actions, for example carriage return or new line commands for printers.

At a much higher level of complexity, control codes are used as security aids, and as components of the communication 'envelope' which surrounds a data 'package', determining its destination and enabling error correction routines to be established and operated. Typically, the 'header' of a message will contain:

Synchronising characters enabling bit and character synchronism to be established
Address information, singling out one or more destination
Information about the nature of the message, which may contain data or may only be asking for a status report
An indicator of the start of data

Figure 2.2. Store board module. Note the refresh store, which occupies the right-hand third of the board.

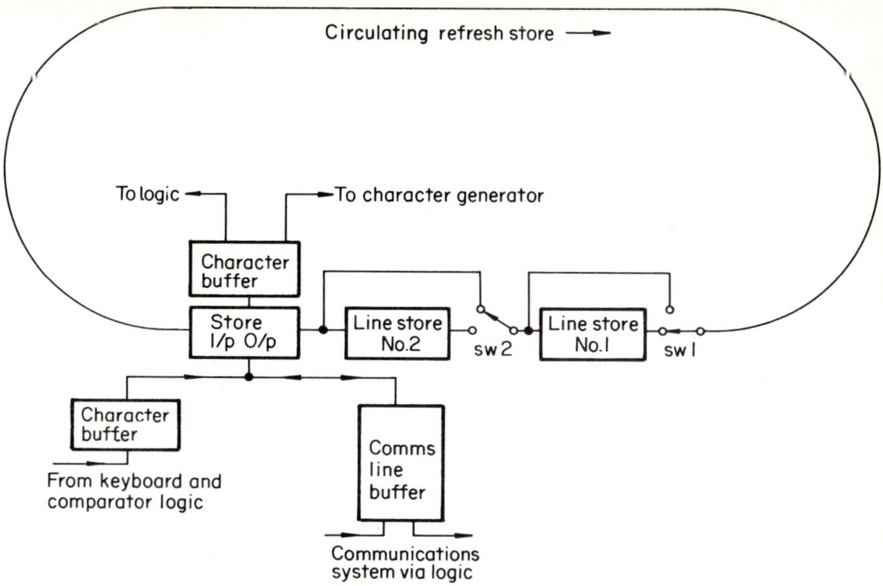

Figure 2.3. Typical refresh store showing logic and control characteristics.

An equivalent number of special characters are usually included in the 'tail', particularly an error character which allows the receiving device to check that its received information is free of errors.

Embedded in the envelope is the message which was the reason for the transmission. It usually contains a high proportion of data characters, which are transferred into the VDU data store. There will, however, be a significant number of control codes scattered in the data (carriage return for example) and these have to be recognised and acted upon, and, depending on the nature of the code, they may be stored with the data or not. At the front of the store there must be a logical decision-making unit which determines whether incoming characters are data or control. A store board module is shown in Figure 2.2.

Thus the basic concept of the data store is a capability for storing 8-bit characters (or 7-bit if parity is discarded, as often happens), and provision of a logic comparator to determine whether any incoming character should be stored or actioned or both. By whatever method this is achieved, the stored data are economically packed into a serial circulating store, or into a random-access store which can be serially addressed (*see* Figure 2.3).

Usually, all the data which are stored are read cyclically so that information can be passed to the character generator and thereby displayed on the CRT screen. This must be accomplished at the refresh rate of the system, typically 50–60 times per second, and in this time all the stored data are reviewed and displayed.

Figure 2.3 shows a typical arrangement for data storage. As indicated above, the store may be cyclic (a long shifting register) or static but cyclically scanned (for example a core store). The two systems are analogous, except that there will be, in the dynamic store, a finite waiting time for information to appear at the input–output window, whereas it is possible to direct the core scanner to an appropriate word with minimum delay.

As information is presented at the window it is subjected to several possible actions. The first of these is that the character, if it is displayable, will be passed to the character generator for display. If it is not, then the control unit will determine what action is consequent and command that it should be carried out. The display operation may then be suppressed.

Another action is to present, when commanded to do so by control, the information to the transmission system for passage to the external world. Again, the information may be disposed of, to be replaced by new information coming in from the outside world or from the local keyboard. Finally, if it is dynamic it is clocked, re-established and sent back round the store.

In a system in which all characters are equal, some method of singling out one for special action is vital, so a tag, usually called a *cursor*, is placed against this character and a special symbol is displayed on the screen. In some designs, an extra bit is available with each character and only one of these is filled to identify the character which is the current object of the logic operation.

Most VDUs now have a cursor register, which is compared with a counter that is synchronised with the store, so that coincidence is achieved for one unique character slot. The most elementary use of this information is to tell the operator at which point any keyboard action he or she initiates will affect the displayed data, and, as keying actions are carried out, the cursor moves ahead to identify the next working slot. The cursor also usually identifies the point at which transmission will commence, or end, when information is committed to the outside world. Movement of the cursor is initiated by a special set of cursor control keys, which can move it anywhere on the screen quickly and silently.

Special editing effects are also part of the function of the data store. Reversing the movement of the cursor, for example, is vital if typing errors are to be corrected. The ability to insert or delete characters is a feature of most VDUs and the re-timing of stored information which makes these actions possible is a combined function of the store and the logic unit. A character can be deleted simply by reducing the store by one character length for one character duration. Similarly, a space can be inserted by adding a character length artificially. These actions are usually, though not always, limited to extending and reducing data on one line.

Figure 2.3 represents the action of two line stores which are in the cyclic path. With one store included and one not, normal display is achieved. If both stores are inserted electronically for one line length, then the effect will be to add a whole line (of spaces) to the store, moving all data from there as far as the end of the store down one line, the last line being lost. Similarly, if both lines are shorted out, then the total store length is reduced by one line, all the following data are moved up one line and the last line filled with spaces. Logical operations of this kind are relatively easy to achieve in an electronic store.

Control characters which are actioned and displayed fall into a special group. The most useful of these is a protected field limiter/delimiter method, in which stored characters are logically recognised and interpreted so that any attempt to change characters between them on the screen is totally inhibited. This control system is commonly used, and variations of it can give greater and more flexible control, as *tabulation markers*, or column setting devices for example.

Typical of control action is a NEW LINE symbol entered from the keyboard or by the processor which will:

Insert a distinctive marker
Clear the remainder of the line to space
Re-position the cursor to the start of the next line
Restrict transmission to data, suppressing the spaces

Other control keys and computer-based commands can, for example,

Erase the rest of the line
Erase the rest of the display
Re-set cursor to top left
Set the 'start of message' marker (when there is one)

The character generator

In the early days of development, most alphanumeric development projects were concerned to drive the electron beam round the character by scan control — this is known as *vector drawing*. The system takes considerable power since there is no energy recovery and a linear wide-deflection bandwidth is required. As a result, more recent VDUs are based on regular scanning methods which incorporate some energy recovery technique in which the high-speed variable is reduced to turning the brightness up and down at appropriate times.

Two basic methods are commonly used. The first of these is the ubiquitous *television scan system*, which is based on the domestic television set, and the other is a regular scan system of horizontal bands with a vertical deflection system superimposed to allow the painting of characters during left to right deflection. There are variants of both but the basic principles of scanning are illustrated in Figure 2.4.

The television system is now very common, and can appear as a true television-compatible raster using standard components, or as an enhanced television raster system in which more lines, or bunched lines, are used to improve definition. The reason for the development of the latter is that the basic television raster is barely capable of sustaining the vertical resolution which present display performance requires. For reasons hinted at above, interlace cannot be used without exposing unacceptable flicker, and the uninterlaced raster has less than 300 lines in which to write information. Allowing for space between lines this reduces the total number of displayable lines to about 24.

To achieve comparable resolution horizontally, approximately 400 bits of information must be written on each line. Since a line on some displays takes about 60 microseconds to write, the requisite bandwidth can be deduced.

The alternative method is to scan the tube face in stripes, each stripe being the height of the letters and numbers contained in the line. In one manufacturer's design, the stripes are written by a vertical scanning waveform — a minor scan or '*diddle*' — and components of the character are formed during this minor scan. For a 25-line VDU, refreshed at 60 times per second, writing a line takes about 650 microseconds, and during that time it must, of course, write 80 characters, each approximately 10 bits wide, if inter-character space is included. The vertical scan rate is therefore 800 per line, excluding any allowances made for scan return, and it has a repetition rate in excess of 1 megahertz.

It is usual to use a sawtooth scan in preference to a simple sinusoid in order to preserve the highest character quality, and the vertical scan must sustain the ability to write up to 14 individual dots in order to maintain the highest resolution. The bandwidths of the two systems are roughly comparable, but it may be claimed that the stripe scan makes more effective use of the CRT face than does the open raster of the television scan. Since the information is used in different ways by the two systems, there are logical implications for the associated character generators.

Earlier VDUs employed as *character generators* (Figure 2.5) either *vector drive systems* or some form of *facsimile reproduction*. Many of the latter still survive in working situations. Basically, facsimile uses a master copy of a character set which is systematically interrogated by a scan raster, yielding

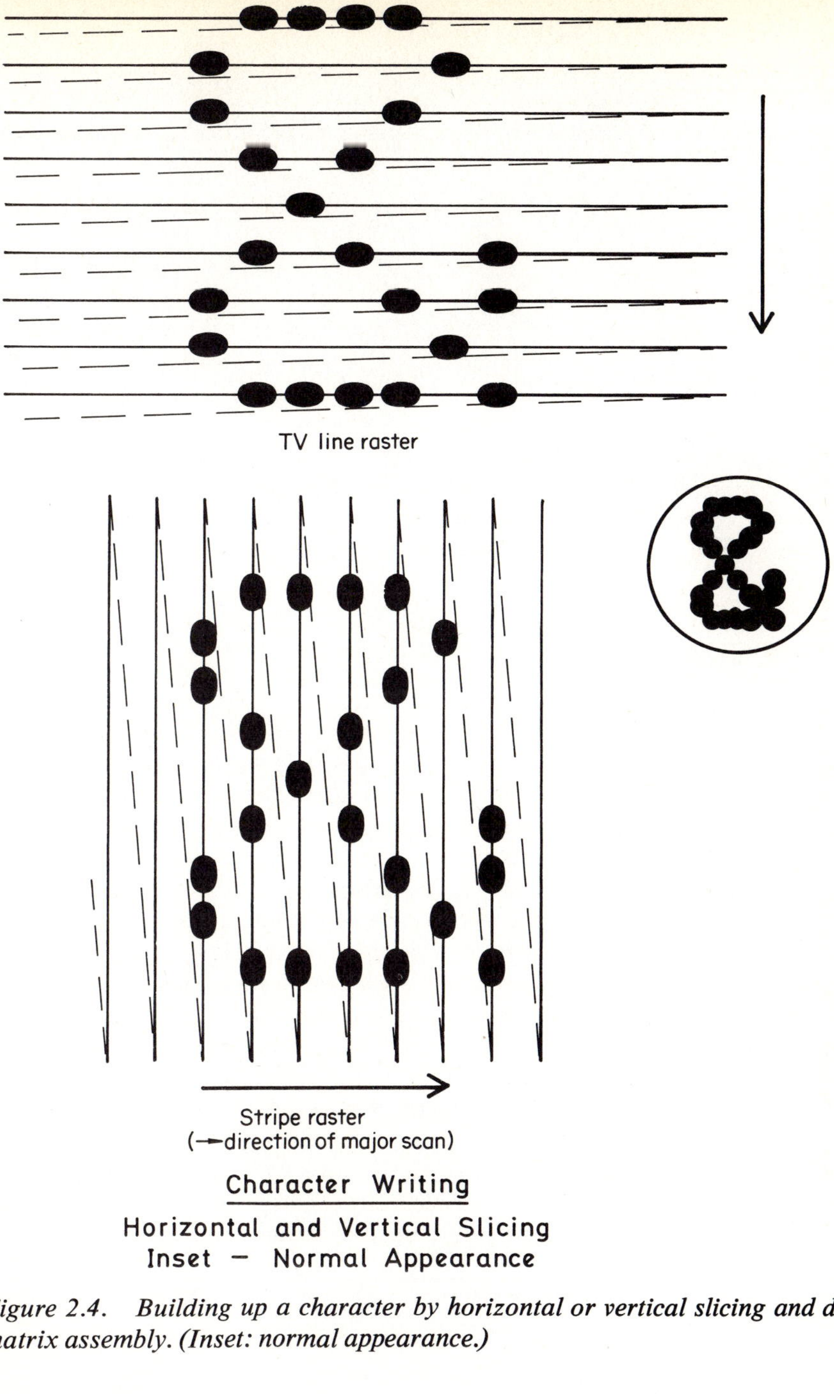

Figure 2.4. Building up a character by horizontal or vertical slicing and dot matrix assembly. (Inset: normal appearance.)

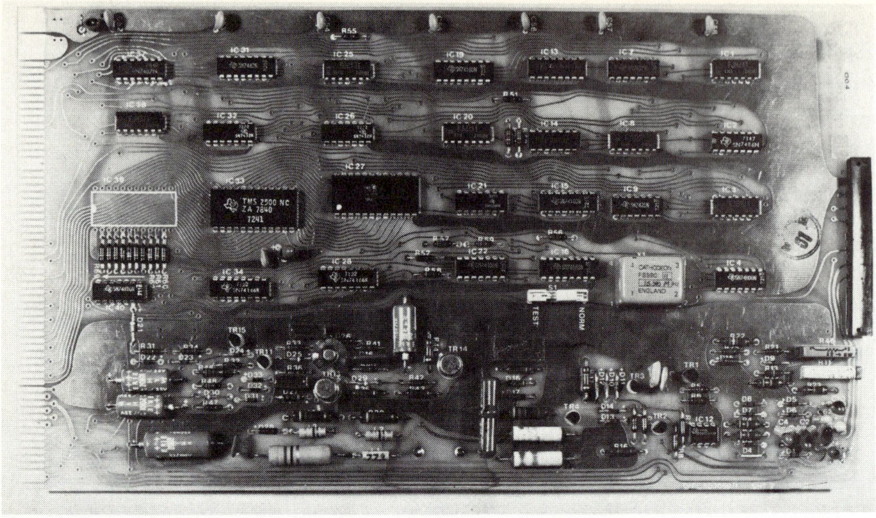

Figure 2.5. Character generator board showing, centre left, the read-only memory source for dot information. (One memory is not occupied — it is used to add lower case as required.)

information which can be 'copied' by a similar display raster occurring at the same time. The one-for-one search of the character provides an exact duplicate for the CRT screen. The facsimile is usually held in a CRT especially adapted for internal scanning by an electron beam. The *Monoscope* and *Symbolray* tubes were examples of this technique.

In recent years a synthetically generated matrix of dots has been adopted almost universally for character writing. In this method, for any character, a master store giving the required dot positions is interrogated synchronously by a search waveform coupled to the scanning system of the CRT. Dot information is released to control the brightness of the CRT beam, and the sequence of dots builds up into the preferred character shape. There are basic dot matrices of various resolutions (7 × 5, 7 × 7, 9 × 7, 12 × 5, 12 × 7, etc.) which can be used at the designer's choice (Figure 2.6).

Upper-case only displays are less demanding, in terms of resolution, than are displays with upper and lower case. Lower-case characters have descenders (below the baseline) and they extend vertically to the same height as upper-case characters. However, most lower-case characters can be accommodated in a five-dot-wide format; only 'w' and 'm' give any real problems. It is possible to treat 'm' and 'w' as special characters, and similar treatment can be given to ',' and ';', which are both conventionally in the upper-case characters set but ideally should have descenders.

The two basic scan techniques referred to above each have their own impact on the scanning logic. The stripe scan in effect writes the whole of one character before passing on to the next. It is ideally suited to facsimile reproduction, in which access to the required character may be relatively slow, but then the search motion for information is small and easily controlled. A television scan implies that the tops of all characters in a line are written first, followed by successive horizontal slices until the bottoms are reached some ten lines later. In order to make this possible, a display based on television scan needs a *single-line buffer* of all the characters to be written which can be scanned ten times (say) before all the characters are released and replaced by the next line.

Pre-packaged *dot matrix memories* are readily available, providing characters of various forms and resolutions, and are supplied with access control logic by component manufacturers. The availability of *programmable read-only memories* makes it possible for special character founts and shapes to be co-opted with relative ease. There is also the possibility of using a random-access store as the dot source, making a variety of characters available under software control.

Techniques for *enhancing* the basically sparse dot matrix character have

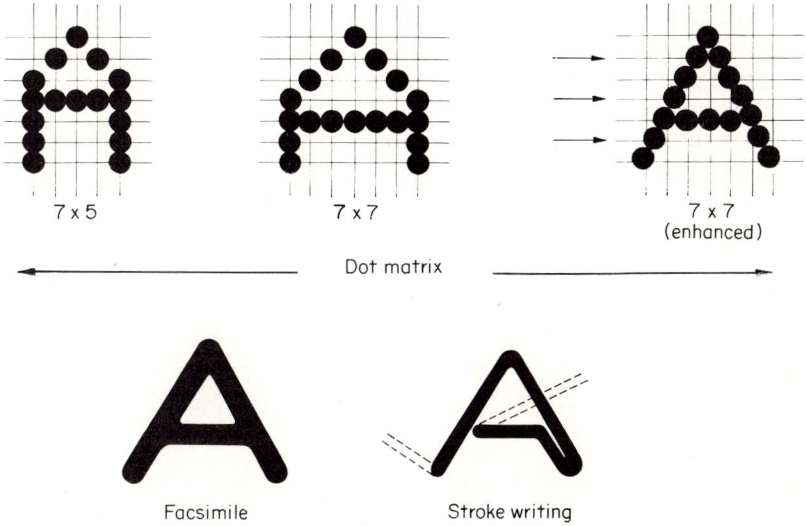

Figure 2.6. Various ways in which a character can be built up.

been developed and are commonly employed. The most familiar of these is 'half-shift' enhancement. The effect of this, as shown in Figure 2.6, is to move, selectively, some of the horizontally disposed dots half of the dot separation to the right or left as required. Well rounded characters are achieved by this method, and the technique has the merit of being simple. Other techniques, including dot stretching, achieve comparable improvement of appearance.

Cursive characters (those of the Middle East for example) and character sets with special accents, of which there are many, are still difficult to deal with, not the least of the difficulties being that the normal code set cannot accommodate all the variants within the 128 range. Hard copy devices commonly avoid this difficulty by providing two basic keystrokes superimposed to build up an accented character. The CRT, which is a real-time device, cannot write two different characters simultaneously, so the two shapes have to be collated electronically before being presented and then the limit is set by the display resolution. There are other, fortunately simpler, problems; writing text from right to left for example, coupled with the ability to write strings of numbers from left to right!

The keyboard

The keyboard (Figure 2.7) is the human interface, the means by which the operator makes demands on the system or contributes new information for the system to use. It therefore differs from the components which have been discussed so far in that many of its characteristics are determined by the needs and limitations of a human being.

The alphanumeric key layout is conventionally a copy of the layout designed (without conspicuous success) to provide even loading for the fingers of nineteenth-century typists in the early days of the mechanical typewriter. What now seems to be an arbitrary, if not positively random, distribution of the characters, has been maintained in the face of determined efforts to improve it, and is so strongly established that there is little likelihood of its being usurped.

Minor variations exist — for example, the French prefer to place 'A' where the British and Americans have a 'Q' — but basically the international layouts for typewriter keyboards are adopted without demur by VDU manufacturers.

A few special applications have been catered for by highly specialised developments. These include:

A keyboard with letters alphabetically arranged
A number block only

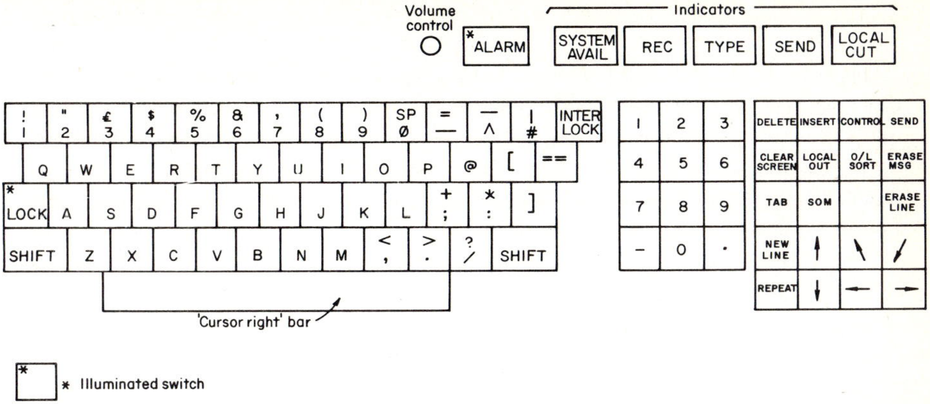

Figure 2.7. Typical complex keyboard layout, including number block and a selection of control and function keys. Indicator lights are included.

Touch-sensing devices which can be labelled by software for use in situations where disciplined and rapid action is called for, as in air traffic control situations, or where the entry is by a totally untrained operator.

The standard keyboard also embodies a number of specialised keys which permit the editing and cursor movements already referred to, and included are the keys which initiate any conversation between the terminal and the outside world, other than the local operator, for example 'SEND' or 'TRANSMIT', which are the release operations which consign data to communications lines.

Each key has to be identified to the VDU logic, and it is common to arrange for the key to generate, either directly or indirectly, the appropriate ASCII code. A number of techniques permit this. The most commonly employed device is for the key contact to be encoded by a logic section which has a discrete input for each key, and a corresponding 8-bit output when strobed.

Single make or break contacts can be provided in a number of ways and ingenious designs have been evolved. A *magnetic reed relay*, in which the operating magnet is carried on the stem of the key movement, is very popular, but other devices such as *capacitive sensors* or *Hall effect sensors* are also used.

The encoding logic must also include exclusion circuits which determine which, if any, of two or more keys simultaneously depressed take precedence; and, more exotically, whether *two-key rollover* or *N-key rollover* is permitted. Rollover occurs when two keys depressed in the time sequence A then B with simultaneous overlap, and then released in the same order, will record the characters in the sequence A then B when they are released. The commonly accepted standard is to permit *N*-key rollover (certainly to the level where *N* is 2) but to exclude simultaneously depressed keys ('two-key lock out').

The alternative to single-contact keys and subsequent encoding is to employ key mechanisms which are fully encoded during manufacture. The usual method of achieving this is to use multiple-winding magnetically coupled key plungers which generate a full coded output when depressed. A trigger mechanism is often included which allows the output to be substantially independent of key depression rate.

The keytops are important ergonomically. A selection of shapes, sculptured to varying degrees, is available and commercially assembled keyboards are comfortable and effortless to use. Some manufacturers introduce an artificial click sound which restores the audio feedback mechanism that operators often like. The pitch and disposition of the keys is more or less determined by standard practice, and there are preferred layouts provided by the European Computer Manufacturers Association which are bringing a high measure of conformity to keyboard layout, appearance and operation.

Most keys are expected to be durable for a long and arduous life, and they are '*two-shot moulded*', that is, the character is deeply recessed in the key top and indelibly filled by a second colour during the two-stage moulding process. This yields a key top which is virtually immune to wear. Engraving, followed by a filler, is often used for special characters where the cost of two-stage moulding tools is not warranted.

The keyboard is usually detachable from the VDU, as a matter of convenience. The separation distances from eye to screen and from hands to keyboard are not always best served by a rigid assembly, and frequently the screen is raised while the keyboard remains at surface level. This separation also makes possible the concept of shared displays, in which more than one operator can make use of the VDU, with one or more keyboards available for control.

The keyboard can also conveniently carry a number of system indicator lights which are provided for operator information. These are not always sited on the keyboard; some of them are related to the screen information and can be sited alongside it, but illuminated action keys which indicate that the required operation has been initiated are convenient and helpful at keyboard level.

Alarm sounds and lights can be mounted at this point, as can system indicators — indicating that the terminal is being polled, for example, or that the line communication system is operational.

Communication interface

There are a number of ways in which communication with the outside world can be established and maintained, and all of them have been employed by VDUs at one time or other. They divide into two main groups.

Unbuffered

Each key depression is consigned to line as it occurs, and an appropriate character (where relevant) is placed in the screen slot designated by the cursor either by the key operation OR by the processor. This latter method is known as *echo mode* and is commonly used in interactive teletypewriter operation.

Buffered

Each key depression enters data, or control, characters into the terminal only, the data appearing on the screen and remaining available for editing. Consignment to line is a deliberate control function initiated by the operator.

In the buffered mode the need to buffer transmitted information is not directly related to the need to buffer the data for refresh purposes, already dealt with above, but, as a matter of convenience, the information is often retained in the buffer store already provided for refresh. In some cases, all the stored information is visible, but there are VDUs in which more data storage is provided than is needed for refresh, from which selected sections can be made visible.

Transmission is possible at a great variety of data rates, dependent on available media and networks. Data can be transmitted at bit speeds up to 9600 per second with relative ease, and it is also possible to interface 48 kilobit per second lines, or to consign data to the input/output lines at speeds up to the synchronous bit rate of the refresh store, which may be two million bits or more per second.

However, there are difficulties introduced by the serial circulating store, which is almost universal. Characters appear at the input/output window in serial order at a fixed rate. This rate is not in any way related to the rate at which the line can accept or give information. Suitable buffering is required to match the two different speeds. This takes the form of a short buffer which accepts information as it appears at one end and yields it up as required at the other. More or less information is taken in depending on the rate of transmission, and this is electronically controlled.

For example, a line operating at 2400 bits per second can accept or deliver

300 characters of data per second. During a single cycle of refresh (at 60 times per second), five characters may, therefore, be needed or have to be accepted. A short buffer of say seven characters can deal with this rate, taking characters as required from the line and making them available in bunches of five or so to the refresh store, and vice versa.

It is clear that at higher data rates more and more characters are involved, so longer buffers are needed to achieve a match. This requirement makes a data rate of say 48 kilobits per second particularly arduous. At much higher rates, it is possible to reach synchronism with the refresh store, and strip data off (or put it on) at refresh rate, but in these circumstances there is an implicit requirement for the other end of the line to be flexible enough to deal with this independently clocked medium. Some elasticity can be introduced by a serial buffer under dual control, which can make the designer's life a little easier.

In its simplest form, a communication line carries data only to and from the host system. The basic Teletype-compatible VDU is elementary in just such a way. Single characters can be despatched at a time totally under the terminal's control, and characters can be received from the line at a rate not exceeding the capacity of the terminal to accept them. No additional characters are involved in enveloping the message, and the only security check permitted is the addition of a parity bit per character. These basically simple transactions are in common usage on time sharing systems, and they rely on a single dedicated line per operating terminal, though this dedicated line can be a dial-up line at lower data rates.

In more complex networks, many terminals can share a higher-speed data line for economic reasons. Higher-data-rate lines cost more than lower-rate ones, but if terminals can share the lines the advantage rapidly reverts in favour of the shared high-speed line. Sharing a line brings its own range of requirements, and typically the very least of these would be twofold:

- A system which prevents more than one terminal from engaging the communication system at any one time
- An address system which determines which of many possible devices is actually engaged in conversation at a given time

These requirements led to the development of '*polling systems*' in which conversations are always under the control of, and instigated by, the central site, which therefore has the ability to eliminate confusion and simultaneous conversations on the communications network. To complicate matters, the basic polling system can also be used to shape the system and to seek information about the system usage; these are refinements over and above the necessary minimum.

In simple polling routines, the terminal is required to indicate that it has a need to converse, and then it is sent an instruction that it may do so. Two terminals cannot therefore simultaneously engage the line unless the central site instructs them to do so. Since this is unlikely to be fruitful, the central site guards against this possibility. The central site can despatch a message to any terminal at any time, since it is aware of the state of the lines and totally in control of them.

It is immediately evident that there may be times, because of operator involvement, when it would be inconvenient for the terminal to become involved in a transaction with the host system. To meet this system refinement, *status polls* have been generated in which the basic poll, saying 'go ahead, it's your turn', has been modified, by characters contained within it, to send a message more like 'what is your present state — do you wish to converse?'. Responses to messages of this kind may be automatic, or they may be operator-initiated. For example, if the keyboard is being used for data preparation, a status reply saying so will usually be automatic, as also will be a request to involve a *hard copy unit* which is unable to comply, either because it is already involved in an incomplete transaction or for some more basic reason like not having any paper loaded or not having its mains power switched on.

Polling systems can be quite complex, and each mainframe manufacturing company has evolved a procedure most appropriate to its system needs. It does not surprise the development engineer that they are all different.

Addressable polls are not all similar either, even in the relatively straightforward need to provide discrete identification of the terminal under control. Single- or double-address characters are used, and the range of addresses more or less confined by system requirements. For example, in one such system odd addresses are interleaved by even addresses, the terminal responding to either equally; the sequence odd, even, odd, even, etc. provides a continuous monitor that the previous transaction was processed. This is sometimes known as '*toggling*' or '*toggle polling*'.

Because the polling of each terminal in a system is time-consuming (the '*polling overhead*'), especially as in a practical situation most terminals which are polled have no wish to negotiate any transaction, site polling systems have been devised in which all the terminals at one site are grouped to a controller, or line sharing device, which can act on behalf of all of them. Any terminal requesting a transaction will be recognised by the controller, and, on receipt of the next site poll, will be connected to the system. In the event that more than one terminal is in the request state, the controller resolves the contention by designating only one of them to enter the transaction. The other remains in a queue which will include other terminals as they come into the request state.

Figure 2.8. General rear view, cover removed, showing modules in situ.

The whole assembly (Figure 2.8)

In addition to the above basic elements of the VDU other items are necessary, as will have been inferred by the reader. An adequate power supply system is one of these, and this will be returned to later. The other is, of course, the logic pack. In earlier VDUs, the logic elements were often dispersed. Decisions and control outputs were made by discrete components with defined performance suiting the need, mounted freely throughout the assembly as and where required. This form of construction gave an amorphous assembly, having complex interconnections, and frequently it was not susceptible to modular breakdown either for manufacturing and testing or for subsequent maintenance.

Modular construction was necessary for the reasons given, and VDU design has become correspondingly tauter and more disciplined. It is well known that modularity generally carries with it a modicum of redundancy, particularly in the areas where deliberate breaks are necessary in order to provide modular independence. The number of plugs and sockets usually increases, for example.

The solution to modularity in the computer industry has been the subject of intensive development for many years and the growth of minicomputers and, more recently, microcomputers has forced the pace. It was logical therefore to

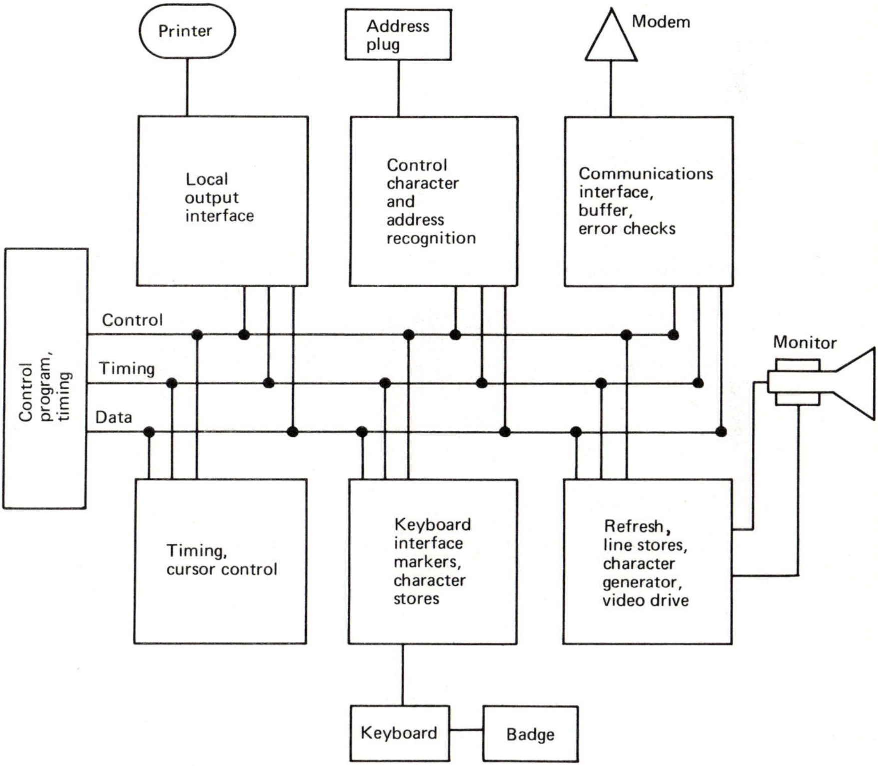

Figure 2.9. Typical simplified block diagram showing the conventional layout of a minicomputer system. Highways carry all necessary data and controls from each module as required.

conceive of the VDU as a mini-controlled device, and most present-day designs are based on this concept.

In effect, as can be seen from Figure 2.9, the VDU comprises a number of functional sections, which to a large extent are synonymous with the peripherals and other internal elements of a mini-processor system. They are connected by *highways* carrying the three basic elements of control: data, timing and control information. Transfers internally between sections of the VDU and between the VDU and the outside world are organised by the control logic section, and take place by movements on the various highways.

This step also introduces the concept of control by program, since it is relatively simple to place the control of transfers logically at the disposal of a series of logical instructions, similar to a computer program. Most modern designs employ this principle and stored-program VDUs are commonplace (Figure 2.10).

Programmable read-only memories have made possible a calculated variety of program capability without too high an economic penalty, and VDUs can be produced having a preferred range of characteristics almost to order.

Figure 2.10. Control program board, showing top right, the control elements, four programmable read-only memories, with space for the addition of two more. More still can be included for extended program control.

The power supply

The power requirements for a VDU are complicated by the need to provide a number of different potentials, some of them at comparatively high current. Three or four voltage rails are needed to energise the semi-conductor elements employed, and of course there are EHT voltages for the CRT, a low voltage for its heater, and an adequate supply for the illumination of indicator lamps.

Reasonable stability is called for in order to maintain the display performance under variable load conditions, and close protection is desirable in order to protect the circuitry from damage.

Transformer-coupled supplies were common, and their use made it necessary to adopt quite elaborate magnetic screening techniques to reduce the spot deflection induced by stray magnetic fields to acceptable levels.

Energy-regulating supplies are gradually supplanting the iron cored component version, and, although the design of these supplies is more difficult, successful units are available, and they bring the benefits of:

Higher efficiency, and therefore lower dissipation
Less magnetic radiation
Much lower weight

By careful design it is also possible to secure stable conditions in spite of wide variations of input power, and to meet the requirements of British Standards for immunity to interference, and for safety in use.

Summary

It is of course quite natural to extend the concept of programmability, making the devices more flexible, and in processing terms more powerful. The display described in this chapter is what is now termed a stand-alone display, that is, a device which is self-contained and needs only a power source and a communication line in order to fulfil its functions. There are other ways of combining the basic building bricks, and other chapters will deal with them. It is sufficient here to state that the various elements detailed above can be combined in an endless variety of ways, giving advantages in cost or performance for some applications.

Centralising the control and refresh and buffer storage, for example, permits the design of cheap monitors which can be shared by a powerful controller. This development can also permit the attachment of a variety of other peripherals — printers, tape units, communication lines, etc. — which can sufficiently enhance the performance of the system so as to reduce its dependence on the host system.

The distribution of logical power, and shared facilities, in this way is beyond the scope of the present chapter, but it should not be overlooked that cost-effective techniques of this kind are in a continual state of flux, and no single optimum solution for universal use is either possible or likely in the foreseeable future.

The short-term future holds the prospect of intensive developments along the presently acceptable lines to reduce the cost or increase the effectiveness of VDUs in the field. New components are under development, as are new ways of interconnecting systems, and these will add considerably to the ease, flexibility and acceptability of terminals in general applications.

In the longer term, it is possible that more direct human interfaces will be developed but these are scarcely predictable by present technology. The VDU is an acceptable medium for use and its further development will extend its influence by improving its performance and reducing its effective cost in response to the needs of the computer-based society.

3 Communications

Peter Burton

Introduction

The effectiveness of visual display terminals as a means of access to a computer depends at least as much on the speed, cost and reliability of the communication network linking the terminals to the computer mainframe as on the design of the terminals themselves. Not only is the network likely to cost some two-thirds as much as the VDUs, but its characteristics will critically affect the performance of the complete system, particularly the speed with which the computer responds to an input by the VDU operator.

The system designer therefore needs to take great care in specifying the communication network lest the costs become needlessly high and user acceptance turn out to be poor owing to human frustration caused by excessively slow response from the computer.

There are two fundamentally different ways of linking VDUs to a computer: direct *parallel connection*, treating the VDUs as peripherals in much the same way as tape or disc drives; and serial transmission. Parallel connection can be used if the terminals are installed in fairly close proximity to the computer, that is, usually within a couple of thousand feet (600 metres) at most. Data transfer rates of many thousand characters per second are easily achieved and the computer can usually service the VDUs rapidly, with little noticeable delay in data transfer, although of course the speed of response to an operator's input may be limited by other factors such as disc access times.

Direct parallel connection requires a number of parallel paths, usually at least 10, between terminal and computer to transmit the data characters and control signals. When distances are short and on the user's own premises a multi-way cable easily meets this requirement. When longer distances must be covered, however, or terminals are off the premises, the user has no alternative but to use telephone, telegraph, or other special circuits provided by a 'common carrier' such as the British Post Office. Each circuit provides at best only a single path in each direction and cannot be used for parallel data transfer. For transmission over such circuits the serial transmission method must be used. The principles of serial transmission are described in the next section and the rest of this chapter is entirely concerned with communication networks using this technique.

However, before we leave the subject of direct parallel connection, it is worth emphasising that there is no commonly accepted parallel interface standard for linking terminals to computers. Two well-defined interfaces, BS 4421 and CAMAC, are ignored by most suppliers of computers and VDUs, and some independent terminal suppliers do not offer a parallel interface at all on their equipment. Unless they are prepared for a great deal of special work on both hardware and software, most users will find that direct parallel connection is feasible only with the larger data processing systems, using the mainframe supplier's own terminals or a 'plug-compatible' version thereof. Users who want to use minicomputers or to have an unrestricted choice of terminals, particularly the lower-cost varieties, will usually find it easier to use the serial communication method even for local connection to the computer.

Serial transmission of digital data

Serial representation of data — the start–stop method

Data characters in a computer system are represented by a data code, each element of which consists of a group of bits (binary digits), each one of which can take the value 1 or 0. The group of bits is called a word or byte. The object of *serial data transmission* is to send these bytes from point to point along a single line or channel.

The method used is to define successive short intervals of time as representing successive bits in the byte, as in Figure 3.1. Two possible conditions, termed *mark* and *space* (from telegraph terminology), are imposed on the line by the transmitting terminal to represent binary 1 and 0 respectively. If the receiving terminal samples the line at the same intervals starting at the same time, it will be able to re-create the byte at the receiving end. (Note that we have used the word 'terminal' to designate either end of the line. In practice the 'terminal' at one end is usually the computer.)

To allow the receiver to start its sampling at the correct instant, the transmitter always reverts to a mark condition for at least one interval at the end of each byte and always goes to a space condition for one interval before starting to send the next byte, as in Figure 3.2. The eight time intervals have now been increased to ten. There is always a transition from mark to space at

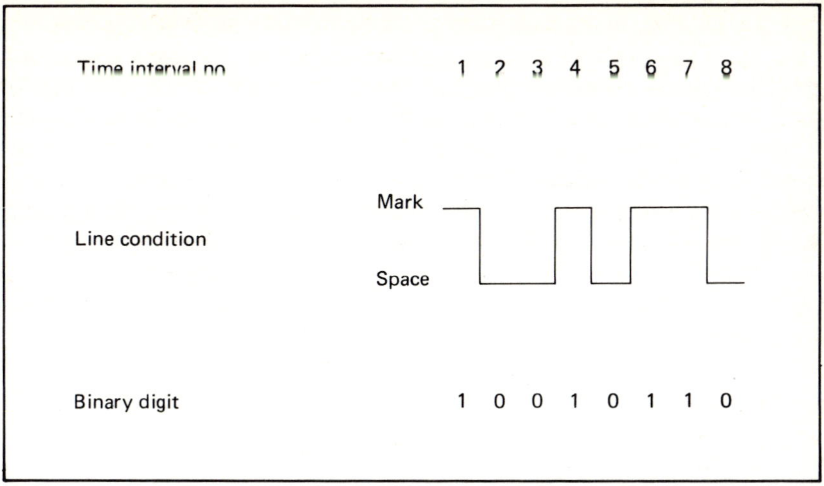

Figure 3.1. The start–stop method of serial data transmission.

the start of the first interval and this is used by the receiver to indicate that it must start sampling at the second interval. After this, the receiver continues to sample until the ninth interval whereupon it re-sets itself and waits until it sees another transition from mark to space. The first and tenth intervals are called respectively the 'start bit' and 'stop bit'. They do not convey data but serve

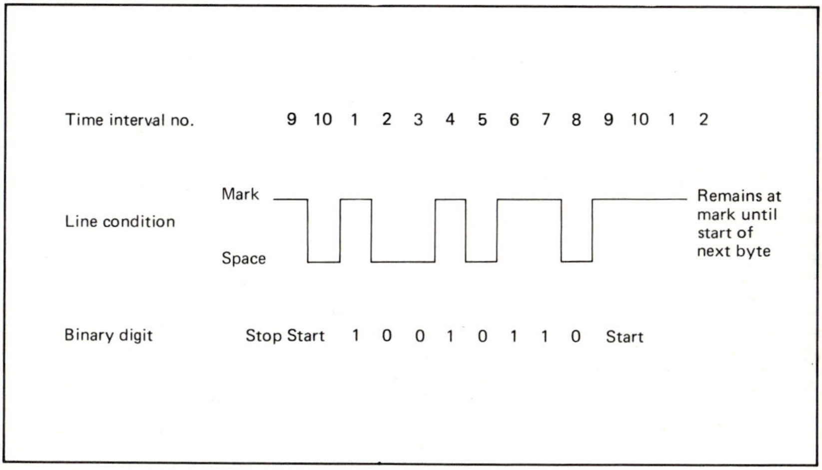

Figure 3.2. Transmission of a 10-bit character.

merely to provide an unambiguous indication that a byte is about to be transmitted. The complete sequence is often referred to as a 10-unit envelope or 10-bit character. Certain mechanical terminals require more than one time interval to reset after each byte. For example, the model 33 teletype uses an 11-unit envelope including two stop bits, and the same 11-unit envelope is often used by Teletype-compatible VDUs.

To ensure correct operation, the time intervals used by transmitting and receiving terminals must obviously be the same. The transmitting and receiving rates, usually expressed in bits per second (bps) are controlled by internal timing devices, termed *clocks*, on the two terminals. In the method of transmission just described the receiving clock is started afresh for each byte received and there may be a gap of any length of time between bytes. This technique of data transmission is known as '*start–stop*' operation.

Synchronous transmission

Although it is relatively simple to implement, start–stop transmission is inefficient because 10 or 11 bits have to be transmitted to convey each 8 data bits. Better use of the channel would result if only the data bits had to be sent, the start and stop bits being eliminated. This can be achieved by the technique known as *synchronous transmission.* It uses fundamentally the same method as start–stop but instead of re-starting on each byte, the receiver clock is allowed to run continuously and is synchronised with the transmitter clock. Bytes are transmitted continuously without gaps so long as the transmission lasts, and if there are gaps in the data stream the transmitting terminal must insert 'idle' bytes as 'padding'.

Clearly, for correct operation, the receiver must start to sample the line at the correct instant, that is, on the first data bit of the first byte, otherwise it will be out of step and will misinterpret every succeeding byte. The necessary 'byte-synchronisation' is achieved by inserting before the data stream two or more SYNC (i.e. synchronisation) bytes having a predetermined bit pattern which can be recognised by the receiving terminal and used to identify the start of the first data byte.

The synchronisation of the receiver clock with the transmitter clock is usually achieved by carrying the transmitter clock information down the channel with the data. A channel which can carry clock information in this way is called a *synchronous* or *isochronous* channel and is described more fully in a later section. A channel that cannot carry clock information is called *asynchronous* or *anisochronous.*

It may help the user if we point out that there is a confusing overlap in the terminology used to describe the method of transmission between terminals with that used to describe the characteristics of the data channel itself. A synchronous terminal is one using the byte-synchronous method as distinct from the start–stop method. Although most synchronous terminals are used on synchronous (isochronous) channels some models can also be used on asynchronous (anisochronous) channels. Start–stop terminals are sometimes called 'asynchronous' terminals but in fact many of them can operate on either asynchronous (anisochronous) channels or synchronous (isochronous) channels.

In the remainder of this chapter we shall use the terms *synchronous* and *start–stop* to describe the terminals and *isochronous* and *anisochronous* to describe the data channels.

Synchronous or start–stop?

Both the start–stop and synchronous transmission methods are widely used with VDUs. The Teletype-compatible models are start–stop, while most of the data-orientated VDUs supplied by the mainframe manufacturers are now synchronous. A number of independent suppliers offer VDUs with the option of either type of operation. Although many designers will probably opt for synchronous transmission in data entry and enquiry response applications, users of minicomputers may still find (in early 1976) that hardware and software costs are significantly lower when start–stop operation is used. At the end of the day, it is a matter of balancing speed of response and communication channel costs against possible savings in hardware and implementation costs.

Data codes

The great majority of VDUs are designed to use one of two international data codes, the ISO 7-bit code (Table 3.1) or the EBCDIC 8-bit code (Table 3.2).

The ISO code promulgated by the International Standards Organization provides for minor national variations. The United States version of the ISO code is the U.S.A. standard code for information interchange, usually abbreviated to USASCII or simply ASCII, and the user will find that most terminals available use this code. The major exception is IBM terminal equipment, which increasingly uses the EBCDIC code. EBCDIC, short for 'extended binary coded decimal interchange code' (so called because it is an extension of the 4-bit binary coded decimal representation), is an 8-bit code giving 256 combinations. ASCII is a 7-bit code giving 128 combinations of

Table 3.1. The ISO 7-bit coded character set

Bits b_7					0	0	0	0	1	1	1	1
b_6					0	0	1	1	0	0	1	1
b_5					0	1	0	1	0	1	0	1
b_4	b_3	b_2	b_1	Row \ Column	0	1	2	3	4	5	6	7
0	0	0	0	0	NUL	(TC$_7$)DLE	SP	0	(@) (3)	P	` (4)	p
0	0	0	1	1	(TC$_1$)SOH	DC$_1$	!	1	A	Q	a	q
0	0	1	0	2	(TC$_2$)STX	DC$_2$	" (6)	2	B	R	b	r
0	0	1	1	3	(TC$_3$)ETX	DC$_3$	£ (2)(7)	3	C	S	c	s
0	1	0	0	4	(TC$_4$)EOT	DC$_4$	$ (2)	4	D	T	d	t
0	1	0	1	5	(TC$_5$)ENQ	(TC$_8$)	%	5	E	U	e	u
0	1	1	0	6	(TC$_6$)ACK	(TC$_9$)SYN	&	6	F	V	f	v
0	1	1	1	7	BEL	(TC$_{10}$)ETB	' (6)	7	G	W	g	w
1	0	0	0	8	FE$_0$(BS)	CAN	(	8	H	X	h	x
1	0	0	1	9	FE$_1$(HT)	EM	)	9	I	Y	i	y
1	0	1	0	10	FE$_2$(LF) (1)	SUB	*	(8)	J	Z	j	z
1	0	1	1	11	FE$_3$(VT)	ESC	+	; (8)	K	([) (3)	k	(3)
1	1	0	0	12	FE$_7$(FF)	IS$_4$(FS)	,	<	L	(3)	l	(3)
1	1	0	1	13	FE$_5$(CR) (1)	IS$_3$(GS)	–	=	M	(]) (3)	m	(3)
1	1	1	1	14	SQ	IS$_2$(RS)		>	N	^ (4)(6)	n	‾ (4)(5)
1	1	1	1	15	SI	IS$_1$(US)	/	?	O	_	o	DEL

1 The controls CR and LF are intended for printer equipment which requires separate combinations to return the carriage and to feed a line. For equipment which uses a single control for a combined carriage return and line feed operation the function FE$_2$ will have the meaning of 'New Line' (NL). This substitution requires agreement between the sender and the recipient of the data. The use of this function 'NL' is not allowed for international transmission on general telecommunication networks (Telex and Telephone networks).

2 For international information interchange, $ and £ symbols do not designate the currency of a given country. The use of these symbols combined with other graphic symbols to designate national currencies may be the subject of other Recommendations.

3 Reserved for national use. These positions are primarily intended for alphabetic extensions. If they are

not required for that purpose, they may be used for symbols and a recommended choice is shown in parentheses in some cases. Some restrictions are placed on the use of these characters on the general telecommunication networks for international transmission.

4 Positions 5/14, 6/0 and 7/14 of the 7-bit set table are normally provided for the diacritical signs 'circumflex', 'grave accent' and 'overline'. However, these positions may be used for other graphical symbols when it is necessary to have 8, 9 or 10 positions for national use.

5 For international information interchange position 7/14 of the 7-bit set table is used for the graphical symbol (overline), the graphical representation of which may vary according to national use to represent ~ (tilde) or another diacritical sign provided that there is no risk of confusion with another graphical symbol included in the table.

6 The graphics in positions 2/2, 2/7, 5/14 of the 7-bit set table have respectively the significance of 'quotation mark', 'apostrophe' and 'upwards arrow'; however, these characters take on the significance of the diacritical signs 'diaeresis', 'acute accent' and 'circumflex accent' when they precede or follow the 'backspace' character.

7 For international information interchange position 2/3 of the 7-bit set table has the significance of the symbol £. Within a country where there is no requirement for the symbol £, the symbol # may be used in that position.

8 If 10 and 11 as single characters are needed (for example, for Sterline currency subdivision), they should take the place of 'colon' (:) and 'semicolon' (;) respectively. These substitutions require agreement between the sender and the recipient of the data. On the general telecommunication networks, the characters 'colon' and 'semicolon' are the only ones authorised for international transmission.

Table 3.1 and the above Notes are extracts from BS 4730, reproduced by permission of the British Standards Institution, 2 Park Street, London, W1A 2BS, from whom complete copies can be obtained.

which 32 are reserved for control functions. In serial data transmission systems the ASCII code is always sent as an 8-bit group, the additional bit being used as a parity check bit (*see* p.84).

Full and half-duplex transmission

A communication channel is described as *full duplex* if data can be transmitted simultaneously in both directions at the same time. If data can be transmitted in either direction but only in one direction at any one time, the channel is said to be *half-duplex*. The process of changing the direction in which data can flow is called 'turning the line round' and the time taken to do this is called the 'turn-round time'.

Many terminal networks which do not actually require data to be transmitted both ways at the same time nevertheless use full duplex data channels, because the turn-round time of the channel would lead to unacceptably long response times from the computer. Another reason for avoiding half-duplex operation is that to turn the line round needs special functions in the computer software and in the terminal and computer interface hardware. Networks using low-cost minicomputer and/or simple Teletype-

Table 3.2. EBCDIC code

EBCDIC	Bit Configuration	EBCDIC	Bit Configuration	EBCDIC	Bit Configuration	EBCDIC	Bit Configuration
NUL	0000 0000	SP	0100 0000		1000 0000	PZ 7/11	1100 0000
SOH	0000 0001		0100 0001	a	1000 0001	A	1100 0001
STX	0000 0010		0100 0010	b	1000 0010	B	1100 0010
ETX	0000 0011		0100 0011	c	1000 0011	C	1100 0011
PF	0000 0100		0100 0100	d	1000 0100	D	1100 0100
HT	0000 0101		0100 0101	e	1000 0101	E	1100 0101
LC	0000 0110		0100 0110	f	1000 0110	F	1100 0110
DEL	0000 0111		0100 0111	g	1000 0111	G	1100 0111
	0000 1000		0100 1000	h	1000 1000	H	1100 1000
RLF	0000 1001	.	0100 1001	i	1000 1001	I	1100 1001
SMM	0000 1010	¢ [	0100 1010		1000 1010		1100 1010
VT	0000 1011	.	0100 1011		1000 1011		1100 1011
FF	0000 1100	<	0100 1100		1000 1100	⑁	1100 1100
CR	0000 1101	(	0100 1101		1000 1101		1100 1101
SO	0000 1110	+	0100 1110		1000 1110	⑇	1100 1110
SI	0000 1111	|	0100 1111		1000 1111		1100 1111
DLE	0001 0000	&	0101 0000		1001 0000	MZ 7/13	1101 0000
DC1	0001 0001		0101 0001	j	1001 0001	J	1101 0001
DC2	0001 0010		0101 0010	k	1001 0010	K	1101 0010
TM	0001 0011		0101 0011	l	1001 0011	L	1101 0011
RES	0001 0100		0101 0100	m	1001 0100	M	1101 0100
NL	0001 0101		0101 0101	n	1001 0101	N	1101 0101
BS	0001 0110		0101 0110	o	1001 0110	O	1101 0110
IL	0001 0111		0101 0111	p	1001 0111	P	1101 0111
CAN	0001 1000		0101 1000	q	1001 1000	Q	1101 1000
EM	0001 1001		0101 1001	r	1001 1001	R	1101 1001
CC	0001 1010	!]	0101 1010		1001 1010		1101 1010
CU1	0001 1011	$	0101 1011		1001 1011		1101 1011
IFS	0001 1100	*	0101 1100		1001 1100		1101 1100
IGS	0001 1101	)	0101 1101		1001 1101		1101 1101
IRS	0001 1110	;	0101 1110		1001 1110		1101 1110
IUS	0001 1111	¬	0101 1111		1001 1111		1101 1111
DS	0010 0000	–	0110 0000		1010 0000	RM 5/12	1110 0000
SOS	0010 0001	/	0110 0001	—	1010 0001		1110 0001
FS	0010 0010		0110 0010	s	1010 0010	S	1110 0010
	0010 0011		0110 0011	t	1010 0011	T	1110 0011
BYP	0010 0100		0110 0100	u	1010 0100	U	1110 0100
LF	0010 0101		0110 0101	v	1010 0101	V	1110 0101
ETB	0010 0110		0110 0110	w	1010 0110	W	1110 0110
ESC	0010 0111		0110 0111	x	1010 0111	X	1110 0111
	0010 1000		0110 1000	y	1010 1000	Y	1110 1000
	0010 1001		0110 1001	z	1010 1001	Z	1110 1001
SM	0010 1010	7/12	0110 1010		1010 1010		1110 1010
CU2	0010 1011	,	0110 1011		1010 1011		1110 1011
	0010 1100	%	0110 1100		1010 1100		1110 1100
ENQ	0010 1101	_	0110 1101		1010 1101		1110 1101
ACK	0010 1110	>	0110 1110		1010 1110		1110 1110
BEL	0010 1111	?	0110 1111		1010 1111		1110 1111
	0011 0000		0111 0000		1011 0000	0	1111 0000
SYN	0011 0010		0111 0010		1011 0010	1	1111 0001
	0011 0011		0111 0011		1011 0011	2	1111 0010
PN	0011 0100		0111 0100		1011 0100	3	1111 0011
RS	0011 0101		0111 0101		1011 0101	4	1111 0100
UC	0011 0110		0111 0110		1011 0110	5	1111 0101
EOT	0011 0111		0111 0111		1011 0111	6	1111 0110
	0011 1000		0111 1000		1011 1000	7	1111 0111
	0011 1001	6/0	0111 1001		1011 1001	8	1111 1000
	0011 1010	:	0111 1010		1011 1010	9	1111 1001
CU3	0011 1011	#	0111 1011		1011 1011		1111 1010
DC4	0011 1100	@	0111 1100		1011 1100		1111 1011
NAK	0011 1101	'	0111 1101		1011 1101		1111 1100
	0011 1110	=	0111 1110		1011 1110		1111 1101
SUB	0011 1111	"	0111 1111		1011 1111		1111 1110
						EO	1111 1111

compatible VDUs are therefore often constrained to employ full duplex working.

The need to make future systems compatible with satellite communication channels which involve relatively long transmission delays and therefore cannot be turned round quickly means that most will use full duplex techniques.

Network configurations

Minimising communication costs

The telephone lines or other transmission media used for data communication are so costly that most of the techniques used in terminal networks are concerned with ways of transmitting the maximum amount of data through the smallest possible number of lines. The system designer needs to establish the best compromise between line costs and transmission speed by choosing from the network configurations reviewed below.

The point-to-point network

In a *point-to-point network* each terminal is connected to the computer by its own direct communication line, as in Figure 3.3. In some ways this is an ideal arrangement since the terminal and computer have immediate access to each other at all times so that there are no transmission delays. The computer software is simplified, since any data sent from the computer interface to which the line is connected will go to the terminal on that line and to that terminal alone; also, data arriving at that interface is known to have come from that same terminal. The speed of response is maximised, because the full speed and capacity of the line are devoted to the one terminal.

However, for a VDU, point-to-point operation is usually highly inefficient

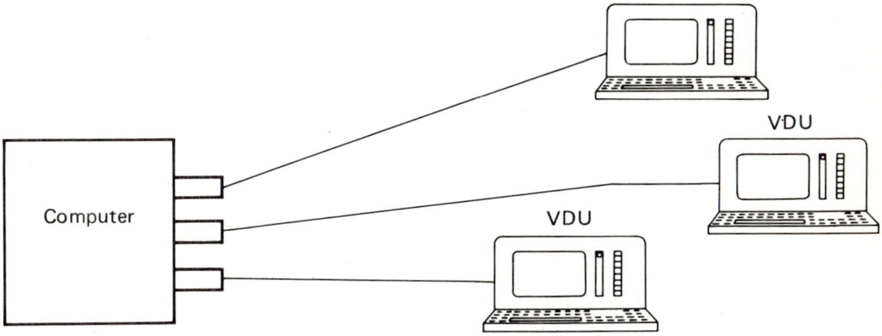

Figure 3.3. Point-to-point network.

because for most of the time the VDU is neither transmitting nor receiving data. Instead, the operator is keying, or just thinking about his or her response to the latest information displayed. The utilisation of the communication channel rarely exceeds a small percentage of the maximum possible.

The polled network

An obvious way to improve the utilisation of a point-to-point communication line is to connect a number of terminals to the same line. This can be done by *clustering*, that is, connecting several terminals to the line at the same point; by *multi-dropping*, that is, connecting terminals to the line at different points along its route; or by a combination of the two methods. The arrangement is shown in Figure 3.4.

The economics now look much better, since a number of terminals can be served by only one line and one computer interface. However, to avoid confusion on the line, the computer software must determine when each terminal is allowed to transmit and must also be able to 'select' each terminal uniquely before sending data so that only the appropriate one receives the information. This technique is known as *polling*.

The polling method has the advantage that each terminal gets the benefit of the full speed of the line when transmitting or receiving but has the limitation

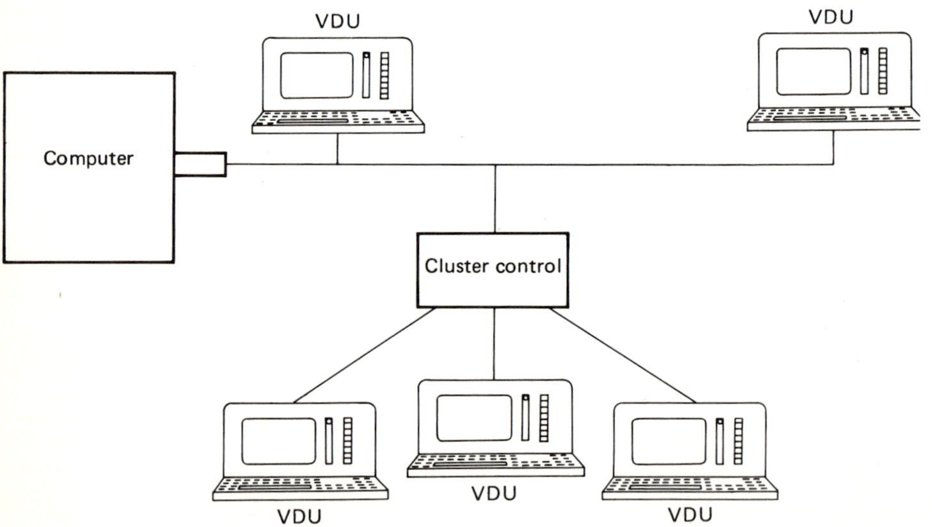

Figure 3.4. A polled network.

that there may be a delay in response from the computer when several terminals need to transmit or receive at the same time. The probability of any given delay can be estimated mathematically (by queuing theory) given the number of terminals, the speed of transmission of which the line is capable, and the length of the data blocks or messages flowing between terminals and computer. In many practical systems at least four or five terminals can share a line without the response time becoming unacceptably long. It often turns out, however, that the factor limiting the number of terminals on one line is the need to protect the system from the consequences of a line failure, rather than the speed of response.

The weaknesses of the polling method include the need for more complex and expensive VDUs, precluding the use of the low-cost, Teletype-compatible devices, the requirement for special software, and the dependence of several terminals on the reliability of one communication line.

Multiplexed networks

A technique which allows a number of simple, low-cost VDUs to share a communication line, introduces almost no delay and requires no special computer software involves the use of multiplexers.

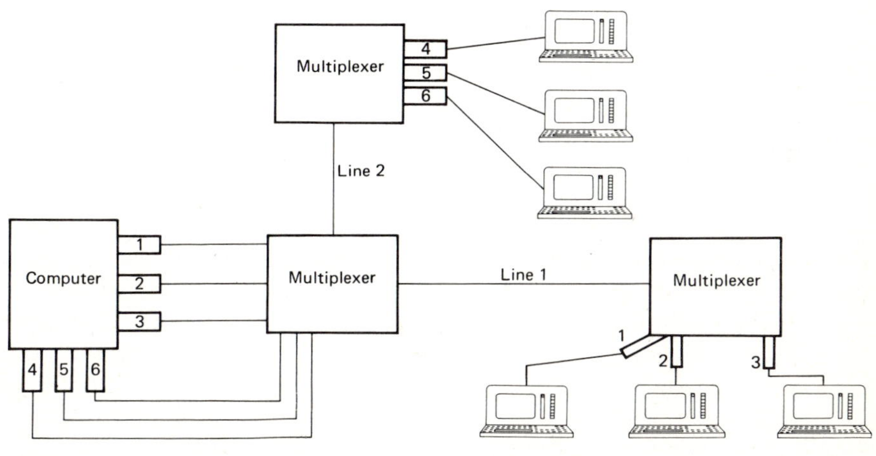

Terminals 1,2,3 share line 1; terminals 4,5,6 share line 2

Figure 3.5. A multiplexed network.

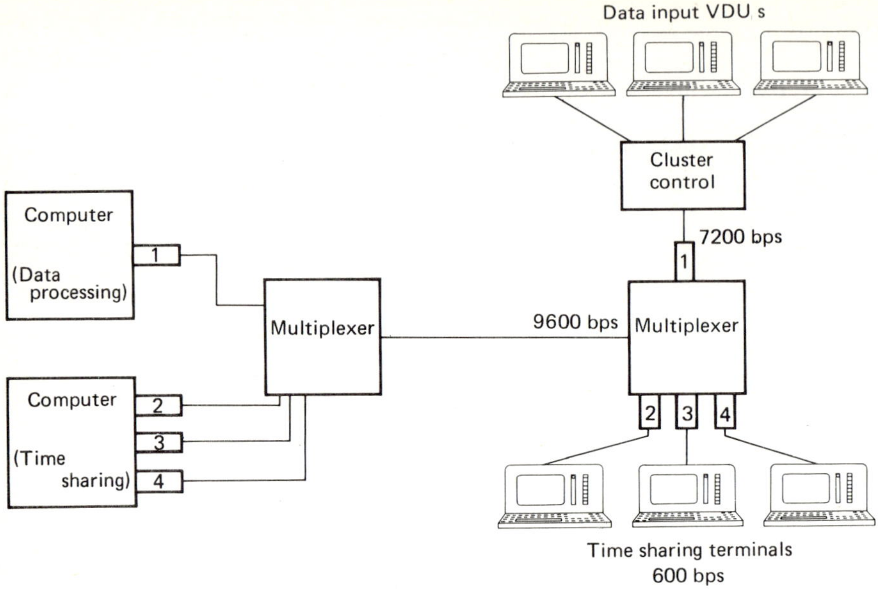

Figure 3.6. Network combining multiplexing and polling.

Multiplexing has the effect of dividing the communication line into a number of independent subchannels, all of which operate simultaneously but at a lower speed than that of the line itself. Each subchannel is connected to a terminal at one end and to a computer interface, or 'port', at the other end, so that unlike the polled network, the multiplexer network does not economise on computer hardware. Figure 3.5 shows the principle.

The relatively low speed of the subchannels (approximately equal in modern systems to the speed of the line divided by the number of subchannels) makes the technique unsuitable for those VDU applications where whole screensful of data must frequently be transmitted, since the operator would rapidly become frustrated waiting for the page to build up. But for applications where short messages are exchanged, as in general-purpose time sharing and simple enquiry applications, channel speeds of 300 bps (30 characters per second) or 600 bps (60 characters per second) are often quite adequate. At these speeds 20 to 40 subchannels can be obtained from an ordinary telephone circuit.

The major benefit of multiplexed networks is undoubtedly the simplicity, low cost and ease of implementation. Modern multiplexer systems are totally 'transparent' and may be added to an existing minicomputer or time sharing system without any modifications to hardware or software. They are particularly useful in networks of simple, low-cost start–stop terminals.

The techniques of multiplexing and polling may of course be combined in one network. Multiplexing is simply a technique of splitting a communication channel into a number of subchannels of the same or differing speeds. A subchannel so derived may have several terminals connected to it controlled by polling. It is beyond the scope of this book to deal with all the possible types of network configuration, but an interesting practical case, shown in Figure 3.6, is the use of a multiplexer to enable several low-speed time sharing terminals to share a line with a cluster of polled VDUs, which are controlled from a different computer. Users on the remote site get the benefit of access to two types of computer service with the use of only one telephone line working at 9600 bps. All terminal users appear to have independent access to the computer. The data input VDUs have a high data rate (900 characters per second, with an isochronous 7200-bps channel to the computer) which can write a screenful of data in 1 or 2 seconds, while the time sharing users have access to a standard computer service using low-cost Teletype-compatible VDUs at the very satisfactory rate, for them, of 60 characters per second, with no noticeable delays in transmission.

Concentration

Multiplexing, as we have seen, is the technique of dividing a communication channel into a number of subchannels. In practical systems these subchannels are rarely loaded to capacity all the time. The total capacity of the channel can be substantially increased by dynamically allocating channel space to each subchannel according to the data throughput actually occurring on each one. The net effect is either to increase the capacity of each subchannel or to increase the number of available subchannels, or both.

The technique is called *concentration* and the equipment employed is called a *concentrator.* Concentrators, usually consisting of a minicomputer with a program specially written for the particular network, have been in use for some years but suffer from certain disadvantages compared with multiplexers. Reliability of hardware and software is lower and the devices are usually not 'transparent'; that is, their use implies modifications to the interaction between computer and terminals, with software modification being needed in the computer. Recently, however, a new form of concentrator, the ***intelligent multiplexer*** or *network processor*, has appeared on the market. This type of device is fully transparent and by making extensive use of firmware the reliability is made comparable with that of the best multiplexers. The intelligent multiplexer also brings other advantages, including detection and correction of errors.

Switched networks

Large users of computers often have a need to support more terminals than they have 'ports' on the computer. Also, they may have several different classes of service offered on several different computers which they require to be available to all terminal users. In these cases a switched network is required, with built-in *contention* to provide service on a first-come-first-served basis.

Switching and contention can be provided by using an ordinary telephone PABX (private automatic branch exchange) for each group of computer ports. The terminal users then dial the number of the service they require, using the Post Office telephone network; if all ports are in use they obtain a normal 'engaged' signal.

Alternatively, line switching equipment specifically designed for computer users, often termed 'PACX' for 'private automatic computer exchange', may be used. A PACX is generally much smaller and more reliable than a traditional PABX, can work at higher speeds with a lower error rate, and can establish a communication link from the terminal to the computer much more rapidly than is possible by dialling. When the computer service desired is fully occupied the PACX sends an explanatory message to any user who tries to obtain access.

Message switching systems designed for control of teleprinter networks handling administrative traffic can sometimes be used to switch terminals between different computer services. If the message switcher has a so-called line-switching or conversational connection feature and supports ASCII-coded terminals it will probably be suitable for that purpose. Each group of computer ports is given an 'address code' and the user can access the service simply by typing in the appropriate code. Message switchers usually provide only anisochronous channels at relatively low speeds and are likely to handle only start–stop VDU terminals used on time sharing applications.

Communication lines and services

Lines for data transmission

So far in this chapter we have referred to communication lines or channels without being precise as to their physical nature. In fact the most commonly used medium for transmission, both nationally and internationally, is the telephone system. Links may be established by dialling on the Post Office switched public network or by leasing lines from the Post Office and international 'carriers'. Of course, in neither case does a physical line exist in the sense of copper wires joining the two points, except for very local connections. Telephone channels for transmission other than locally are grouped together in carrier systems using co-axial cable, microwave, or even satellite links. The copper wires exist only at the two ends, and ironically it is these relatively short 'tails' or 'local loops' which are subject to the electrical interference which produces much of the noise and consequent data errors in telephone transmission.

The *telephone network* is designed, naturally, for voice transmission and it turns out that channels giving the most acceptable voice quality cause serious distortion of the 'square waves' (*see* Figure 3.2) used for serial digital data transmission. Much of the complexity in high-speed data transmission equipment arises from the need to compensate for line distortion, a process known as *equalisation.*

The Post Office and other 'carriers' will provide leased lines especially equalised or 'conditioned', which improves the quality of data transmission to some extent, but nothing can be done to improve the quality of channels established by dialling on the public network; in this case the communication equipment must be able to tolerate or correct for transmission errors.

Some users may be able to lay their own private telephone wires for transmission of data within their own building or site, and this has the advantage, as we shall see later, of removing restrictions on the equipment that may be connected to them.

Leased telephone lines are available either as '4-wire' or '2-wire' circuits. The former provides in effect two independent channels, one in each direction, while the latter provides one channel usable in either direction. A dialled connection is always 2-wire, although a 4-wire connection can be made by dialling two calls on separate telephones.

In some countries the 'carriers' are starting to provide networks especially designed for serial *digital data* transmission. In the U.S.A. there is AT & T's 'DDS' service, offering leased channels, and Datran's 'Datadial', offering very fast (less than 1 second) dial-up connections. There are also some so-called 'value-added' networks which detect and correct errors that occur in transmission and guard against loss of data. Many of these networks operate on the *packet switching* principle in which the channels are shared by all users and data is transmitted in short, interleaved blocks, each accompanied by its own destination code. Examples are TELENET in the U.S.A., TRANSPAC in France, and the Post Office's experimental network, EPSS, in the U.K.

The specialised *digital data networks* have a much lower error rate than the telephone network although, as previously mentioned, the local loops connecting the user to the network can introduce errors even when the main system is well-nigh perfect. One cannot generalise about error rates on different networks since the spread is very large even on lines of the same type or on the same line at different times of day. The system designer should consult one of the specialist works on the subject, since error rate can have a dramatic effect on data throughput and hence on response time in a VDU network. However as a guide, the telephone network in the U.K. is commonly taken to have an error rate of the order of 1 bit in 10^5, with a spread of 10^4 to 10^7. Digital data networks, depending on whether they contain built-in error correction, can be expected to be several orders of magnitude better. (But remember the local loops.)

The oldest digital data network is of course the telegraph network, including its dial-up service known as Telex. It is not much used for computer data transmission since the maximum operating speed is very low, typically 50 bps, corresponding to $7\frac{1}{2}$ characters per second. The physical transmission methods used in the telegraph network are, however, often used for data transmission over private wires (*see below*).

Transmission methods

The physical method of transmitting the type of waveform shown in Figure 3.2 depends on the type of network employed. On private wires for transmission over short distances, up to a few miles, a voltage can be applied directly to the line, say positive for '1' and negative for '0'. Alternatively a current can be made to flow for '1' and switched off for '0'. These methods, often known respectively as 'double-current telegraph', and 'single-current telegraph' or current loop, are simple and involve only low-cost hardware at the interface between the terminals and the lines. They are well suited to minicomputer systems using low-cost, start–stop VDU terminals and can be used up to quite high speeds, for example, 9600 bps if distances are reasonably short.

Such signals cannot however be sent over the *telephone system.* For telephone transmission the digital waveform from the terminal must be converted into signals within the voice frequency band, which extends from about 400 hertz to 3000 hertz. This process requires the connection of a *modem* between any terminal and telephone line. The higher the speed of operation, the more complex and costly is the modem. In 1976, prices range from £50 or less for a 30-bps modem to over £3000 for a 9600-bps modem.

The complexity of high-speed modems arises directly from the problems of compressing the signal into the relatively narrow voice channels of the telephone system, of minimising the effects of line distortion and noise, and of preventing interference to adjacent telephone lines or channels. Where private wires are available many of these limitations are removed and a simplified form of modem costing much less can be employed for transmission at up to 9600 bps or higher over distances of several miles. These devices are variously referred to as *baseband modems, limited-distance modems, line adaptors* and *long-line drivers*.

Limited-distance modems are also used for connecting terminals to some *digital data networks*. The DDS network, for example, employs such devices and calls them 'data service units' or DSUs. The DSU is a relatively low-cost device, much cheaper than a modem at speeds of 2400 bps and above. Note however that some value-added digital data networks such as the U.K.'s EPSS use the telephone network for some or all of their communication links. In these cases the user may still need to use modems for access to the network.

Specialised digital data networks usually provide facilities for both *isochronous* and *anisochronous* channels (*see* p.66). In the case of the telephone network or private wire networks it is the modem which determines whether the channel is isochronous or not. Modems operating at 2400 bps and above are almost always isochronous, whereas those working at lower speeds are usually not. One reason for this is that the higher-speed modems use a data-encoding technique which requires the transmission of 'clock' information to allow the receiving modem to restore the data to a form comprehensible to the terminal. Limited-distance modems, designed for operation at 2400 bps and above, even though they may not need the 'clock' for their own operation, are usually designed to permit transmission of clock information for use by the terminals.

The system designer should also be aware that the modem, rather than the telephone line, can determine whether the channel is half-duplex or full duplex (*see* p.69). At speeds of 2400 bps and above, full duplex transmission needs a 4-wire circuit. At 1200 bps and below however, modems are available that can establish two channels, one working in each direction, on a 2-wire circuit. With these modems, full duplex working can be achieved on a dialled telephone connection.

Standards for modems

International standards for modem operation in the form of the V series recommendations of the CCITT exist for speeds up to 2400 bps. (CCITT is the Comité Consultatif International de Télégraphie et Téléphonie, an international body belonging to a United Nations organisation, namely the International Telecommunications Union.) Recommendations for 4800 and 9600 bps operation may be agreed in 1976 but at present there is no standardisation at these speeds, and a variety of techniques are in use by different modem suppliers. This should cause no difficulties for the designer of private networks using leased or private lines since compliance with the standard is important only when modems from different suppliers are to be mixed on the same line, as when carrier-supplied modems are used at the ends of an international link.

Conditions for using transmission lines

Post Offices and other telecommunication carriers impose certain restrictions on the use of their lines for data transmission. Unfortunately the rules vary from country to country and the designer of an international network should be sure to understand the limitations that will apply in each area.

The purposes of the restrictions include: prevention of interference with other users of the carriers' facilities, prevention of damage to installations or injury to maintenance staff; and, in cases where the carrier himself provides modems or other equipment, elimination of competition from other equipment suppliers.

The restrictions vary from complete prohibition of the use of privately supplied modems or related equipment on all or part of the carrier's network, to a requirement that all equipment to be connected be approved by the carrier. In the U.K., the principle generally applied is that private equipment, provided that it has been approved for connection, can be used on leased telephone lines but that only Post Office-supplied equipment may be used on the public dialled network. There are a few exceptions, but these apply only where the user can prove that he has a genuine need which cannot be satisfied by Post Office equipment.

Pricing of transmission facilities

Prices of national and international *leased telephone lines* terminating in the U.K., including those conditioned for data (the *Tariff T circuits*), may be obtained from the Post Office. As an example, a 200-mile 4-wire Tariff T circuit within the U.K. at 1976 prices is charged at about £3000 p.a. To this must be added the cost of the modems which for 9600 bps operation would add another £1000 p.a. at each end, making a total of £5000 p.a. for the complete link. Expressed in capital terms, the cost of this link would be about £20 000, equivalent to the cost of perhaps 10 VDUs, illustrating the fact that the cost of the communication links can be comparable with the cost of the terminals they support.

No digital data links are publicly available in the U.K. at present but it is interesting to compare the cost of the 200-mile telephone link just quoted with the cost of a 200-mile link using DDS in the U.S.A. Although the vastly greater distances covered by telecommunication networks in the U.S.A. make direct comparison with the U.K. somewhat unfair, the fact that the cost of the DDS link is only about one-third that of the telephone link does emphasise the advantage of the specialised service. A significant factor is that the DSU connecting users to the DDS network is very much cheaper than the 9600-bit modems needed on the telephone link, but the charges for the line are also much lower.

Communication interface standards

A true international standard — CCITT V24

The CCITT recommendation V24 which defines an interface standard for connection of data terminals to modems for serial data transmission is extremely important. It is the only interface standard that is accepted internationally by all computer manufacturers. Using this interface, system designers can be sure at least that their terminals will be compatible with the computer at the hardware level.

The CCITT specification (and its U.S. version the EIA specification RS 232) does not however lay down the method to be used for controlling the flow of information across the interface. This is a function of the computer software and varies from system to system (*see* p.83). What the CCITT specification does define is a set of control functions and the way each function is to be used. A standard pin position on the interface connector is given for the circuit controlling each function; another specification defines the electrical characteristics of the control circuits. Most data terminal equipment, however, makes use of only a small number of control circuits selected from the full list of over 40.

Local connection to the computer

Although the V24 interface is intended for transmission of data over telephone links equipped with modems, it can be used for local attachment of terminals to a computer if the cable run is no more than about 50 feet. Used in this way the V24 interface allows the system designer to connect almost any terminal to any computer giving him an unrestricted choice of equipment. Note that if control signals, as well as data and clock information, are to be transmitted across the interface it is necessary to connect the devices together through a 'modem simulator', a simple unit which interconnects the control circuits so that each device 'thinks' it is connected to a modem.

Operation with modems — leased lines

In addition to the circuits used to transmit data and clock signals in both directions between the terminal and modem, the circuits most commonly used in leased-line operation are REQUEST TO SEND, READY FOR SENDING and CARRIER DETECTOR. This is not a comprehensive list but will serve as an example of the control functions at work.

REQUEST TO SEND is used to turn the modem transmitter on and off. For example, in a multi-point polled network a terminal recognising its own address must turn on REQUEST TO SEND in order to turn the modem transmitter on before it can send its response to the computer. In fact the terminal will be designed not to transmit until it has received from the modem the signal READY FOR SENDING, indicating that the modem has had time to establish contact with the receiving modem at the computer end and is ready to transmit. When the terminal has finished sending data it must turn off REQUEST TO SEND to turn off the modem transmitter, thus freeing the line for transmission from another terminal attached to another modem.

The CARRIER DETECTOR circuit is turned on when the modem receives a signal from the modem at the other end of the line and has prepared itself to accept data. The terminal is designed such that CARRIER DETECTOR must be present on the interface before it will accept data; this is a safeguard against disturbances on the line being interpreted as data by the terminal before the modem to modem link is actually established.

Operation with modems — dialled connections

Where the computer must automatically answer a dialled call made by the terminal user, additional CCITT V24 circuits are used, including CALLING INDICATOR, DATA TERMINAL READY and DATA SET READY.

The presence of ringing current on the line causes CALLING INDICATOR to turn on. If the computer is functioning, it will be programmed to have DATA TERMINAL READY already on; this being so the modem will automatically connect itself to the line, equivalent to lifting the receiver on a telephone and so answering the call. The modem at the same time turns on DATA SET READY, telling the computer that the modem is connected to the line. The computer then turns on REQUEST TO SEND, switching on the modem transmitter which responds with READY FOR SENDING. The terminal user can hear the carrier tone emitted by the modem transmitter and can connect his own modem and terminal to the line by using the pushbuttons provided on his telephone. The computer senses the presence of this modem by the CARRIER DETECTOR and thereby knows that the link is now established in both directions.

When the user has finished and hangs up, this action disconnects his modem from the line. CARRIER DETECTOR at the computer end thus turns off, indicating to the computer program that the call is finished. The computer turns off REQUEST TO SEND and DATA TERMINAL READY. The latter action causes the modem to disconnect from the line, equivalent to 'hanging up'. The modem then turns off DATA SET READY, confirming to the computer that the disconnection has been made, whereupon it turns DATA TERMINAL READY on again to prepare for the next call.

Other V24 interface functions

The two preceding sections give an idea of how the V24 control circuits can be used. It is impossible in this book to cover the full range of possible functions, which include, for example, circuits to change the modem operating speed and to control automatic dialling equipment.

The system designer needs to have a clear understanding of the control sequences involved in half- and full-duplex, point-to-point, and multi-point operation, and to be aware of the time delays involved in these sequences when using different types of modem and different types of circuit, since these factors can greatly influence the response times and line utilisation of his system.

Information flow control

The purposes of flow control

Information flow control has two main purposes: to ensure that information is transmitted when and only when the communication channel is free and the appropriate terminal devices are ready to receive it; and to prevent corruption or loss of information during transmission.

Communication protocol

The term *protocol* is used to describe the set of rules governing information flow in a communication system. The simplest protocol is that used by Teletypes or Teletype-compatible devices, sometimes called *free-wheeling* terminals. In this method, data can be transmitted at any time, without preamble. The computer transmitting the data does not know whether it is received or not, or whether it is received correctly. Each data character has a 'parity bit' which is added to the 7 data bits of the ASCII code to form either an odd number of '1's (odd parity) or an even number of '1's (even parity). The parity bit allows the receiving device, if suitably equipped, to detect errors in individual characters involving corruption of a single bit, but not corruption of pairs of bits. However there is nothing in this simple protocol to inform the sending terminal if an error is detected.

If greater data security is required, additions may be made to the protocol, for example, an 'answer back' check. Here, the computer, before transmitting any data, sends a control character usually known as ENQ. The terminal is designed to respond automatically with its own 'answer back code', a sequence of characters which identifies the terminal uniquely, enabling the computer to check that the communication channel is open, that the terminal is switched on and working, and that the right terminal has been selected. It represents a big advance on the simple method, but data can still be lost or corrupted during the subsequent transmission.

Let us now consider a more complex protocol which includes a *polling* routine as well as more comprehensive error control. In polling, the computer transmits a predetermined sequence of control characters, plus the 'address' of the terminal consisting of one or more characters. This message is recognised by all the terminals on the channel but only the one recognising its own 'address' is arranged to respond. Different messages are used to invite the terminal to indicate whether it has data to send or not or whether it is able to receive or not. Until an appropriate message is sent to a terminal it will neither transmit nor accept data. Thus confusion on the line is avoided, only the desired terminal is selected, and the computer can ensure that nothing is sent unless the terminal is ready and working correctly.

Automatic repeat request systems

A method of checking the subsequent transmission of data is needed, and also a means of informing the transmitting terminal or computer when an error occurs, so that the transmission may be repeated. The solution is to break up the transmission into blocks each of a convenient number of characters, and to add to each block a check character or characters computed from the data characters according to a predetermined process. By re-computing the check character(s) at the receiving end, it can be determined, to a certain level of probability, whether an error has occurred. The receiving terminal can then send a control character to indicate either that the block was error-free, or that an error occurred and a re-transmission is required. These two responses are usually designated 'ACK' for acknowledgement (i.e. all is correct) and 'NAK' for 'negative acknowledgement' (i.e. an error has been detected).

This protocol also guards to a high degree against total loss of data: if the terminal receives nothing or becomes inoperative it will respond with neither ACK nor NAK; the computer can of course be programmed to take appropriate action in such a case.

The error control system just outlined is one example of an ARQ system, standing for *automatic repeat request*. We will return to this subject later in the chapter.

Error-detection systems

One fundamental requirement of an ARQ system is the transmission of additional information with each character or block of data, such as the parity bit or the block check character (*see above*), which allows the receiving terminal to have a chance of detecting errors. This additional information is sometimes called 'redundant' and the techniques of error detection *redundancy checking*. There is a direct trade-off between the amount of redundant information and the probability that an error will be detected. Highly redundant systems not only give good error detection; they can also perform error correction without re-transmission, a technique sometimes called 'forward error correction'. However, most commercial communication networks rely on ARQ for error correction and employ only one or two characters of redundant data per data block.

The simplest system is called LRC (*longitudinal redundancy check*) or 'block sum check', and uses one 8-bit check character or byte per block computed by calculating a sort of lengthways parity bit; that is, on the assumption of even parity, the most significant bit of the check character is chosen to make the total number of '1's in the most significant bit positions of all characters in the block an even number, and so on with all the other bit positions.

The LRC check, combined with a parity check on each character, is quite a powerful error-detection technique but the bursts of noise that occur in telephone channels can create error patterns which pass undetected by this technique. A more powerful method, the *cyclic sum check* or *cyclic redundancy check* (CRC) is now very commonly used, most often with a check 'character' of 16 bits. Conceptually, the cyclic check works by using each bit several times in computing the check character rather than only once as in the LRC method. As a result, the chance of the error pattern produced by a noise burst remaining undetected is much smaller. It can be shown theoretically that all errors involving odd numbers of bits and all error patterns shorter than the check character will be detected by a CRC check. It has been estimated that the improvement in error rate compared with an unchecked system obtained by the CRC 16-bit method on typical telephone circuits is a factor of about 50 000.

There is a CCITT recommendation (V41) for a CRC 16-bit error detection system.

More complex protocols

The ARQ system described above is sometimes called a 'half-duplex' protocol because after each block is transmitted the sending terminal waits for a response from the other end. In satellite links, which have a long transmission delay time, the use of these protocols wastes considerable channel time while terminals wait for the responses. Throughput drops dramatically. To overcome this problem a full-duplex protocol is used. The sending end transmits block after block without delay and takes action only when it receives notification of an error. By this time, of course, several more blocks will have been sent. The system must therefore number the blocks individually and must keep blocks in storage for the time necessary for an error notification to arrive. The error notification must indicate which block is in error.

Two methods of error recovery are commonly used: either the erroneous block is re-transmitted by itself, or the sending terminal goes back to the erroneous block and sends it and everything that followed it, the receiving terminal discarding any block previously correctly received. The latter method is often called the 'go back N' technique.

Modern protocols specify more details concerning the exchange of data between terminals and computers than we have referred to so far, including for example the 'flag' or character used for synchronising the receiving terminal or padding the data in isochronous transmission; block length information and information about the purpose of the block (data, control function, etc). *Packet switching* networks have particular need of quite complex descriptive information about each block or packet to be included in the block.

Standardisation of protocols

At present (early 1976) there is no standardisation of protocols. Almost every mainframe computer manufacturer has his own, and some industries, such as airlines, also have their own protocols. Packet switching and other value-added networks (*see* p.77) have their own. There are considerable differences between these various protocols. The widespread use of programmable or 'intelligent' VDUs and other terminals in which the protocol can be written in software or firmware to the required standard is one way the industry is coping with this confused situation, but many users still feel themselves 'locked-in' to the mainframe supplier's own terminal equipment.

In truth, although commercial considerations have undoubtedly slowed progress towards a standard, the task of defining a universally usable protocol is exceedingly complex and there is a danger that the standard could be unwieldy and wasteful of communication channel capacity. Work on standards in proceeding under the auspices of several international bodies including the ISO and CCITT. A draft standard for the ISO 'High Level Data Link Control' or HDLC is available and IBM have already announced their 'Synchronous Data Link Control' or SDLC, which closely resembles it. It seems that SDLC, like its IBM predecessor 'Binary Synchronous Communication' protocol, may become a *de facto* standard for the industry.

The designer of a VDU network should certainly acquaint himself with HDLC and evaluate its relevance to his project before settling for one of the proprietary protocols.

Outlook

Forecasting the rate of progress of new techniques in a high-technology field like communications network design is a foolhardy exercise for a mere practitioner, and will not be attempted here. Important developments, however, are likely to include the wider use of *intelligent multiplexers* and network processors to achieve better channel utilisation and improved error performance on the telephone network; the increasing use of specialised *digital data networks*, both public and private; and a dramatic fall in the costs of satellite ground stations making very high-speed, virtually error-free digital data channels available at modest cost. This last development could have very profound implications for computer networks, perhaps allowing the use of distributed data bases and totally changing the economics of real-time data base access and processing.

4 Intelligence

Ian Richards

Introduction

Until fairly recently nearly all alphanumeric display units were *hardwired.* This means that three logical functions, namely (a) screen handling, data editing, etc.; (b) communications line handling; and (c) hard copy printer handling, were performed by hardware logic elements designed to perform those and only those particular functions. Thus the user of one of these alphanumeric display units was constrained to a single communications line protocol, a single set of data entry and editing facilities, and a printer facility which could give a hard copy of the screen contents to a fixed set of formatting rules.

If a particular application required special facilities then either difficult and expensive modification processes had to be carried out on an existing display unit or the display manufacturer had to develop a new display unit with facilities unique to that application.

Many of the problems of hardwired display units have been overcome by *soft-centred* terminal controllers which, in addition to emulating existing hardwired devices, can provide intelligent user-defined functions and in some cases provide off-line type facilities.

Programmable and intelligent terminal controllers are defined below.

A *programmable* terminal controller is defined as one whose responses to commands from either a terminal operator or any other external stimulus is specified in part or in whole by an internally held program capable of being changed. Terminals in which the program is held in storage elements which are read-only and difficult to change are essentially the same as hardwired terminals.

Programmable terminal controllers may be divided into two subgroups. *Non-intelligent* terminal controllers are capable of driving peripheral devices and of transferring data from one peripheral device to another. Any change made to the data, whether in content or format, has to be very simple and is carried out according to fixed rules. Emulation of existing hardwired devices falls into this class.

Intelligent terminal controllers are capable of all non-intelligent functions but also capable of modifying the data or their format according to program instructions and/or data content as specified by the user for the particular application. Additionally, intelligent terminals are sometimes capable of stand-alone, off-line operation.

Obviously there is an ill-defined dividing line between an intelligent terminal and a small stand-alone processing system. Certainly the intelligent terminal may be capable of capturing, processing, storing and retrieving data; in principle the only difference between an intelligent terminal and a small stand-alone processing system is its dependence upon a host processor. In this context, an intelligent terminal is considered as a device which, whilst operating normally, is connected to and is usually dependent upon a host mainframe computer. Any stand-alone off-line working is considered as an abnormal situation and used in the event that access to the mainframe is denied.

The reasons for intelligent terminal systems

Owing to the advances made in semiconductor technology, particularly in semiconductor storage elements, *large-scale* and *medium-scale integration* of components have now had a considerable impact upon terminal system design. Small 8-bit processors and storage elements are quite cheaply available on a single chip.

The situation is now such that terminal systems can be implemented having the same functional capability as previous hardwired solutions at lower cost. Decrease in cost is by far the major reason for the current trend to so-called 'intelligent' terminal systems. Many of the disadvantages of the hardwired approach are minimised if not eliminated with the more flexible programmed or microprogrammed systems.

Thus for the first time, the following truly essential functions of a terminal controller can be realised:

- The ability to use and share expensive peripheral facilities in a flexible and user-defined manner e.g. communications channel, printing facilities, backing stores
- The ability to perform expansion/compression and formatting of data, thus making more efficient use of backing store and communication lines
- The ability easily to interface specialised peripheral devices — point of

sale devices, ticket printers, etc.

The ability to perform user-defined processing functions

It must be emphasised that many applications do not require this degree of flexibility and sharing capability and therefore unless an 'intelligent' solution to a particular problem is somewhat cheaper than the present hardwired solutions, a user is unlikely to tolerate the additional operational problems which an 'intelligent' solution poses.

Thus intelligent terminals are now required by the market basically because they can perform the same functions as hardwired devices at a lower cost. Cost is undoubtedly of the essence.

The structure of intelligent terminal systems

Figure 4.1a shows the interfaces to a conventional display unit which is connected to a host mainframe processor and has connected to it a hard copy (printer) unit. Whether the unit is a stand-alone (i.e. single) display unit or a cluster of such units depends entirely upon the number of interfaces provided. The functions of this unit are simply defined as (a) providing a visual display of keyboard-entered or host mainframe-generated data; (b) providing data editing facilities; (c) providing a hard copy of display screen contents; and (d) providing transmission and reception facilities for data between the display and the host mainframe. Such displays could be, and usually were, implemented in random logic, that is, specialised and dedicated logic arrays.

Figure 4.1b shows the interfaces to an intelligent display unit (or cluster of units). In this case the number and type of interfaces is much larger. In addition to the interfaces shown in Figure 4.1a and mentioned above there could be (a) a second mainframe interface; (b) a backing store interface; (c) a supervisory operator interface; and (d) other peripheral interfaces.

Hardware

A possible hardware configuration of a terminal controller to implement these functions is shown in Figure 4.2.

The diagram shows a generalised *arithmetic and logic processor*, which is referred to as the *processor unit.* The processor unit drives two hardware interfaces, namely the store interface and the programmed input/output interface.

The store interface is a fast interface which may have connected to it (a) program store holding instructions which are to be executed by the processor

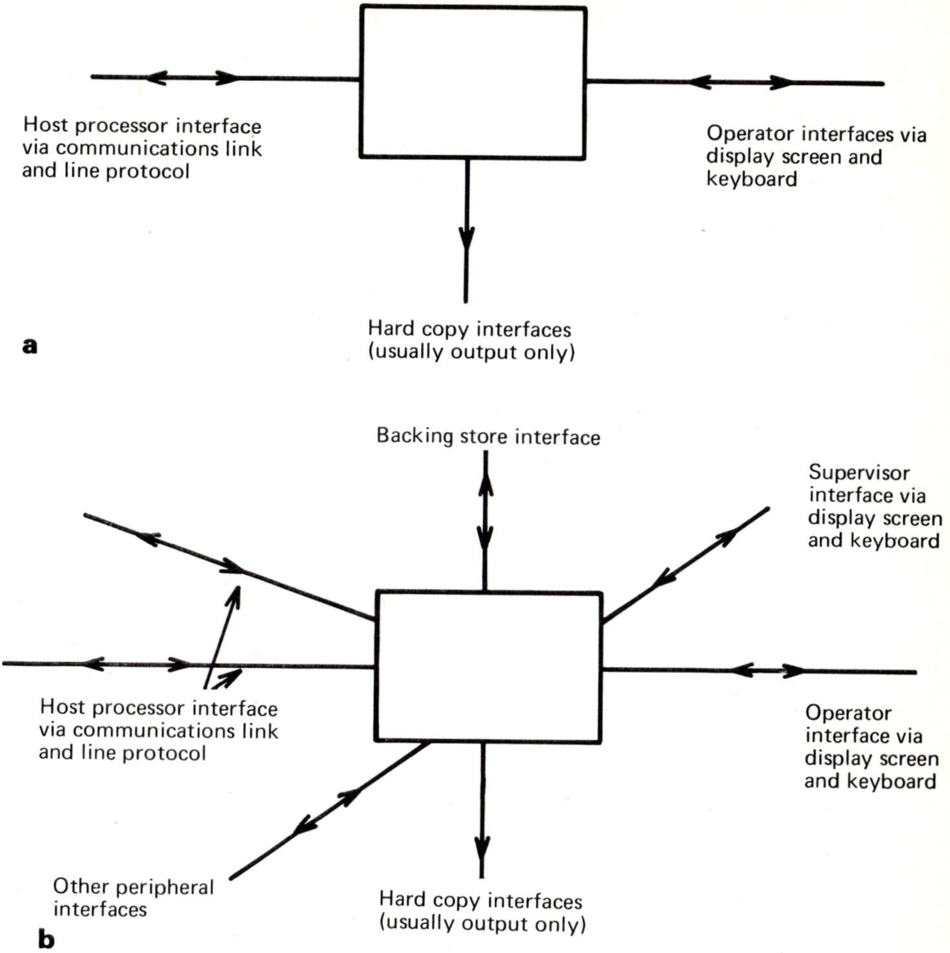

Figure 4.1. External interfaces.

unit; (b) a data store, for example buffer areas which may be temporary stores for blocks of data; (c) autonomous input/output processors such as a disc controller, which itself may drive a dual floppy or cartridge disc system.

The programmed input/output interface is a slow character-by-character interface to which the drive cards for various slow peripheral devices are attached, such as a line driver card to a modem, printer driver. Transfers across

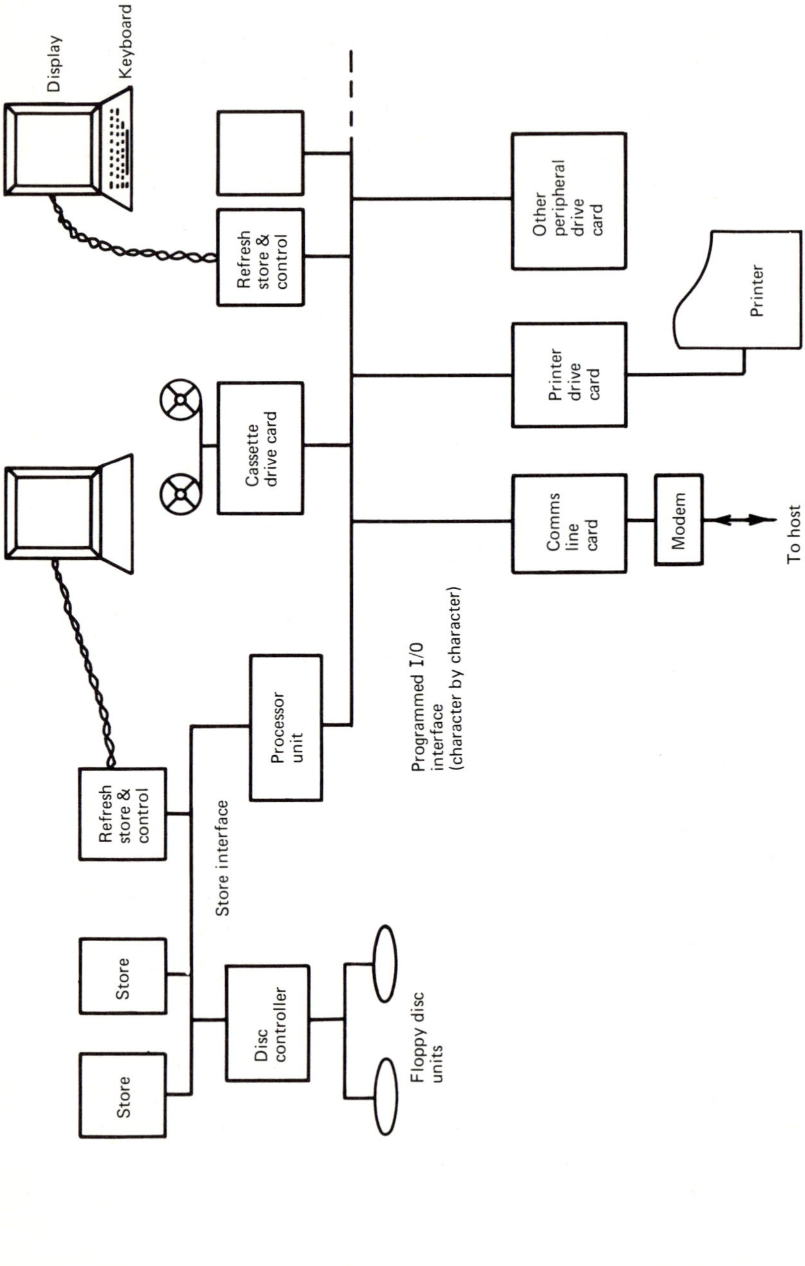

Figure 4.2. Possible hardware configuration of a cluster of intelligent alphanumeric VDUs.

this interface are effected under direct program control. Usually the fastest device connected to the programmed I/O interface is a communications line which may be operating at 9.6 kilobauds. This represents a transfer rate of 1200 bytes per second, which is usually the fastest transfer at which it is efficient to use the programmed I/O interface.

In Figure 4.2 the refresh stores for the alphanumeric displays are shown connected to both the store interface and the programmed I/O interface, since connection to either is viable. In the case where the refresh stores are connected to the store interface, reading and writing to and from the displays are merely normal store transfers; where the refresh stores are connected to the programmed I/O interface, then the equivalent reading and writing operations are merely normal peripheral transfers.

Software

In addition to the hardware configuration shown in Figure 4.2, there is obviously an equivalent software configuration, which is shown in Figure 4.3.

The *executive* or *organiser* provides a framework within which a number of systems and task programs may operate and provide the necessary control and communication between these programs. Additionally, the executive will provide facilities for interrupt handling, program scheduling, dynamic working store management, timer facilities, etc.

The *line control module*, together with the line driver hardware and modem, etc., provides the communication link to a host processor. The module will be entered either on timed activations or on request of an interrupt from the line driver hardware.

Typical facilities of the module would include:

Recognition of line control characters
Code conversion from line code to internal machine code
Decoding of terminal address
Organisation of responses to polls
Control of *transmission block checking* ('cyclic redundancy' check, 'vertical and longitudinal redundancy' check; *see* p.85).

The display control or *edit module* enables data for display and transmission to be edited in the refresh store of the display under control of the display keyboard. This module is entered on timed activations to read the display keyboards, and performs the functions of editing and echoing of characters to the displays. This module typically provides the following facilities:

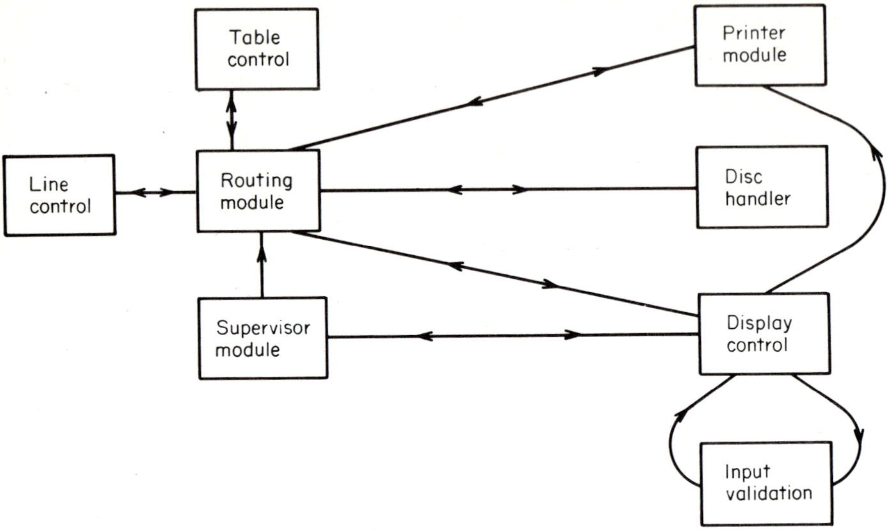

Figure 4.3. Possible software configuration of a cluster of 'intelligent' VDUs.

Display of alphanumeric characters and symbols
Cursor movements
Editing facilities (insert/delete, tab, selective erasures, etc.)
Definition of protected and unprotected fields
Execution towards displays of commands from the host processor

Each peripheral in the cluster can be defined by a *device control cell*, and for a display the cell would include the following information:

Cursor position
Control character/start of message positions
Keyboard status
Device status
Peripheral number within cluster
Physical I/O address

The printer module controls the printers connected to the system and is responsible for the formatting of data to be sent to the printer. Data for the printer could emanate from the display control or edit module (hard copy of screen contents) or the line control module (direct online printing).

The modules described above would be required for a non-intelligent application such as the emulation of an existing hardwired system. Intelligence could be added to the system by incorporating the following modules into the structure:

Standard applications programs for data *validation, formatting, spooling*, etc.

User-specified and/or written programs for, say, special application-dependent processing

Disc-handling and simple file-handling software for the support of the above programs

A *supervisory control module* whereby a designated display may be given extra control facilities in order to change the mode of operation of the whole cluster

A *table control module*, which receives data from the host processor as if it were itself a physical device; the data which it receives is used to update tables and lists which are accessed by other modules (principally the validation module) which require tables for the processing of data

The way that such a hardware and software structure may be used is discussed later in the chapter. The structure of the soft-centred terminal described in this section is not intended to be representative of any particular implementation nor is it necessarily exhaustive. It does, however, provide a general framework against which other implementations may be compared.

The first use of soft-centred terminals was to emulate existing, hardwired devices. Many intelligent terminals are based around these emulators, since they provide a basic vehicle for communication with a host mainframe and a defined and known operator interface. The reason for this is that in using intelligent terminals any repercussions on mainframe hardware and software ought to be avoided. The mainframe interface with the remote intelligence ought to be at application or user program level and not below that. Thus an intelligent display unit to be remotely connected to an ICL mainframe, say, should appear to the mainframe as an ICL-type device and not use a line control procedure and display control facilities alien to the ICL environment.

Program storage and program loading

Soft-centred terminals may have their programs held within both read-only and read/write storage elements. Read-only memories are non-volatile and may be divided into two types, *read-only memories* (ROMs) and *programmable read-only memories* (PROMs). In the case of ROMs the program instructions are incorporated into the device by means of a special mask during the manufacture of the semiconductor. PROMs are encoded by the application of electrical signals subsequent to the manufacturing process. Programs residing in ROMs or PROMs are often known as firmware. Any change which has to be made to the program in this case necessitates the creation of new ROMs or PROMs. Soft-centred controllers having this kind of program storage are, for all intents and purposes, hardwired and unintelligent.

The traditional means of read/write program storage was *core store*, which is now being replaced by semiconductor *random access memory chips* (RAMs). These elements are volatile and hence have to be loaded with the program instructions whenever power is removed from the device.

The problem then arises as to which is the most cost-effective way to load the program into an intelligent controller. Clearly if the controller has a disc or magnetic tape unit connected to it, for reasons other than program loading, then the program can be held on and loaded from that device. Any updating or new release of the programs may necessitate the distribution of discs or tapes to the relevant controller locations. There is no fundamental reason, of course, why the distribution of new programs should not take place via the communications link. Thus whilst the programs are stored more or less permanently on a disc, say, connected to the terminal controller, changes to the program are sent from the host mainframe to the terminal controller and written to the disc.

The distribution method outlined above is available only where the terminal controller has a suitable backing store. Many applications do not require those facilities and often the cost of a local loading device is prohibitive. One program loading scheme which can be used for exclusively on-line controllers is that of *teleloading*, in which the host mainframe sends the program to the terminal controller on demand, there being no local loading device. The line control program or a subset of it must of course be held in read-only memory in this case so that the controller and host mainframe may communicate at least at a level sufficient to allow the correct teleloading of the main program.

The power of terminal controllers

Clearly a terminal system designed specifically to be capable of 'intelligent' operation will carry some cost penalty when competing against a terminal system designed specifically, say, to emulate existing hardwired systems and consequently having inherently less power. The corollary is also true; a lower-powered programmable system will be overloaded and probably incapable of meeting the requirements of an application requiring remote intelligence.

The picture is, however, confused when connectivity is considered since system 'power' is consumed either by the servicing of large numbers of devices or by the performing of 'intelligent' functions. Consequently a spectrum of terminal system power can be conceived as follows:

Low power:	Low connectivity;	no intelligence
Medium power:	Low connectivity;	limited intelligence
High power:	High connectivity;	limited intelligence
	or low connectivity;	high intelligence

Connectivity

The average number of cathode ray tube terminals per cluster installed in the U.S.A. some time ago ranged between eight and nine units. The median cluster size is between five and six; half of all clusters have five or fewer terminals with a minimum of two.

It is expected that the number of small clusters, typically 4 devices, will grow more rapidly since this represents the installation of systems by new users. Large clusters, those with 8 or more terminals, will grow both in the number of installations and the number of devices per installation as current large-cluster users expand their applications and grow in volume. As a result the average number of devices per cluster will grow from 8 or 9 units in 1972 to about 11 or 12 units in 1976.

The above statistics have been generated from a survey of purely interactive clusters, primarily display-based. For applications of the *remote job entry* and *remote data terminal* type, connectivity is less of a problem since only one particular type of peripheral device is usually connected. This may be a line printer, card reader and punch or paper tape reader and punch or a mix, cassette tape, interactive display or keyboard printer (for remote job entry applications).

The coming of remote intelligence has, however, brought with it the possibility of mixed interactive and bulk systems, so that a user can work interactively during normal working hours with displays and then can use the same equipment (i.e. terminal controller) at night for, say, bulk printing. Thus while it may be unusual to require a terminal controller with sufficient power to run concurrently a large interactive cluster of displays and bulk peripherals, the terminal controller may have to have the physical capability of having such a mix of devices connected.

In general, it appears that a terminal controller should have the capability of simultaneously servicing at least 8 interactive devices but carry little cost penalty when only, say, 4 are connected. The capability should also exist for connecting the usual mix of bulk peripherals either alone or in some mix with the interactive devices.

Intelligence

Computer users are often conscious of the limited and poor performance of mainframe hardware and software components.

Dispersing intelligence outwards from the mainframe to the terminal system reduces the load on the mainframe and leads to a more efficient overall system. This approach is often very attractive to users capable of specifying and/or writing programs resident within the terminals. The theoretically correct approach to reorganise and sometimes rewrite some mainframe software is very expensive, probably not within the user's capabilities and usually will not be undertaken by the mainframe manufacturer.

The reasons for concentrating 'intelligence' within the mainframe rather than dispersing some of it to the terminal subsystem are very powerful, and include the following:

- Increase in system intelligence also increases intelligence to all terminals
- Cheap uncomplicated terminals can be used; this allows low maintenance and installation costs
- The number of terminals on system can be increased cheaply and quickly

Against these, however, are the advantages of remote intelligence:

- Reduction in communications line loading
- Reduction in mainframe loading
- Reduction in operator loading, i.e. the system is easier to use
- Possibility of a degree of stand-alone working in the event of a central site failure
- The terminal system need not necessarily be changed if host mainframe is changed

Large users are now demanding, not unnaturally, terminals which can work to any of their mainframes and having different line protocols at the flick of a switch. Indeed systems have been implemented which require the terminal controller simultaneously to communicate with two different host mainframes, having different line disciplines, with the connected displays being allocated to one or the other mainframe. The particular example in mind gives a good illustration of a relatively high-powered terminal controller in a high-connectivity, limited-intelligence mode. This particular controller is simultaneously remotely connected to IBM and Univac mainframes at speeds

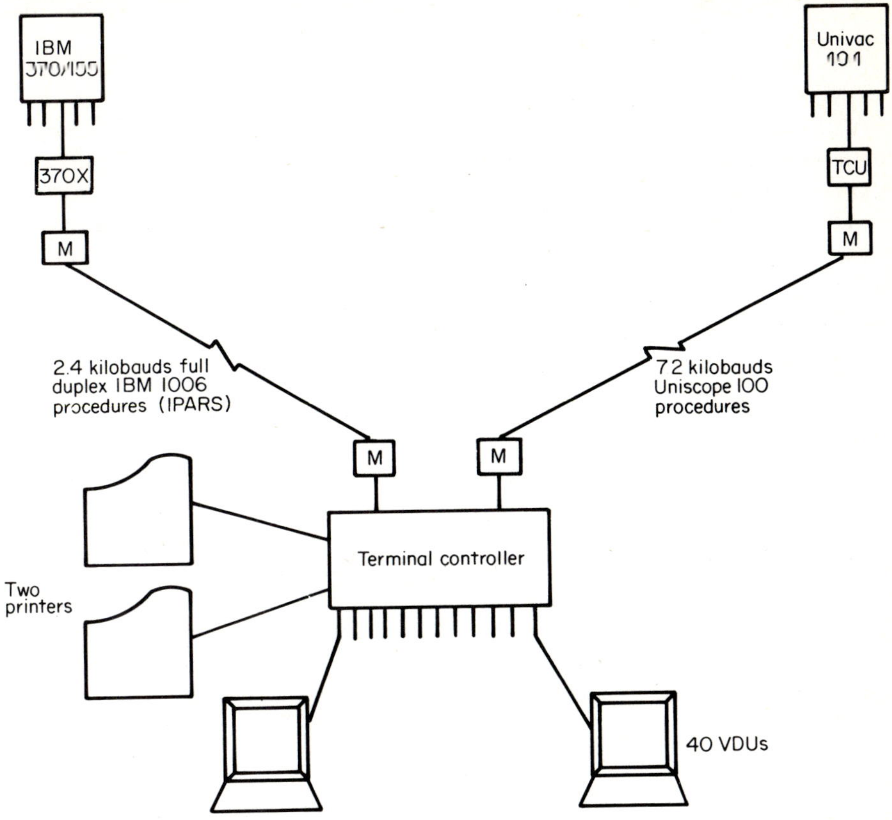

Figure 4.4. Large VDU-based cluster with simultaneous access to two host processors.

of 2.4 and 7.2 kilobauds respectively and supports 40 display units and two printers. Figure 4.4 shows the configuration.

The performance of soft-centred controllers

The phrase *soft-centred controller* has been introduced in order to define a class of terminal controllers which (a) are conventionally programmable, or (b) whilst having the appearance of being hardwired may in fact not be implemented in random logic but are more likely to be implemented with a generalised microprogrammed structure.

Inevitably and justifiably, the performance of a soft-centred terminal will be compared with the performance of an equivalent hardwired system in carrying out the same function. In such a comparison the soft-centred terminal does not usually match the performance of the hardwired counterpart. This is not particularly surprising since flexibility and enhanceability have to be paid for in some way. It is a fact that a generalised processor-based logic system cannot possibly emulate a specialised hardware-only system designed specifically to undertake a particular function, as far as speed of operation is concerned. Fortunately, however, the manifestation of poor performance in soft-centred systems is largely disguised owing to the fact that human operator responses are very slow in these terms.

Most hardwired display systems could perform all their editing functions within two screen scan times, i.e. two cycles of the re-circulating store, normally about 40 milliseconds since screens are usually refreshed at about 50 times per second. Thus, for instance, if the CLEAR SCREEN key was depressed, the erasure of all characters on the screen would be completed within 40 milliseconds. Additionally, if there were many displays clustered together, the performance of one display was not affected by the performance of any other since each display usually had logic dedicated to it. Consider now the case of a cluster of displays driven by a soft-centred controller which performs all logic functions by software. Thus, for VDUs having a capacity of 2000 characters, a CLEAR SCREEN operation consists of writing a null character into 2000 locations in store. Assume that a store write, etc., may be completed in 12 microseconds, then a CLEAR SCREEN operation should be capable of being completed in $2000 \times 12 \times 10^{-6}$ seconds, i.e. 24 milliseconds. However, this time is dependent upon *processor utilisation* and assumes that the processor is dedicated to the work of clearing the single screen. In practice, only 10%, say, of the processor utilisation may be available for this so that the elapsed time fully to clear a particular screen could well be ten times as long, that is, 240 milliseconds.

The CLEAR SCREEN example given above is by no means the worst that could have been chosen. Consider a rackup-type operation whereby the top line of the screen is discarded, the remaining lines shifted one position upwards and the bottom line left clear. Again a hardwired display can accomplish this within 40 milliseconds. For a soft-centred display, a rackup operation involves a minimum of 80×24 read and write operations plus 80 write operations. If we assume 20 microseconds per operation and a 10% utilisation, then the elapsed time to perform the rackup would be $2000 \times 2 \times 20 \times 10^{-6} \times 10$ seconds $= 800$ milliseconds.

Consequently the emulation of a hardwired device which is capable of supporting up to 32 display units and which may be connected to a host processor by a link of speed 9.6 kilobauds is no mean task. Indeed few, if any, soft-centred devices with a single centralised processor, as described, are capable of emulating such a device without a considerable decrease in performance.

Implementations of course exist which do not depend upon a single centralised processor and which overcome some of the performance defects mentioned above. These are discussed more fully later in the chapter.

The uses of intelligence

Given that technological advances have made soft-centred terminals both technically and economically viable, the user must evaluate the benefits of remote intelligence with respect to his particular application. A user will consider remote intelligence only if it can be shown that real financial savings result.

Possible rich savings are:

- Reduction in line loading, i.e. cheaper, slower lines and modems, or fewer lines and modems through greater line sharing
- Reduction in mainframe loading, i.e. better throughput and response times
- The degree of autonomy given to remote sites, i.e. off-line data entry type environment if the host mainframe or communications line fails, can result in the operators being used more fully
- In certain applications, a small, secure database may be maintained remote from the host mainframe which cannot be accessed by any operator other than the local ones

It is necessary now to look in detail at how some of these benefits are achieved. The user's requirements for intelligence fall into various general categories as dealt with below.

Validation of input data

In many systems, any attempt by a terminal controller to perform validation checks on data input by an operator would be wasted since either (a) the mainframe software will perform the same, plus more comprehensive checks, on receipt of the input message; (b) the validity checks are such that reference to main files is required in order to perform the check. The checks which a terminal controller is capable of performing are intra-field checks and, perhaps, some inter-field checks.

Intra-field checks are checks that may be carried out on any data field which do not require reference to information not contained within the field itself. Examples would be to check that a field (a) is all numeric, (b) lies within a given range, (c) is all alpha, and (d) contains the correct check digit. Inter-field checks are more difficult and only simple checks of this type are likely to need carrying out within a terminal. Such checks are (a) control total accumulation over designated fields, (b) alternative checking rules for field N, depending upon the contents of field $N-1$.

Data formatting

Data may be transposed or otherwise changed on transfer from one peripheral device to another, the communications line being for these purposes considered a peripheral device. The reformatting rules concerned with the communications line cannot usually be changed by the user since they are usually governed by the emulator procedures in use. For example, only modified unprotected input fields may be transmitted back to the host mainframe. In general, however, the user may want to delete, re-order or merge data streams on any other transfer. The most common example is a 'hard copy' operation, which involves printing out the contents of the screen. Obviously the format of the data required on the printout may not be the same as that on the VDU screen; indeed, preprinted stationery may well be used in the printer and any protected fields on the screen may have to be suppressed.

Journalistic and editing-type facilities

There is often a requirement for some kind of log or tally roll operation at the terminal controller for audit and/or security purposes. The operation consists of writing to, say, a cassette tape (admirably suited to this type of slow serial operation), a subset of the main transaction data together with some terminal controller-generated data, such as transaction number, transaction type, date, time, control totals, etc.

Local generation of screen formats

If the number of formats within which a display operator inserts input data is small, or for any application there are a few frequently used formats, then much central processor unit activity and line traffic can be avoided by not soliciting formats from the mainframe, but storing them locally to the terminal controller. Cassette tape is not a suitable medium for holding these formats because this would involve serial access. Floppy discs (random access) are ideal.

Supervisory functions

The more 'intelligent' the VDU system, the more intelligent must be the user to take full advantage of it. The control of the various intelligent functions is best carried out from the *supervisory display station*. The supervisory facilities could include:

- Allocation of displays to either on-line interactive working or off-line data entry mode
- Initiation of *despooling* of data previously spooled to a backing store
- Initiation of printing of print files previously sent from host mainframe and held on backing store
- Acquisition of statistics of operator performance and available free space in files, etc.

Operator assistance

As terminal systems become more widely used it is almost certain that the number of untrained people with access to displays will grow. Frequently these people will require assistance in completing a transaction. An intelligent terminal could satisfy these requirements fairly easily by providing a simple input type of device, that is, a *menu selector* such as touchwires, a touch-sensitive panel and indicator lamps under program control.

Off-line operations

Many users cannot tolerate display operators being idle in the event of a failure in the mainframe or in access to the mainframe. Consequently it is often necessary to maintain some sort of operator service, albeit degraded from that which is normally available on-line. Usually the degraded form of service consists of operators working in a data entry mode whereby data is entered into formats which are held locally on a backing store and the data generated is temporarily held in files on that backing store. When access to the mainframe is restored the data held on backing store is sent to the mainframe for processing and operators then continue in normal on-line fashion.

It is perfectly possible for an application to demand simultaneous on-line and off-line data entry working from displays connected to the same intelligent controller. In this case a special routing program is added to direct messages between the display and their required destination according to their mode of operation.

Additionally, truly off-line operations such as data verification, media conversion, etc. are quite feasible.

The user interface for a typical application

The purpose of this section is to describe the user's interface with an intelligent on-line display system. The form of the 'intelligence' in this example is that of a display controller containing within its program store a set of generalised software routines which may be invoked by parameters appearing within a data stream. In order not to overcomplicate the example, a single form of the intelligence is discussed in detail, that of input data validation.

The necessity for input validation

It is well known that the further or deeper into a processing system that keying errors go undiscovered, the more likely they are to remain undiscovered. If possible, keying errors need to be detected as they are made and whilst the source document from which the input is being made is still immediately accessible. Obviously a host processor is as well or better placed to validate the input data as an intelligent, remote controller. However, since with untrained operators keying errors per transaction can be quite high, the host processor can be relieved of a significant processing load if simple validation can be performed remotely. Additionally, communications line utilisation is reduced by reducing the number of messages and error responses which have to be transmitted.

The number of keying errors which may be generated by untrained operators should not be underestimated. A recent application study estimated that in the initial phases of operation, up to 70% of all input messages contain three or more keying errors.

Format and format composition

Usually all data input by an operator is entered into a format or pro-forma which has been called up by that operator. All formats contain within themselves parameters required to invoke validation checks. Thus when a format is being designed and laid out, it is necessary to include the required parameters in the sequences of data. This is not a new idea, being merely an extension of the way in which protected and unprotected fields are defined.

Thus a field definition sequence, which does not appear on the display screen, is included in each unprotected field. The parameters are stripped off and stored until they are required.

Usually only a single character position is used to delineate fields.

Basic field definition

Each field on the screen has several basic physical and logical properties which must be defined. Physical properties are:

Displayed *or* blank. 'Displayed' is obviously the normal state, 'blank' used for security passwords, etc.

Steady *or* flashing. 'Steady' is the normal state, 'flashing' used for attention status, e.g. system messages, or to signify errors

High intensity *or* low intensity. Used to highlight differences between fields; normal/reverse video and different character fonts are examples of other techniques

Basic logical properties of fields are more open to user choice but could include:

Unprotected *or* protected. 'Protected' fields cannot be altered by the display operator and are used for heading and identification data; 'unprotected' fields are the fields into which data is entered by the operator and on which validation checks are performed

Variable *or* fixed length. Applies only to unprotected fields; fixed-length fields must have data entered into each and every position

Mandatory *or* non-mandatory. Applies only to unprotected fields; mandatory fields must have data entered into them, they cannot be skipped over

Validation definitions

How the field is to be validated is defined by including a *parameter symbol* with the basic field definition data. This parameter symbol invokes at the required time (e.g. when a field has been completed by the operator) a routine stored within the controller which performs a check on the data within the field.

The type of checks which can be performed with a terminal controller fall into three groups.

Group 1. These checks are simple character-by-character check routines which can be performed as data is entered. Typical of these checks are 'alpha only', 'numeric only', 'integer only', 'alphanumeric', etc. (Some of these very simple checks have in fact been implemented with hardwired displays)

Group 2. These checks involve the whole field and are performed when all data has been entered into the field. Typical of these checks are 'range check', 'dictionary check' (where a field is compared against a list of permissible fields), 'check digit' (various moduli and weighting systems), 'check field' (against a value in an accumulator), etc.

Group 3. Whilst not strictly checks, this group performs simple routines which are invoked by the same mechanism. Typical of these routines are 'determine sum', 'difference', 'product', 'quotient of two fields', 'add to accumulator', 'display accumulator', etc. These routines can be used for hash totals.

For this type of intelligent system, therefore, the user interface is fairly straightforward and consists of inserting into the normal format data stream some parameters which invoke checking routines within the controller as the format is progressively filled.

The future

There appears to be little sign that the current trend towards 'intelligent' terminal systems will not continue. Indeed the whole concept of large, centralised mainframes and their attendant databases is now being questioned in all cases except where such configurations are imperative, such as airline seat reservation systems. Currently it appears that the industry is at a peculiar half-way stage on the road to distributed processing systems. Some of the simpler functions are being removed from the host mainframe and performed in intelligent terminal controllers. Gradually, more complex functions will be dispersed until a hierarchical structure of processing units can be envisaged with each processing unit having a sufficient database for the greater proportion of its work, and rarely needing to refer to a central site. Clearly such a hierarchical structure is applicable only to large nation-wide systems. Nevertheless the trend to dispersion of intelligence is quite clear.

It seems likely also that greater numbers of untrained people will have access to alphanumeric displays in the future. The display unit is ergonomically ideal for such people to use and interact with. 'Intelligence' applied to the display unit could greatly ease the problems of an untrained public trying to use these devices by guiding such users smoothly through an enquiry or transaction.

The performance of soft-centred controllers was mentioned earlier, and the structure of a typical controller was given. In the future, several changes in implementation will be evident and in some ways these will improve the speed–performance characteristics of current implementations. Instead of having, within the controller, a classical multi program environment with several task programs (each allocated to a particular function) running under an Executive or Organiser, multi-processor implementations are likely to be common: a small chip processor will be allocated to a particular function (rather than a program) which interfaces with other similar processors, each performing their allotted tasks. Such implementations are even now beginning to appear on the market.

The cost of intelligence or processing power has obviously decreased dramatically over the years. Conversely the cost of telecommunication facilities has increased equally dramatically over the equivalent period of time. Whilst the former trend continues, with semiconductor manufacturers producing larger, cheaper storage elements and faster, cheaper processors, unfortunately the latter trend shows no sign of reversal. Consequently system costs will be decreased by minimising the number and speed of telecommunications links. The most important contributor to that reduction in costs as far as display-based systems are concerned will be the integration of the display units and their intelligent control.

Further reading

Intelligent Terminals — Quantum Science Corporation, 1973.

Guide to Intelligent Terminals — Auerbach, October 1974.

The European Market for Minicomputer Equipment 1874 to 1983 — Frost & Sullivan Ltd, May 1974.

A Syndicated Survey of the European Market for Computer Terminals — Logica, May 1972.

EDP Market Studies — Intelligent and Remote Batch Terminals — IDC Europa Ltd.

5 Software

Brian Larbalestier

This chapter discusses the various software aspects of handling alphanumeric display terminals, known as VDUs. The main topics are (a) layered software, (b) terminal handling, (c) formatting and field definition aids and (d) multi-tasking software. It will be apparent to the reader that much of the discussion is equally applicable to other types of terminal, such as keyboard printers:–

Layered software

The software in the central computer that drives the terminals can be viewed as consisting of successive levels, each level performing a separate function in the process of mapping applications programs onto terminals (Figure 5.1). At the highest level exist the applications programs and at the lowest level the software handlers which regulate input/output (I/O) to the terminal devices.

An operating system or transaction processing executive provides overall system control and general services. The levels are as follows.

1. *The I/O handlers.* These control the I/O devices to which the terminals are attached. They transmit data and control messages from the protocol-handling software to the communications line and will pass hardware status and data arriving at the hardware interface back.

2. *The protocol handlers.* Above the I/O handlers are the line control modules which are dependent upon the different communications protocols used to control the terminals.

3. *Network control.* This is concerned with setting up the logical transmission paths between applications and terminals. It may for instance map terminals onto a communications line where several are attached to one line, establish a connection over a switched telephone line or generate polling messages.

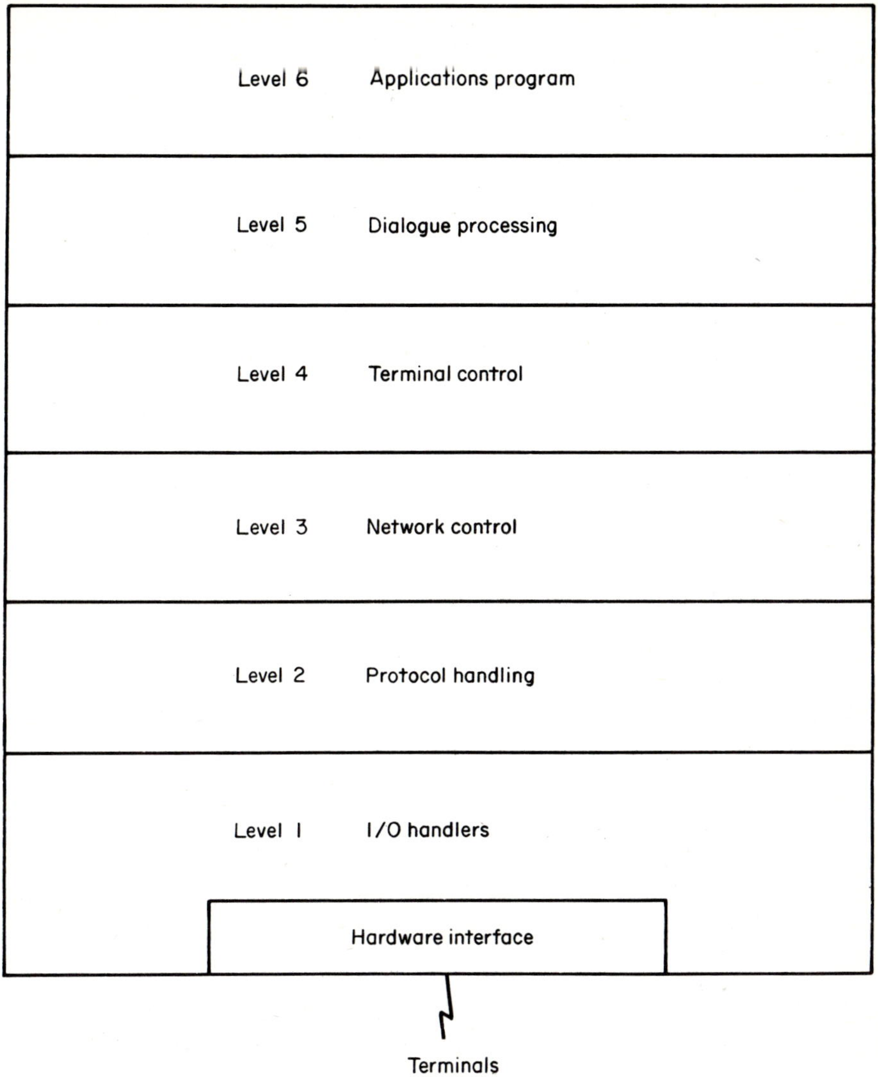

Figure 5.1. Software levels.

4. *Terminal control* will take messages and format them as required for a specific terminal type. This might involve code conversion or message reformatting. At this level the commands supported by a dialogue are made specific to a given terminal type.

5. *Dialogue control.* Between the applications are the terminal control programs which handle the specific terminal dialogues. Screen formatting and report-generation facilities may be provided here and more than one dialogue could be used to access the same applications program.

6. *Applications programs.* At this level are the programs which perform the applications processing.

Terminal handling

Introduction

This section discusses the basic software functions which can be provided and how they might be achieved for the different terminals.

Historically the terminals in use today include:

Unbuffered terminals such as teletypewriters, which communicate a character at a time
Buffered devices, which communicate a block at a time
Intelligent terminals

We shall see how the system designer can overcome the different problems that these devices present.

Data transmission

VDUs may be situated locally to the computer and attached directly, or remotely from the computer and attached via telephone lines. The telephone links may be leased or established by dialling on the public switched network. There are three ways that data may be transmitted, namely 'serial asynchronous', 'serial synchronous' and 'direct parallel'. The latter can be used only for local connections.

The line on which the data is transmitted may be operated in full duplex mode, in which case data may be transmitted in both directions simultaneously, or half-duplex, where data may be transmitted in both directions but only one at a time.

The transmission method, mode and speed are usually defined by hardware constraints. Each has advantages and disadvantages for particular applications and seriously affects the software in the computer. Most terminal dialogues are in fact half-duplex, as the messages are dependent on each other, though to improve response a full duplex communications facility is often used.

A basic I/O device handler

The function of the handler is to send and receive specified messages between terminals and applications programs. To do this it sends the messages to the communication line and receives messages from it interfacing directly with the I/O hardware of the computer and handling device interrupts. Exactly how much work it must do will depend on the sophistication of the hardware, for example whether the hardware/software interface is in terms of block, single-character or single-bit transfers. Consider a message being sent to a terminal.

1. On receiving a request to transfer a message, the handler will check to see if the request is valid and if so the message will be queued for the line specified.
2. The handler, if it is not transmitting on that line, will initiate the transfer.
3. The handler will process the interrupts as they occur.
4. On completion of the transfer the handler will perform the end of message processing before informing the requesting software that the transfer has been completed.
5. If there are any further messages awaiting transmission on that line it will initiate the next one, etc.

This is a simplified view which ignores the handling of errors and other factors.

Messages arrive irregularly from applications and VDUs, are of different lengths and are transmitted at varying speeds. The handler will reflect this unpredictability, providing queues for buffering messages and specific software modules for the different functions. To control the transfer the handler will need to have access to static data, which defines the characteristics of the device, and will also need to maintain dynamic data, which reflects the current states of the transfers queued or in progress. The designer will provide common structures which are used to store this data. The design and content of these structures will reflect the features of the devices supported, such as transmission speed, modem control, etc., and the number and type of devices supported. The I/O handler itself may be interrupted so care must be taken to provide mechanisms to ensure the integrity of the data, for example by turning interrupts off, queueing the requests, or by semaphore locks.

Figure 5.2 illustrates the possible structure of a handler and also indicates the control and information flow.

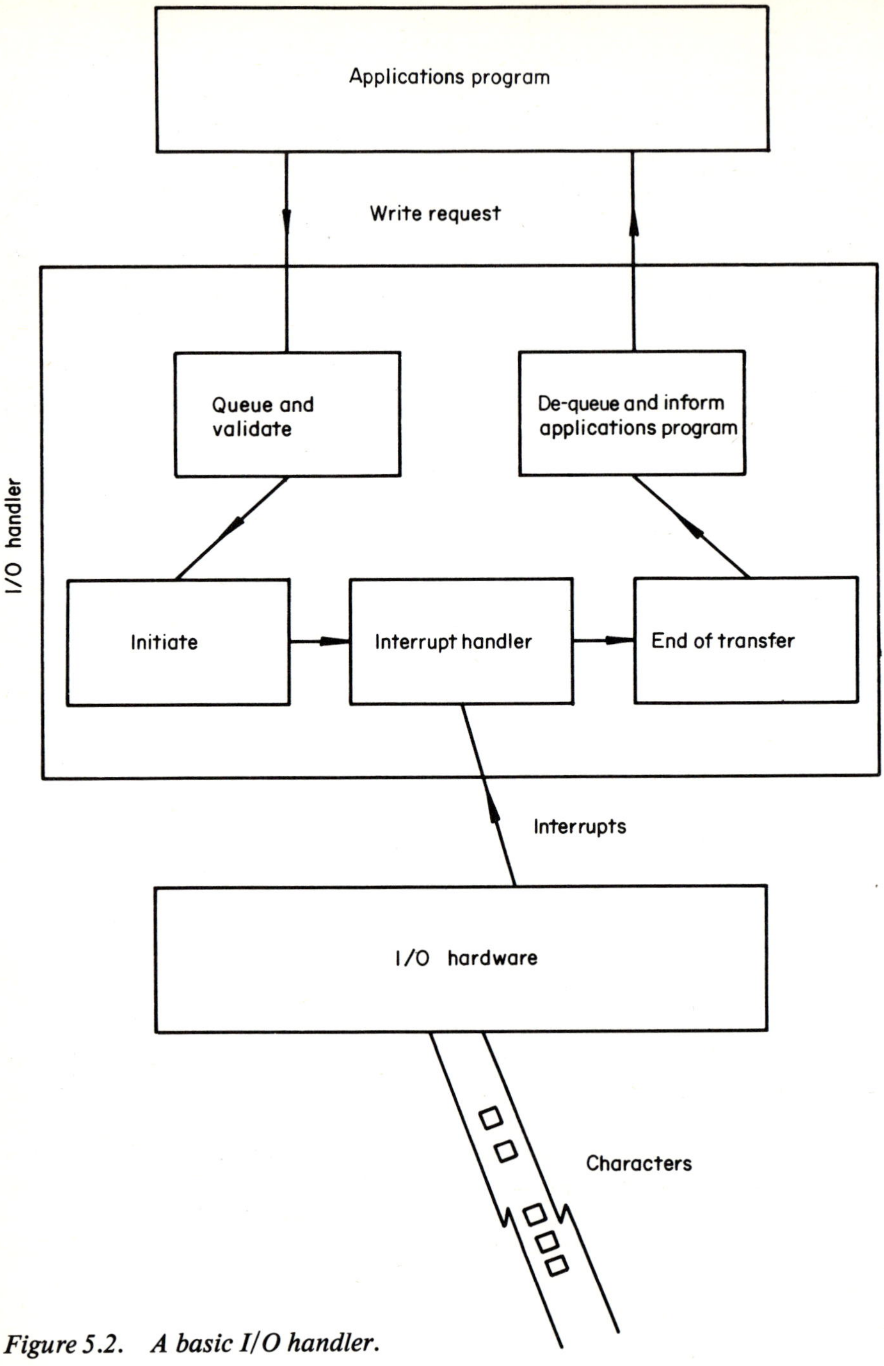

Figure 5.2. A basic I/O handler.

Further functions of a terminal handler

Listed below are functions that might typically be performed by a handler for both input and output.

- To assemble or break down the data into characters and messages
- To perform any code conversion necessary, e.g. EBCDIC to ASCII or 5-bit to 8-bit code
- To check for any errors in transmission, e.g. parity or block check, and to take remedial action if at all possible, or to inform the requesting program
- To perform any editing required, i.e. to rub out characters or delete lines
- To look for the end of the message, e.g. carriage return, and to perform any necessary processing

Driving Teletype-compatible terminals

The first interactive terminals closely resembled the typewriter, having the familiar 'QWERTY ...' keyboard and a paper roll on which characters were printed as they were typed or received from the computer. They were unbuffered devices and so characters were transmitted to the computer as the keys were pressed, typically 2 to 3 characters per second. On output the transmission speed was limited by the electromechanical nature of the devices to 10 to 15 characters per second. Such terminals are still in use but their operation is restricted by their characteristics. They are unbuffered, often hard copy only; slow; electromechanical, except in the case of VDUs; and have limited device status as regards paper out, off-line, etc. This means that transmission is asynchronous, i.e. start–stop, and the terminal operation is half-duplex. Because the device is unbuffered the transmission speed on output is limited by the time it takes to output certain characters, such as carriage return.

A major limitation is the difficulty experienced in detecting and recovering from errors, whether they are made by the operator or occur during transmission. The problem that arises is how much data it is sensible or possible to re-transmit when an error is detected.

For instance, if the terminal is being used to print invoices on pre-formatted stationery and an error is detected, a single character may necessitate the re-transmission of the complete invoice. This can be done because the computer, unlike the terminal, has buffer storage. Character coding techniques make it possible to detect single-bit errors in transmitted characters by using parity. However, the limited device status and lack of a handshake mean that the computer can be outputting characters which are not actually received, and printed, by the terminal. Teletype-compatible terminals are thus not suited for unattended operation.

Where the operator is entering data for storage within the computer it is desirable that he can correct his own errors and those occurring during transmission. To make this possible, an unusual method of working, called 'Echo-plex', is commonly used. It utilises a full duplex communications channel. In this mode the characters typed at the terminal are transmitted directly to the line, not printed, received by the computer and then transmitted back to the terminal for printing or displaying. The operator can then check visually that the characters printed were those typed. Special control characters are provided at the terminal which enable the operator to RUBOUT characters, DELETE LINES, etc., so enabling him to perform limited error recovery. One aspect of this mode of working is that the operator can 'type ahead' of the characters displayed at the terminal.

What are the implications concerning the software in the host?

1. There is a high processing overhead for each character input, as the computer must look for special characters and perform the required action. This will include looking for end of record and echoing each character input.

2. Interrupts are locked out while the character input processing is performed. If many terminals are connected to the processor it will be heavily loaded and non-interruptible for significant periods of time. There is thus a danger that the processor will not be capable of receiving characters transmitted from the terminals and so the characters will be irretrievably lost.

3. Depending on the transmission speed, the software may have to insert 'pad characters' for some terminals to give it time to action those characters for which this takes longer than one character time.

Hence the terminal handling process must be written to minimise the time spent handling each character. This is even more important as nowadays Teletype-compatible visual display terminals are capable of operating at much higher speeds, e.g. 9600 bauds, than the original hard copy terminals, which operated at 100 to 150 bauds.

Often system designers are constrained to support a variety of similar terminals, such as the different Teletype models and visual display equivalents on a variety of communications I/O devices, at varying speeds. This means that a trade-off is made between the character throughput to be catered for and the amount of memory used by the handler. This compromise may cause the software to be implemented as a single unit, so obscuring the various software levels.

Buffered terminals

The original VDUs were made Teletype-compatible for two reasons. First, the software for driving Teletypes already existed and so VDUs could be used as plug-in replacements for them. Secondly, the cost of providing local storage in the terminal to buffer the communications line was comparatively high. Nowadays the cost of electronic components has fallen considerably and buffered terminals are relatively inexpensive.

The term *buffered* refers not to the screen buffer from which the display is refreshed but to a communications line buffer. This buffer may or may not be the same size as the screen buffer. There are many consequences of having a buffer in the terminal. First, the transmission speed need not be limited by the time the device takes to action certain characters, as it is with unbuffered devices. It is thus possible to transmit on the communications line at faster speeds and to use *synchronous* rather than *asynchronous* transmission, so using the line more efficiently. Secondly, the terminals themselves can now be half- or full-duplex in operation. VDUs usually operate in half-duplex because it is not meaningful to have full duplex dialogues. However, if terminals are to receive messages, originating from the computer or another terminal, while a dialogue is in progress then this would require the terminal and the line to be full duplex.

A major advantage is the benefit that the operator experiences with respect to the detection and recovery from errors. Indeed transmission errors are more frequent, owing to the higher transmission speeds used. Individual characters are more susceptible to error at higher speeds and a burst of noise on the communications line lasting a few milliseconds will corrupt many more characters at 9600 bauds than at 150 bauds. Several techniques are available for detecting errors in the transmission of a block of data, for instance LRC (longitudinal redundancy check) and CRC (cyclic redundancy check). As both the computer and the terminal are buffered it is feasible for either end to request the re-transmission of the data should an error be detected. It is common practice to re-try only a limited number of times, often three, before reporting that the line is faulty.

The operator uses the VDU very differently from a Teletype-compatible terminal. He will prepare his data on the screen before pressing the SEND key, which causes the terminal to transmit the message to the computer. He is thus able to edit text, correct errors he makes and to use screen formatting aids. To assist the operator the terminal will have keys which enable the cursor to be moved around the screen, for inserting and deleting lines or characters, for clearing the screen, and many other functions.

In order that the receiver can detect the start and end of a message it is necessary to delimit each message with a unique start identifier, STX (start of text), and end identifier, ETX (end of text).

The software handler in the computer is more sophisticated than in the previous case. Consider a read request issued by an application program in the computer for a particular terminal.

1. The application program will solicit input from the terminal by placing a buffer on the communications line to which the terminal is attached and setting the handler in a state ready to receive the response.
2. The handler will do nothing until the operator at the terminal presses the SEND key. When this happens, the terminal will then transmit all the characters in the message.
3. On detection of the STX character the interrupt handler will input the characters as they arrive until ETX signifies the end of the message.
4. On detection of ETX it will compute the error checking code (LRC, CRC, etc.).
5. If the error code is invalid it will re-try by requesting the terminal to re-transmit.
6. Assuming the error code is valid, the end of message processing will be performed and the calling software informed.

What are the differences in handling the different terminal types? Both the terminal and computer must compute the error detection code, which is expensive in processing time. The character arrival pattern is very different; instead of single characters arriving randomly, complete messages arrive at irregular intervals. These messages might be short (1 or 2 characters) or long (1400 to 1500 characters). The computer must receive them, without character loss, and buffer them in the computer. The processing requirement, or processor power needed, is proportional to the transmission speed and to the number of terminals that can simultaneously transmit. The storage requirement for buffering is dependent on the number of terminals connected. Also, the environment is uncontrolled; resources must be provided to cope with instantaneous peak rather than average demands, so limiting the number of terminals that can be connected.

To spread the load and so make better use of the resources it is necessary for the computer and not the terminal to have control of the situation. A simple solution is for the terminal not to transmit the message immediately the operator presses the SEND key but instead to send a short message saying 'I have something to send'. The computer receiving the message can then inform the terminal when it has both the storage and processing resources to input the message. This enables the processor to share buffers between many terminals and to avoid character loss.

As far as the software levels are concerned, the basic message transfer functions would be handled by the low-level I/O device handler (at level 1), while the error detection and re-tries would be performed with higher-level line control routines (level 2).

Using a communications protocol

The previous sections have assumed that the terminals are connected one per communication line, known as *point to point.* To reduce costs it is common for more than one terminal to be attached to a line, known as *multi-point* or *multi-dropping.*

Each terminal must have a unique identifier or 'address' so that each knows which one the computer is talking to. It is possible to multi-drop Teletype-compatible terminals, as they need to occupy the line for long periods of time thus causing poor response at the waiting terminals.

When more than one terminal is attached to a line only one may transmit at a time. It is therefore necessary to have some systematic operating procedure or *protocol* to control the terminals.

There are two methods of controlling the line, *contention* and *polling.* In a 'contention' situation, a terminal needing to access the computer will bid for the line. If the line is vacant it will be given the line to transmit its message; if the line is busy the terminal will try again at regular intervals until it succeeds. In a 'polling' situation the terminal must wait to be invited before it can transmit a message. The computer will systematically invite terminals to transmit by sending out the address of the terminal invited. The terminal may reply with a message, decline, or fail to reply. If the system has data to send to a terminal it will 'select' it by addressing the terminal for which the message is destined.

The previous section indicated the need for a single format involving unique identifiers, STX and ETX, to delimit variable-length messages and this is illustrated in Figure 5.3. The basic character and block assembly and transmission tasks are level 1 functions.

The level 2 software performs the protocol handling. It is concerned with transmitting and receiving physical blocks of data to and from the

Figure 5.3. A typical message format.

communications line. The functions to be performed include error code generation and checking; re-tries should an error be detected; and the upwards reporting of line errors. This software is unaware which communications lines have terminals attached. When it initiates a transfer there are three possible replies from the terminal: ACK (transmission successful), NAK (transmission in error) and no reply. No reply is detected by timing out the transmission, and so the level 1 software must provide timeout facilities.

Many protocols break messages down into a number of smaller blocks. The reasons for this are to minimise the number of characters to be re-transmitted if an error is detected and to keep the size of the communications buffer down. A problem that arises with message blocking is that a burst of noise on the line may cause control characters to be lost or the end-of-transmission character to be lost or invalidated. It is thus possible to lose a complete block or for two blocks to be merged. Some protocols overcome this by having block sequencing or alternate odd and even indicators stored in the transmission blocks.

The level 3 software provides the networking facilities. It is here that the logical paths are established between the terminals, the communications lines and the applications programs. The software will control the logging on and off of terminal operators, queue messages for the terminals, and poll and select terminals. Additional functions that might be provided include automatic dialling and answering, the disconnecting of calls, and the re-routing of messages. The monitoring and control of the network is provided here. In times of system overload it might control the network by polling fewer terminals or polling them less frequently, or in a priority order.

The polling of terminals is a considerable overhead on the computer. Even when the terminals are not transmitting, the computer will be fairly busy sending out polls and processing the NAKs or timeouts with which the terminals reply. It is common for many terminals to be located near to each other, and costs can be considerably reduced by having several terminals attached to a local *cluster controller*. In this case the computer sends 'general polls' to the controller instead of 'specific polls' to each terminal attached. The controller arbitrates to decide which terminal can use the line. This significantly reduces the processor overhead incurred by polling.

Flexibility

We have already seen how some flexibility can be provided but a brief summary will be useful.

In level 1 software, more than one communications I/O device can be supported by providing as many I/O handlers as required. Each handler can implement, to a different degree, the facilities provided in the actual hardware devices. For instance, they may or may not support varying transmission speeds, or terminals with similar characteristics. Level 2 software can provide support for different communications protocols by having a handler for each. The level 3 software can provide a variety of networking functions including dial-up connection and message routing.

It will be shown below how with a new layer of software, level 4, different though similar terminals may be supported, allowing different terminal types to communicate with one application program.

Direct parallel connection

The terminals discussed so far are connected to the computer via serial communications lines. In this arrangement the display and the keyboard appear as one device although they are in fact two, sharing a single interface. The screen appears as a serial store both to the operator and to the computer and the time taken to write to the screen is limited by the transmission and device speeds. For example, it will take 4 seconds to fill a 2000-character screen at 4800 bauds, which is quite acceptable for many dialogues.

There are classes of dialogue where each character input may require a large amount of processing, file accessing and also significantly change the contents of the display screen. Clearly it is unacceptable for the operator to wait 4 seconds for the screen to fill each time a character is typed. Such applications may require the contents of the screen to be completely changed in milliseconds.

In these circumstances it is common to choose visual display terminals where the keyboard and the display are logically separate devices. The keyboard is connected to the computer using the normal serial interface and the display connected via a high-speed parallel interface. Note that this method is suitable only for connecting terminals which are local to the computer. Applications where this method is used include computer graphics, word processing, high-volume data entry and others.

Unlike the situation for serial interfaces, there is little standardisation. The computer considers the display much as any other block transfer device, such as a tape or disc drive. The complexity of the handler will depend on how much assistance the interface hardware gives it (i.e. whether transfers are under processor control or direct memory access), how compatible the character widths of the device and the computer are, and so on. Some systems are in fact very helpful as the computer sees the display as a specific area of memory. The memory is dual access and the display controller fills the display screen automatically from the memory.

Formatting and field definition aids

Introduction

The discussions so far have concentrated on the software for communicating between the computer and the terminal. This section considers the aspects of implementing different dialogues and is concerned with the communications between the terminal operator and the application program, using the facilities provided by the terminal. These are at software levels 4 (*terminal control*) and 5 (*dialogue control*). Level 5 is often implemented in the applications programs.

There are many different dialogue structures in common use and the approach chosen will depend on the nature of the application, the type and skill of the operator, and the facilities of the terminal. Below is a brief description of some common dialogue types.

1. *Programming languages*. Examples are APL and BASIC.
2. *Fixed-format commands*. These are commonly used for operator communication in many operating systems and for specialised applications such as air traffic control.
3. *Mnemonic*. In dialogues of this type the operator may input a varying number of fields in any order, by preceding each field with a predefined mnemonic descriptor: NAM = F. BLOGGS; DATE = 03/02/76;
4. *Natural language*. Utopia for the user but fraught with problems for the system, owing to the overheads involved in handling large vocabularies and the ambiguities of our languages. Limited-language input is useful for the casual user.
5. *Question and answer dialogues*. The computer asks the operator a series of questions to which he may reply yes or no. Alternatively the computer may ask the user to supply specific items of information.
6. *Menu selection*. A variation on the question and answer technique in which the computer guides the operator through sets of predefined

choices. Each choice has a reference number beside it. The operator replies by inputting the appropriate reference. For example

ARE YOU?
1. SINGLE
2. MARRIED
3. DIVORCED
4. WIDOWED

PLEASE REPLY BY ENTERING THE APPROPRIATE NUMBER.

7. *Form filling* (filling in the blanks). A method of working in which the user enters predefined fields into predefined areas on the screen. This is appropriate only for buffered terminals.

In the first four dialogues the operator tells the computer what to do whereas in the following three the computer guides the operator through the dialogue. The first four assume that the operator has some skill, and has been trained in the use of the dialogue whereas the remainder are more appropriate for less skilled operators. For instance, a command-orientated dialogue, type (2), will be suitable for an air traffic controller but not for a manager who uses the terminal only occasionally, and is always too busy to learn!

Consider a factory floor application where the requirement is to monitor the assembly of motor cars and that at the start and conclusion of a particular task workers have to enter this information through a display terminal. The data to be input might include the chassis number; the time; the task identifier; an indication as to whether it is the start or finish; and the worker's identification. There are a variety of ways in which the dialogue can be implemented. Table 5.1 indicates possible dialogue structures that might be used. In the example, the worker is recording the information that he has just finished putting an engine into the car, identified by chassis number 01234.

The most suitable dialogues would be (5) and (7) as they ensure that all necessary data is entered without relying on the user to remember. In fact in a factory (5) might be preferable as it presents the operator with only one field to enter at a time. Type (7) requires a buffered terminal on which to implement it while type (5) could be implemented using an unbuffered terminal.

Menu selection dialogues are commonly used where there are a limited number of possibilities for each input. This technique has a number of advantages; it guides the operator through the dialogue and can be implemented easily on unbuffered terminals. However, it relies heavily on output, and on slow terminals it can be tedious for the operator.

Table 5.1. Example of a dialogue. Small capitals indicate data output by the computer; larger capitals indicate the corresponding data input

Type 2
ENGINE, END, 11.55, 01234, S. SMITH;

Type 3
TSK = ENG, STAT = END, NAM = S. SMITH; IDNT = 01234, TIM = 11.55;

Type 5
WHAT TASK?,
ENGINE;
START OR FINISH (S OR F)?
F;
TIME?
11.55;
SERIAL NUMBER?
01234;
NAME?
S. SMITH;

Type 7
TASK ENGINE STATUS END TIME 11.55 REFERENCE 01234 NAME S. SMITH

Important factors

In implementing a dialogue the designer must bear in mind certain factors. In order of priority they are:

1. *Minimising line time.* A very significant factor for reasons of response, and cost, is the time that the dialogue uses the communications line. The line time is proportional to the number of characters that are transmitted and the transmission speed; it should be kept to a minimum.

2. *Minimising the data to be re-transmitted following line errors.* It is desirable to minimise the line time used for re-tries when transmission errors occur, particularly on a multi-dropped line. This is one reason why it is common to break messages into smaller transmission blocks.

3. *Ease of use.* The operator must be provided with keys at the terminal which enable him to action the most frequently used functions in the terminal, without interacting with the computer.

A basic assumption is that the operator will make mistakes, and so facilities must be provided to make it easy for him to take correcting action. To do this he needs to be able to move the cursor to a specific place or field on the screen. When he has positioned the cursor he needs to edit the screen. The keys provided may enable him to:

Clear a field, the whole screen, or all unprotected fields
Insert and delete lines and characters

Having given him these facilities the dialogue must now prevent him from misusing them. First, when the computer displays a format on the screen, which may be reused many times, it remembers the position of each field, so the operator must not be able to corrupt the format. Secondly, visual display terminals often have locally attached printers which can output the contents of the screen. These may be used for printing contract notes, or order and delivery documentation. Such printers create a security risk if the operator is allowed to modify the contents of the screen, and so the computer must be able to prevent him from doing this by protecting the characters displayed on the screen.

To summarise, it is necessary:

To constrain the input of characters to specific times in the dialogue, and so it must be possible to lock and unlock the keyboard
To restrict the use of certain powerful keys to specific periods in the dialogue. This can be achieved by having different modes or states, with specific keys being valid only in certain states
To prevent the operator from modifying specified areas of the screen, or sometimes the whole screen

Likewise the computer must be able to build up formats on the screen, set the mode of the terminal, lock and unlock the keyboard and generally control the dialogue. To achieve this the terminal must recognise and obey commands transmitted from the computer.

Terminal aids

The previous section stated that the most important factor when implementing a dialogue is to minimise line time. The terminal must help the implementer in this task by enabling him to express in an efficient manner the commands which are most expensive in line time and most frequently used. It is thus no surprise that even the simplest display will clear the screen on receipt of a short character sequence rather than the computer having to transmit a space down the line for each character position on the screen. On unbuffered VDUs the terminal may not be able to action the command in a single character time and so 'pad characters', which are ignored, may have to be inserted in the stream.

Similarly, pad characters may also have to be inserted on buffered terminals if the communications buffer is smaller than the transmission block.

The structuring of the screen is called *formatting*. At the simplest level it is broken down into areas into which the operator can input characters, called *unprotected fields*, and areas into which he cannot. Figure 5.4 illustrates this for a simple screen. Often other actions can be performed on fields; for instance, they can sometimes be 'flashed'. These actions are called *attributes*.

The actions that the programmer may wish to perform when setting up a screen format are:

Clear the screen
Clear the screen from a specified position
Describe fields and areas on the screen
Clear individual fields
Clear all unprotected fields
Position the cursor at a specific place in the screen buffer
Repeat a character a specified number of times
Position the cursor at the position where the operator is to start inputting

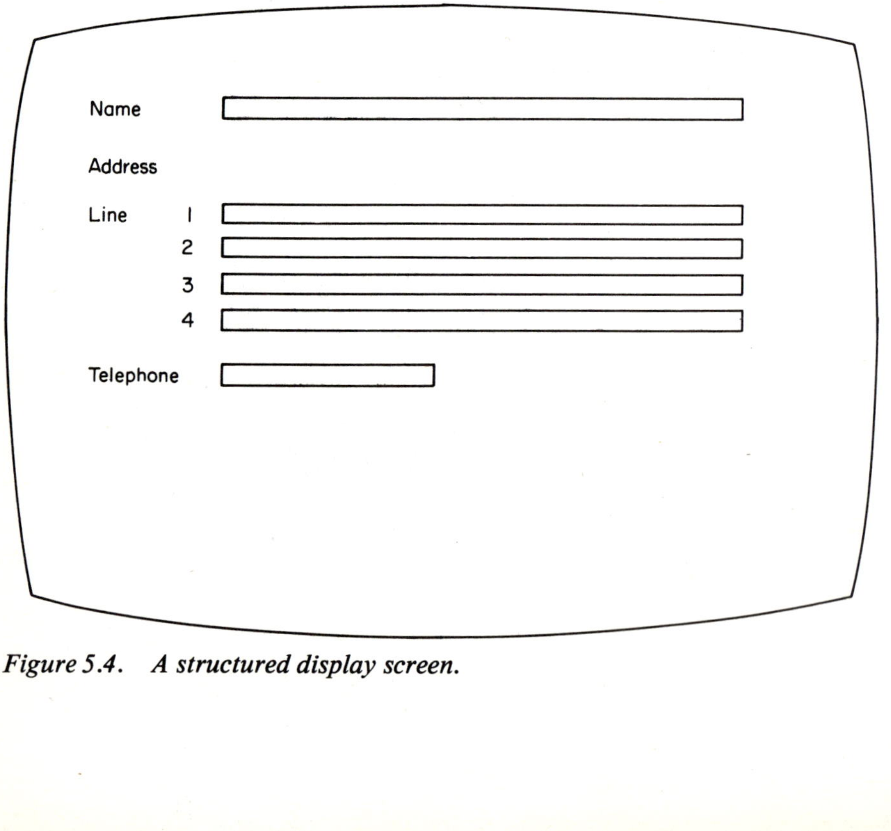

Figure 5.4. A structured display screen.

To minimise the data transmitted on input the ability to read selected areas of the screen may be required, i.e.

A line
An area delimited by a 'start of message' character and an 'end of message' character
Only fields that have changed since the previous command, called 'read-modified'
From the cursor position to some marker

In some applications the same format is used many times consecutively and it is inefficient to re-transmit it each time. To do this, facilities are required to:

Clear all unprotected fields
Clear individual fields
Locate the cursor at a position in the screen buffer
To insert and delete lines and characters
To turn field attributes on and off

The terminal must assist the programmer in describing and setting up field attributes. At the simplest level it must enable him to:

Position the cursor
Turn protection on
Turn protection off

Data input may be invalid, and so on detection of this the computer will need to inform the operator. To do this it might display an error message in a predefined area of the screen and emphasise the field in error, possibly by flashing it.

To aid the programmer, many terminals provide a command-orientated interface. Unfortunately there is little standardisation between manufacturers. It is fairly common to use the ASCII control codes and escape sequences. For instance the command might be specified by transmitting ESCAPE (ESC) followed by the command identifier and any data characters:

ESC N_1 $d_1, d_2 \ldots d_n$

So

ESC A may mean 'clear screen'

and

ESC B X Y may mean 'move the cursor to position *X, Y*', where *X* and *Y* are binary numbers

Software aids

Much of the work in programming on-line systems lies in specifying the many screen formats required by the different transactions.

A tool very useful to the programmer is a dialogue generator, which enables the programmer:

To specify his reports, screen formats and dialogue structure in a high-level language
To add new formats and amend existing ones
To try out different dialogues easily. This allows the user to experiment so that he will have a suitable dialogue

Additional benefits are gained if all dialogue handling is performed outside the applications programs. The applications thus have a simple transaction interface which is independent of the network and the specific terminals.

The primitives of this language will reflect the commands and attributes of the terminals, i.e. 'clear screen', and also the basic dialogue building blocks. The dialogue programs can perform common functions such as range checks, batch control checks, and checks on field dependencies. Aids such as this are gradually becoming available from computer manufacturers and independent software companies.

Using intelligent terminals

'Intelligent' or 'programmable' terminals are increasingly being used with on-line systems. Originally this programmability was exploited in order to emulate particular manufacturers' terminals, enabling independent terminal manufacturers to sell their products as plug-compatible in the same way that Teletype-compatible displays can be substituted for Teletypes. They are now being used as a more powerful tool to assist the designer in implementing dialogues. They provide the designer with the ability to tailor the terminal facilities to suit his requirements either at the time, or later when he understands them more clearly, or they have changed. He must however distinguish between choosing communications protocols for his network (software levels 1–3) and distributing the dialogue (level 4), or application functions (level 5), outboard into the terminal.

In deciding which features to implement in the terminal, he will bear in mind the basic rules, implement the functions that otherwise cost the most in line time and are used most frequently; those that provide a more friendly user interface, especially with respect to response times; not forgetting the cost of the terminal. Additionally he may wish to put outboard functions that are expensive in central processor resources. It must be borne in mind that intelligent terminals have their own limitations. Below are listed some functions that might be placed in the terminal.

Local storage of screen formats

The ability to check more complex fields, such as numeric data only, fixed point number, floating point number, alpha field, alphanumeric field, and fields where the first character is alpha and the rest are numeric

The ability to store data not all of which is displayed at once. The dialogue then turns areas on or off depending on operator actions. For example, suppose an operator fills in a form comprising 15 fields and the computer detects four errors. The computer might send all the error indicators and error messages down the line at the same time but display them only one at a time. Thus the operator would correct each error before requesting the next message

Checks on fields, i.e. check digits and range checks

Checks on the dependencies between fields

Batch control checks

Passwords for people allowed access to that terminal

Commonly accessed reference data, i.e. the fastest-moving stock items or the most frequent customers

and many more.

Multi-tasking software

Introduction

In a *batch system* the user would normally submit jobs to the computer for processing and the computer would then execute these jobs one by one in the one or more batch streams. Resources would be allocated as requested in the job control statements incorporated along with the job. In an *on-line system*, however, the user logs on at a terminal for a 'session' during which he performs one or more 'transactions', each transaction comprising one or more 'message exchanges' with the computer. All this time the operator is under the illusion that the computer is dedicated to his needs while in fact the computer is providing this service for many terminals using the system.

There are a number of aspects concerning this environment which are different from the earlier batch systems.

There is an increase in the number of simultaneous jobs being processed, although each has a relatively low level of activity

The uncontrolled nature of this environment, compared with batch, in respect of instantaneous demands for main store, processing, communications lines, records, files and other resources
The complexity of error control and recovery
The apparent sharing of programs between terminal users

The requirement for main storage to handle the number of simultaneous jobs has increased. This is twofold; first, 'real storage' is required to cope with jobs running at a given instant; secondly, 'virtual storage' is needed for the jobs which appear to the terminals' operators to be running but are inactive at that particular instant. Real storage is limited, so it is therefore desirable to exploit common features between the jobs being processed by sharing programs.

Structuring the software

Three basic techniques can be used to structure the software. We shall first define some basic concepts.

The term *thread* can be used to define the sequence of operations carried out on behalf of a terminal. The duration of a thread may be considered as a message exchange, a transaction or a session, although a transaction is the most common. A *function* can be defined as a program or piece of code that performs a given operation. A *task* can be defined as a program or unit of code which is scheduled or run. At any point in time a task will be performing a particular function on behalf of a particular thread. Where the code can simultaneously be executed by more than one thread then it is said to be '*re-entrant*'. Where it can be executed by only one thread at a time yet be executed by different ones in turn it is called '*serially reusable*'. Thus a task which is re-entrant will have a unique context for each thread which identifies the thread and working storage while a serially reusable task may have the working storage within the code.

This ability to handle more than one terminal user simultaneously is known as *multi-threading*. Three different ways that software may be structured are discussed below along with some implications.

Task per terminal. In this case there is a task for each thread or terminal (*see* Figure 5.5). This is the simplest structure for the programmer as he does not need to be aware of any other users of the system. However, it has the disadvantage that each task requires a copy of all code needed to perform the functions on behalf of the thread.

This type of structure is commonly used for systems with only a few terminals or where no common features are predictable in functions between

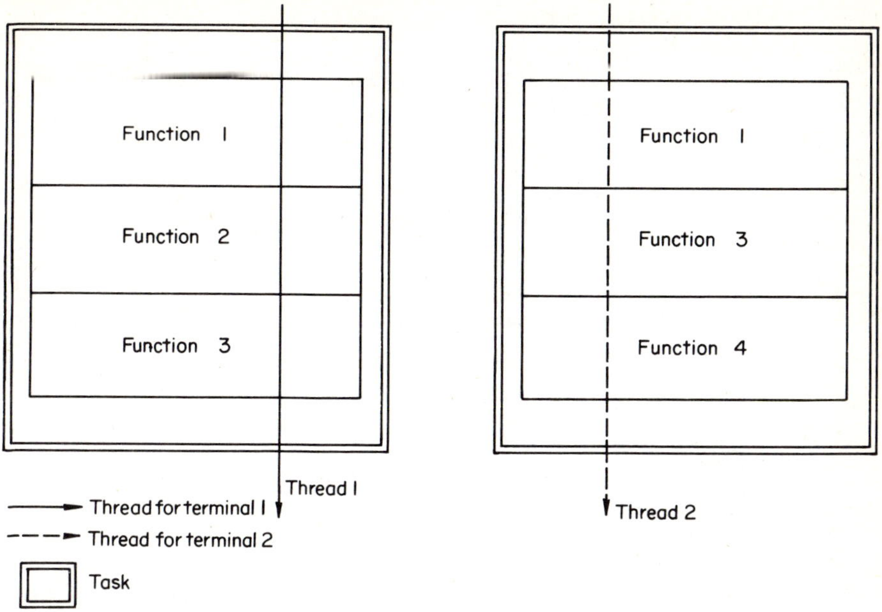

Figure 5.5. Task per terminal.

threads, for instance time sharing. However, holding a copy of the code for each task means that the system rapidly runs out of real store.

Functionally dedicated task. In this scheme tasks are dedicated to specific functions (*see* Figure 5.6). Thus only one copy of the function or code is held, however many threads are being processed. The task performs the function for one thread and on completion performs it again for another thread. Threads are executed by passing messages from one functional task to another. A receiving task may be busy when a message is passed to it, so it is necessary to queue messages for tasks.

This method is more economical in storage than the 'task per terminal' method as only one copy of the code for each function is held. The programmer is also unconcerned that there may be other users. He does, however, have to consider how best to break down a thread into functions. At any time the computer may be processing a number of threads although each task will be performing its function for only one thread. Thus the system code need only be serially reusable and not re-entrant.

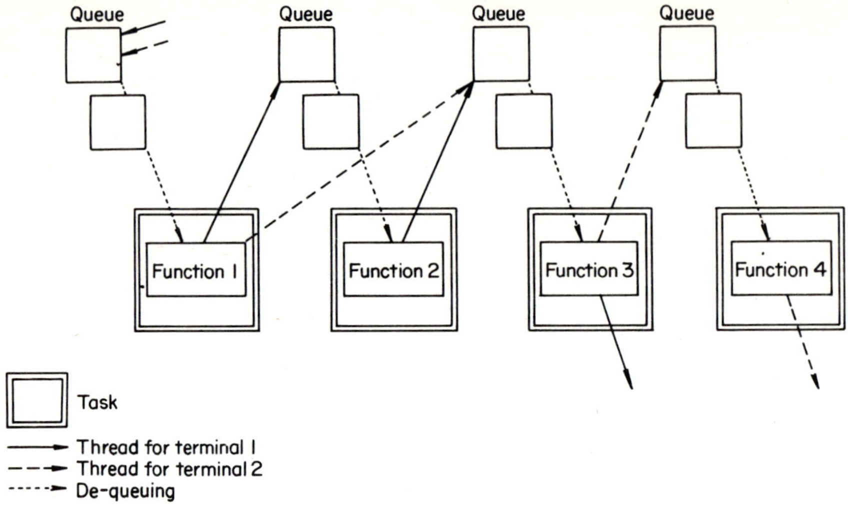

Figure 5.6. Tasks dedicated to each function.

Multi-threaded task. In this scheme a single task will perform its own multi-threading (*see* Figure 5.7). This means that it will itself coordinate the switching between function–thread combinations. To do this it must have its own scheduler built in, which will run particular function–thread combinations and which will schedule another when it has completed. This is a more difficult programming environment for the implementer as he must cater for other threads and take care that threads do not interfere with or corrupt each other.

The 'task per terminal' technique provides the implementer with a simple and protected environment in which to program but is expensive in resource usage, making it unsuitable for systems with many terminals. In the past, where performance and not protection has been the prime aim multi-threaded task architectures were widely used. Nowadays though, there is greater concern to provide protected systems. Many computers have provided hardware protection only on a per task basis, which favours systems based on functionally dedicated tasks.

The main aims of an architecture, then, are to:

Provide an easy environment in which to write applications programs
Protect threads one from another
Minimise main storage requirements

To reduce main storage requirements it is common to implement the basic functions in re-entrant shareable libraries, which is not always consistent with

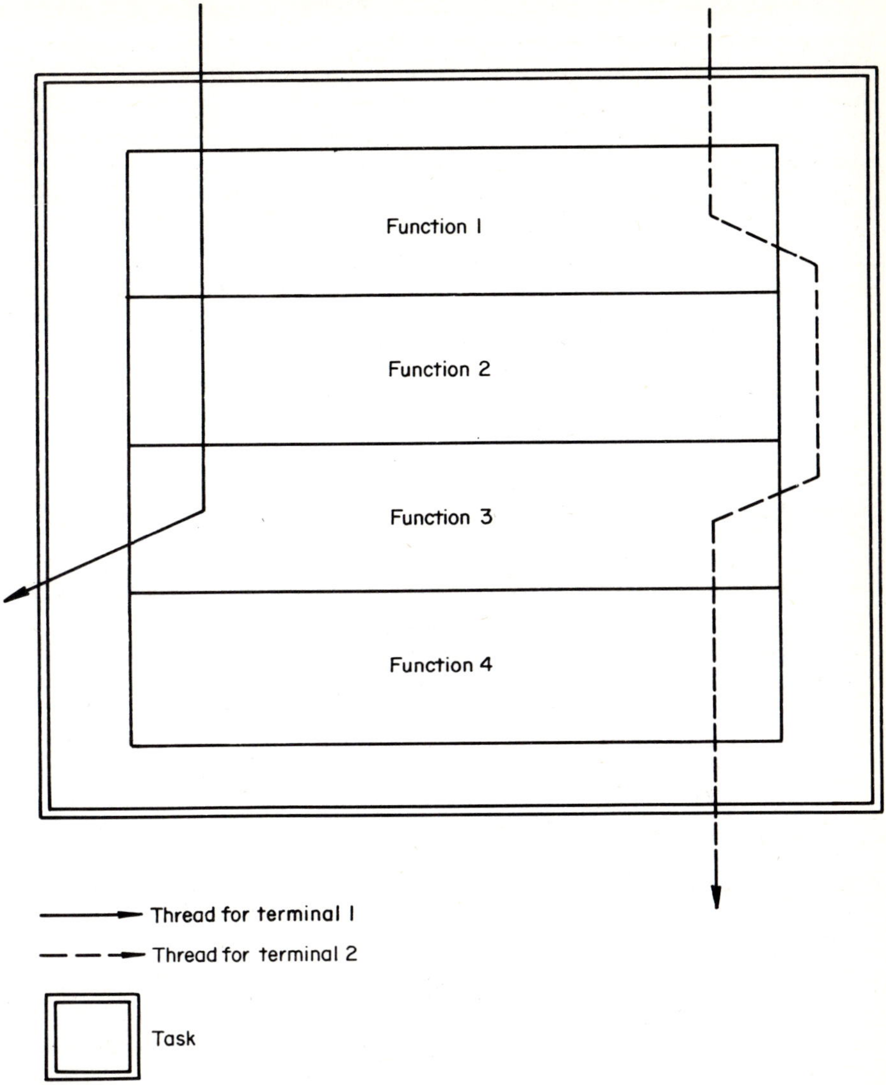

Figure 5.7. A multi-threaded task.

the aim of making it easy for the application programmers. There is increasing tendency to program in high-level languages but unfortunately not all those commonly used are capable of generating re-entrant code. The problem exists primarily because such languages as FORTRAN create their own local storage. Thus the code is only serially reusable.

To reduce the instantaneous demands for main storage it is necessary to have a virtual storage system. In such a scheme the system must be able to store threads temporarily on backing store while the main storage is used to run another thread. This is called *checkpointing.*

In the 'task per terminal' situation a complete thread may be checkpointed as required. Again, with functionally dedicated tasks it is relatively easy to checkpoint a thread by saving the messages that tasks pass between each other. In this case the message queues would be maintained on backing store. Similarly, with multi-threaded tasks all the local data for a particular thread could be checkpointed.

Implementation of the terminal handling software

This section attempts to provide an overall view of how terminal systems, rather than the specific components, may be implemented. Some of the software aims are listed below. It may be a requirement:

- For more than one terminal type to access the same application program
- For the same terminal to access different applications programs
- That the applications programmer is unaware that there is more than one terminal on the system
- That programs are written in a high-level language
- That terminal users, or threads, are hardware protected from each other
- That code should not be unnecessarily duplicated, i.e. should be re-entrant

Historically the design of terminal handling systems has been influenced by the hardware and software technology of the day and not surprisingly our understanding has increased considerably over the years, thus influencing system design.

The first terminal systems were implemented with computers and operating systems designed for batch processing. The basic problems arose because of the computer's inability to multi-thread efficiently and because of failure to provide a protected programming environment. In an early system the terminal handling software would have been added on beside the operating system (*see* Figure 5.8), either within the applications program or as a separate program within the operating system. This was not satisfactory, as devices were allocated to specified application programs at the start of a job and not dynamically as the programs ran. This meant that it was not possible to connect terminals to applications dynamically, except by using dial-up lines or line patching techniques to connect the terminal to another communications

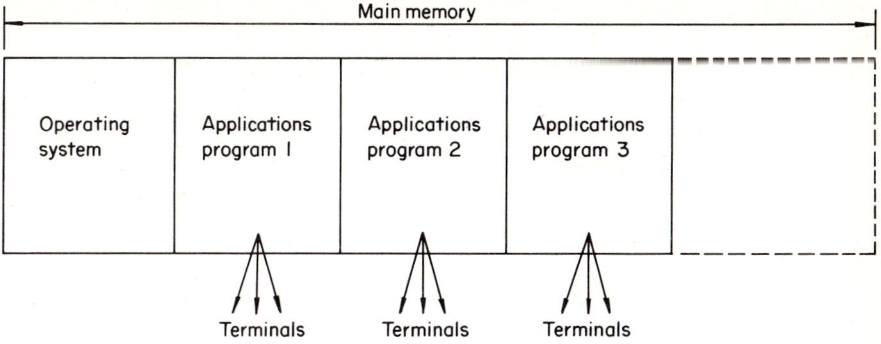

Figure 5.8. Applications handling their own terminals.

line. Unless a task per terminal architecture was used, the programmer had to perform his own multi-threading and so was restricted in his use of high-level languages.

The next development was to have a separate terminal handling program to which all terminals were allocated. This program performs all the terminal I/O on behalf of the applications program and can be considered as being dedicated to the function of terminal I/O (*see* Figure 5.9). The terminal handling is now independent of both the operating system and the applications programs, making it possible to write applications programs in high-level languages, the terminal program taking care of any multi-threading.

There is now a formal interface between terminal handling and the

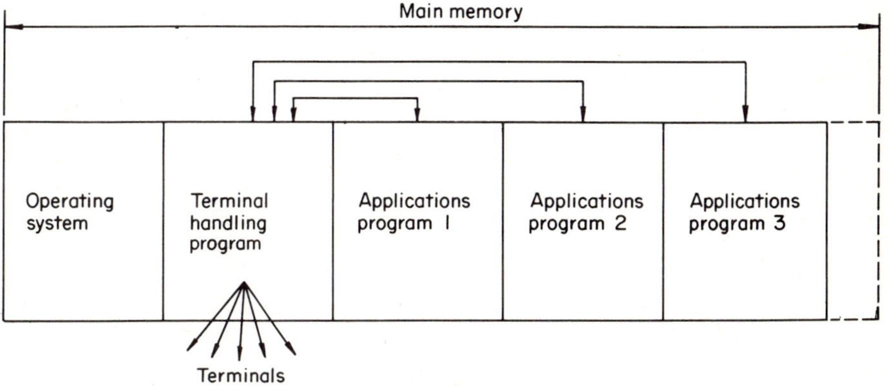

Figure 5.9. Separate terminal handling program.

applications programs. Typically the terminal program would perform the functions associated with software levels 1–3 whereas the terminal-specific functions and the dialogues handling would still be handled within the applications programs.

Freed from some of the problems of terminal and communications handling, the programmer was free to concentrate on writing his applications, or so he

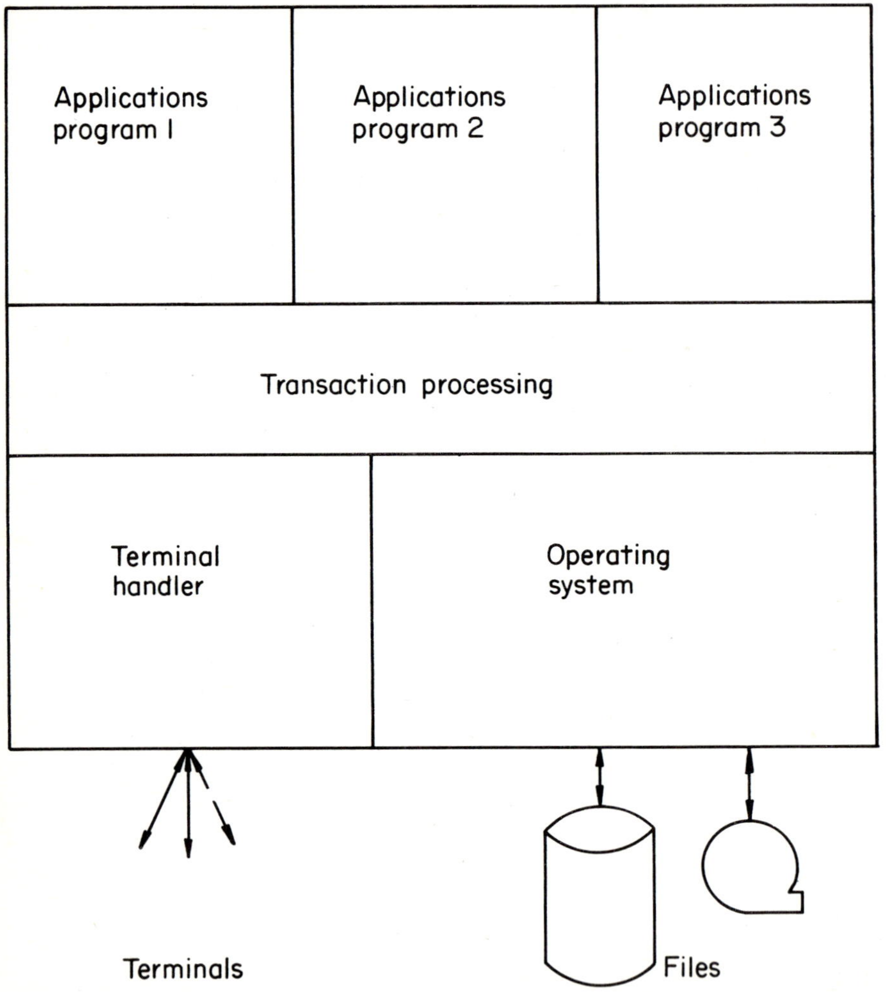

Figure 5.10. Transaction processing environment.

thought! Even with the simplest application he was spending considerable effort coping with other problems. The first was with the many different interfaces with the terminal handling program and the other operating system facilities. Next were the problems associated with more than one terminal, or program, wanting simultaneous access to records and files. Thus to simplify the programming task, to reduce the effort, to minimise and contain errors, and to provide flexibility it was clearly necessary for interfaces which provided an environment orientated towards the applications programmer's needs. This was provided by having another level of software above the operating system and the basic terminal handling software (*see* Figure 5.10). The applications make all requests, whether to files, terminals or other resources, through this standard interface. This software now provides a programming environment more familiar to batch programmers. Indeed the software has taken over many of the services that the operating system provided in the batch system, including the scheduling of programs, the management of main memory, and buffering.

More recently, special software systems have been designed and implemented specifically for transaction processing rather than having transaction processing added as an afterthought. Such systems provide many of the desirable facilities more efficiently than previously. Figure 5.11 illustrates this change of emphasis.

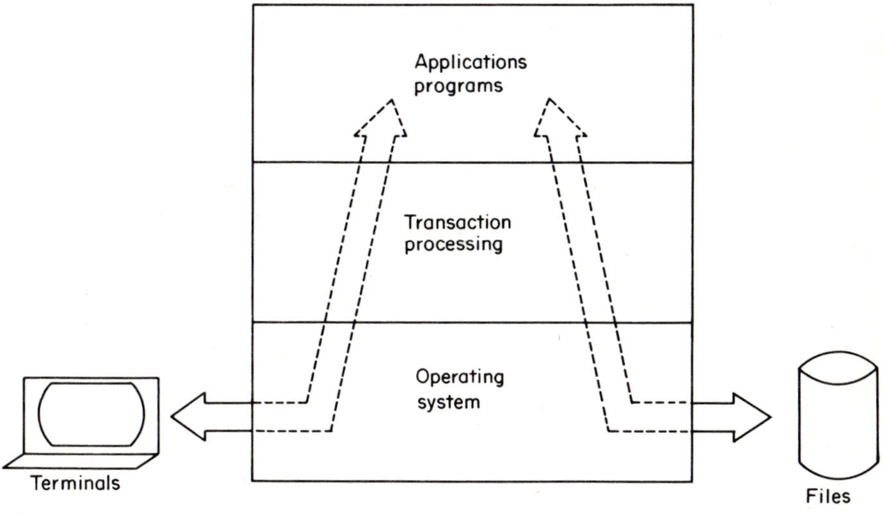

Figure 5.11. Integrated transaction processing system.

Further study

The reader should now be well equipped to pursue the subject and the following suggestions for further study can be made.

Further reading:

J. Martin (published by Prentice-Hall); *Design of man–computer dialogue* (1973); *Design of real-time computer systems* (1967); *Systems analysis for data transmission* (1972)

D.W. Davies and D.L.A. Barber (published by John Wiley): *Communication networks for computers* (1973)

Study the specifications of the many terminals available on the market today.

Study the specifications of the various communications protocols commonly used, such as IBM Bisync, Burroughs BOLD.

Consider the implications of intelligent terminals.

Study the architectures of some of the transactions processing systems in common use, such as IBM CICS, ICL DRIVER, Cincom ENVIRON/1 and Honeywell TDS.

Consider the problems associated with the application program being accessed by both buffered and unbuffered terminals.

6 Human factors in the design of visual display units

Roy Gladman

Introduction

VDUs operate at the interface of computer systems and a variety of human ones, examples being an office clerical system, a shop floor data collection system or a warehouse control system. It is clearly essential that the design of each component of a display system should be considered in relation to its interaction with the operator. This area of analysis is termed 'human factors' and can significantly contribute to operating efficiency. Such things as operator eye strain or muscle fatigue, caused by a poorly arranged keyboard or ambiguous character design on the display, will have an adverse effect on operator performance.

The operator who is comfortable and confident in the working of the equipment will get through more work, and even small gains in productivity are significant in today's environment when a display and its operator will cost between £300 and £400 each month. Perhaps the more significant aspect is that a comfortable and confident operator will make fewer mistakes. If these are not detected and corrected by the operator, but allowed to enter the computer system, they could become very costly to correct.

In this chapter the VDU is broken down into its two major components, the display and the keyboard. Each will be looked at in turn to define the 'human factor' requirements for optimum efficiency and to see how they interact with the design. Lastly, the operating environment of the complete unit is briefly considered.

The display unit

From a human factors point of view the main requirement of the display is *legibility*. This breaks down into two areas: first, how to make the best use of the space available to display information, and second, the quality of the display itself, which is the subject of this chapter.

The requirements for a good-quality display can be defined as follows:

- Easily discernible characters, with an optimum width to height ratio of 0.75–0.8
- Characters as large as possible, both for ease of viewing and to allow a wider range of working distances from the screen
- Well spaced characters and lines — research indicates that there should be a half-character's width between characters and at least one character's height between lines of information, more if possible
- Constant dimension, by which is meant that characters must have the same size wherever they are placed on the display, that the horizontal lines and vertical columns remain straight, and that the spacing between them remains constant
- No discernible flicker of the characters
- A means of indicating position on the screen
- A means of drawing the operator's attention to individual parts of the screen
- A means of accommodating a range of ambient light levels

Employers are tending to ask an increasing number of their staff to spend more of their day looking at displays. What is required is a total effect that allows operators to scan the information on the display. What must be avoided is forcing them to read every detail of it because the lines and characters are crammed together, as this will result in unnecessary fatigue over the working day. Try it for yourself with a double-spaced and a single-spaced typescript page.

The design process begins with the manufacturer selecting the highest-quality cathode ray tube (CRT) within the practical limitations of cost and commercial availability. Such a CRT normally has a 12–15 inch (300–375 millimetre) diagonal measurement.

The second step is to ensure that technical considerations are not in conflict with the basic human requirements. For example, variations in voltage and temperature-compensating elements lead to a variable-size character being presented on the screen. This is obviously less acceptable to the user than a constant-size character. Similarly, misalignment of the electron gun elements is reflected in a lower-quality screen image. The screen designer must also overcome distortion effects associated with variations in tube roundness in order to present the same size and high-quality character at any point on the screen. He will have to select the phosphor coating most appropriate to the user operating environment, taking into consideration such factors as colour, contrast, brightness, use of selector light pens, deterioration of the phosphor and image persistence. These physical properties are covered elsewhere in this book.

Within the real-world limitations of existing technology and cost the boundaries of the image quality which may be attained have now been established. The next step is the detail design. The basic building block, with implications for the quality of the entire display, is the individual dot within the character matrix. A very small, sharp, round dot is required with no overlap and no elongation from the horizontal scan, which would prevent the display of fine detail without smearing of the character. The width of the individual character, while staying within the parameters of quality, is actually proportional to the width of the spot. With dot sizes in the area of one- or two-hundredths of an inch (0.2–0.5 millimetre), a difference of two- to three-thousandths of an inch (0.05–0.07 millimetre) makes a difference of 10–14% in the number of characters per row. The number of characters per row becomes a factor of the size of the individual dot and the responsiveness of the phosphor selected. In other words, for how brief a period of time can the phosphor be excited and still maintain an adequate level of brightness? The spot size is a function of the quality of the scan gun, responsiveness of the circuitry and the phosphor itself.

Most commercially available displays have a line width of 80 characters, while typescript and book pages typically comprise 60–80 characters per line. It is this requirement to place 80 characters on a line within the available width which determines the character size. The amount of space available for character design, together with the requirement to maintain odd dimensions, usually leads to a 5- or 7-dot character width. The ideal width to height ratio is 0.75–0.8 and therefore the corresponding heights must be 7 or 9 dots respectively. An extra line of dots may be required to generate an underline or overline cursor. Allowing a double row for inter-line spacing, we could have 384 or 480 sweeps of our horizontal scan in order to produce an entire screen of data on a 24-line display, if we intend to scan the spacing rows in the same way as the rows participating in character generation.

The phosphor response and the character matrix fix the time required to generate a single character row. The number of rows, therefore, affects the time required to generate the entire screen. In large-capacity displays this places constraints upon the designer to maintain a refresh rate which tends to minimize detection of flicker by the operator. If an adequate refresh rate (generally accepted as just less than 50 times per second) cannot be maintained, then some operators will detect flicker.

There are actually three factors which contribute to what is an adequate *refresh rate* for an individual display. A high-persistence phosphor, within reasonable limits, tends to reduce the rate which is necessary. The brightness also affects the refresh rate required: the higher the intensity, the higher the required refresh rate tends to be. In addition, the concentration of displayed data also affects the frequency required. The more dense the displayed information, the higher the required refresh rate. Therefore, not only does data spacing affect the efficiency of the operator by allowing him or her to scan instead of read, but it also bears on the likelihood of detecting flicker. On the other hand, a refresh rate which is significantly higher than required is unnecessarily costly, and there would be a tendency for the dots to enlarge and the characters to become blurred.

While the effect of intensity on *flicker* was being explored, it was found that a neutral-density filter with reasonable transmission qualities over the face of the CRT could reduce the effects of the intensity on flicker perception without affecting the visibility. It is estimated that this discovery eventually increased the ability to display characters of good quality by approximately 20%. To put it another way, without such a filter, one would be able to display only 19 lines out of the usual 24 while maintaining the same quality of image.

A refresh rate of just under 50 times per second is not attainable on current commercial CRTs where 480 horizontal scans are required to generate a screen capacity of 1920 characters. Manufacturers use one of two techniques to overcome this: either 'interlacing' or 'skipping' as illustrated in Figure 6.1 and described below.

The theory of *interlace* is that a screen refreshed at a rate of 30 times per second is equivalent to 60 times per second if alternate scan lines are refreshed on each pass through the screen. However, this does not appear to be true for all the population since some people can detect flicker under these conditions.

The alternative method to obtain a true refresh rate of 50 times per second is to use a *skip* technique. In this method, the scan is advanced to the next row participating in character generation. As a by-product the skip can be made greater than a single line's width which, as has already been seen, not only helps to combat flicker but also improves the operator interface by making it easier to scan the data rather than reading it. For example, on one VDU which has a 7 × 9 character matrix with underline cursor, only 217 rows (9 per line + 1 per cursor) need to be refreshed at 50 times per second and the inter-line spacing has been increased to 1.8 times the character height.

In the creation of the character matrix, the vertical dot separation needs to be kept as equal to the horizontal separation as possible. If this is not done, either the horizontal lines or the vertical lines will tend to look solid while the

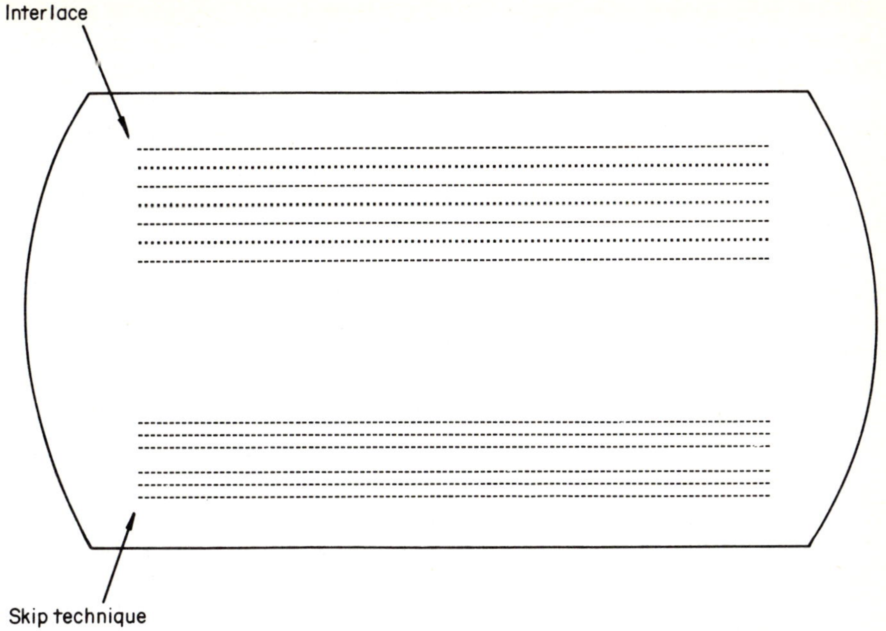

Figure 6.1. 'Interlace' and 'skip' techniques of preventing screen flicker.

others show a dotted pattern. However, even though the designer has achieved this to a typical tolerance of 0.0005 inch (0.012 millimetre), he still has to optimise the design and generation of the individual characters for the best quality. The characters should be discernible, simple and distinctive. Users should reliably be able to tell the difference between such characters as B, S, 8, 5 and 3; or between I, 1 and a vertical bar. It is an aid to easy recognition if in the detail areas in the centre of certain characters there are two unused dots between the detail and the outside.

The requirement for position indication is normally met by a cursor but there are many different types, such as an underscore, an overscore, a solid rectangle, a blinking solid rectangle or a character in reverse image. For attracting the operator's attention similar techniques can be used, for example underlining, blinking or a higher-intensity brightness as well as an audible alarm. User preference will play a large part in deciding what techniques are adopted. I favour an underline cursor, since a block cursor obscures the character and I believe a blinking one is distracting. For the same reason, I prefer a higher-intensity brightness for emphasising information. There may well be a requirement in a particular application to highlight more than one field. I find it most distracting when trying to look at one of these fields if other fields and even the cursor are blinking.

Displays have to be operated in a wide range of ambient lighting conditions. The operators themselves will have differing preferences for brightness levels and for contrast between normal and high intensity. It is therefore important that each display gives an ample range of adjustment for each intensity and that the operator should be able to see the display whilst manipulating these controls.

Another factor to be considered in relation to the operating environment is potential glare from the CRT surface. There are many advantages in having natural lighting in the display area but there can be problems because of its great range of intensity, from less than ambient to well over 10 000 foot-candles (100 000 lux).

It is helpful to orient the displays at right angles to the windows so that natural light will not shine directly on the surface of the display or be in the operator's field of view when he is working at the display. It is also helpful if the top of the screen is tilted forward slightly (preferably in manufacture) so that light is reflected downwards, away from the operator's eyes. If these measures do not overcome glare, consideration should be given to a non-glare screen, although any screen that diffuses light from external sources will also diffuse light coming from within the display and so detract from the quality of the characters.

Lastly, when one is positioning operators at displays, a character height subtending 16 minutes of arc at the eye should be considered a minimum. If the task requires frequent looking back and forth from the display to a source document, it would help if document and display were equally well lit and both were a similar distance from the human eye.

The keyboard

The way in which the keyboard is laid out, how it functions and even how the keys themselves are designed could have a significant effect on operator productivity and error rates. The importance of layout is well recognised and most manufacturers have a range of four keyboard types — operator console, typewriter, data entry and proof. Clearly the first step for every user is to ensure that the correct type is used for each application. There is not the space to argue the merits of the commonly used 'QWERTY ...' keyboard layout versus many other types, so I shall concentrate on the other two aspects mentioned above.

Whatever type of keyboard from whatever manufacturer is selected, it will now be an electronic keyboard rather than a mechanical one such as one commonly sees on the older typewriters. In other words, the depression of a key is detected electronically rather than transmitted mechanically.

The introduction of electronic keyboards has given users improvements in cost and reliability. The elimination of the mechanical linkage has also led directly to improvements in productivity. The keys can be better placed in relation to one another and so there is less operator hand movement; they have a lighter touch, so operators can sustain faster rates. However, the old mechanical keyboards had properties that were useful to the operator and it is important for most users that equivalent functions are incorporated into the electronic keyboard.

The old mechanical keyboards had mechanical interlocks to stop the operator keying multiple characters simultaneously. With the lighter-touch electronic keyboard it is only too easy to have two keys depressed at the same time — indeed an efficient operator frequently hits a second key before the first one is released and a really good operator may even hit a third key. An electronic keyboard must implement a form of *key roll* (to be described later) which ensures that a character is accepted by the system as soon as its key is depressed, and is not 'lost' because other keys are depressed.

With mechanical keyboards the operator could hear when the key hit the paper or was accepted. There was also a difference in the force required to press the key after it had been accepted. If an error were detected (by attachment to a computer) then the keyboard could be physically locked to signal the error and to prevent the operator from continuing. In other words, there were important audible and tactile feedbacks telling the operator what was happening, thus improving confidence. From a human factors point of view it is important that both these feedbacks are translated into the electronic keyboard, for both together are more reliable and timely than either by itself.

Laboratory tests have shown that keyboards without *audible feedback* result in significantly greater numbers of undetected errors on the part of operators. (Undetected errors are those introduced at the terminal by the operator without his being aware of having made any keying errors.) Practical tests with users have shown the same is true for tactile feedback.

In one group of tests the average number of undetected errors from a keyboard without audible feedback was over $2\frac{1}{2}$ times greater when compared to a keyboard with audible feedback. The primary contributors to this increase were omitted key strokes and duplicate key strokes, in that order. It was shown that operators did associate the audible feedback with acceptance of the character and that they were able to detect and correct nearly 80% more of their own errors at the time of entry. It was also shown that the absence of the audible feedback could be used to inform the operator of a disabled keyboard, reducing the need for him to look at the screen to determine whether or not characters were still being accepted from the terminal. The tests were conducted over a range of applications varying from unskilled inquiry to high-speed typing. Audible feedback was still shown to be a factor in performance with keying rates as low as two characters per second. As speeds increase, the difference in performance on different keyboards becomes greater. As the keying rate increases and/or the task becomes more complex, the keyboard has a greater effect on operator-detected errors.

Audible feedback is nowadays provided electronically — the system causes a solenoid to click when it accepts the character, and its absence denotes an error. It is important that this click should occur when the key is depressed and thus correspond to the operator's keying rhythm. In some implementations of keyroll (*see later*) the system clicks late when a second key is depressed before the previous one is released, and this tends to break up the operator's rhythm.

Figure 6.2a illustrates what happens when using keys without *tactile feedback*; the operator presses against a spiral spring with increasing force until stopped. The point at which the character is actually generated is at some intermediate location prior to the bottom of the keystroke. Without some feedback mechanism the operator cannot be certain when the character has actually been generated. If he or she presses the key fully home to make sure the character is accepted then keying speed suffers; if he or she does not press far enough in an attempt to go faster then the character is not generated. Any key vibration, called 'teasing', around the unknown point of acceptance (illustrated as *A*) will cause multiple character generation.

Figure 6.2b illustrates a system with tactile feedback. Here the operator presses against an elliptical flyspring in addition to a spiral spring. The point of acceptance by the system is arranged to be where the flyspring collapses; that is, when it is pressed just past the horizontal. There is a definite change in feel at this point which the operator will detect. He is aware that the character has been accepted and it is not necessary to depress the key further. The result is less pressure, less finger movement and faster operation. The flyspring also ensures that there is a physical change point when the key is released. This point is different from the acceptance point and in terms of finger travel is quite some way from it. Thus teasing does not lead to multiple character generation.

Tests have been carried out comparing the overall production throughput and error rates of one particular microswitch keyboard and an alternative capacitance keyboard (with a tactile key) over a whole range of applications, from enquiry by untrained operators to high-speed data entry by trained

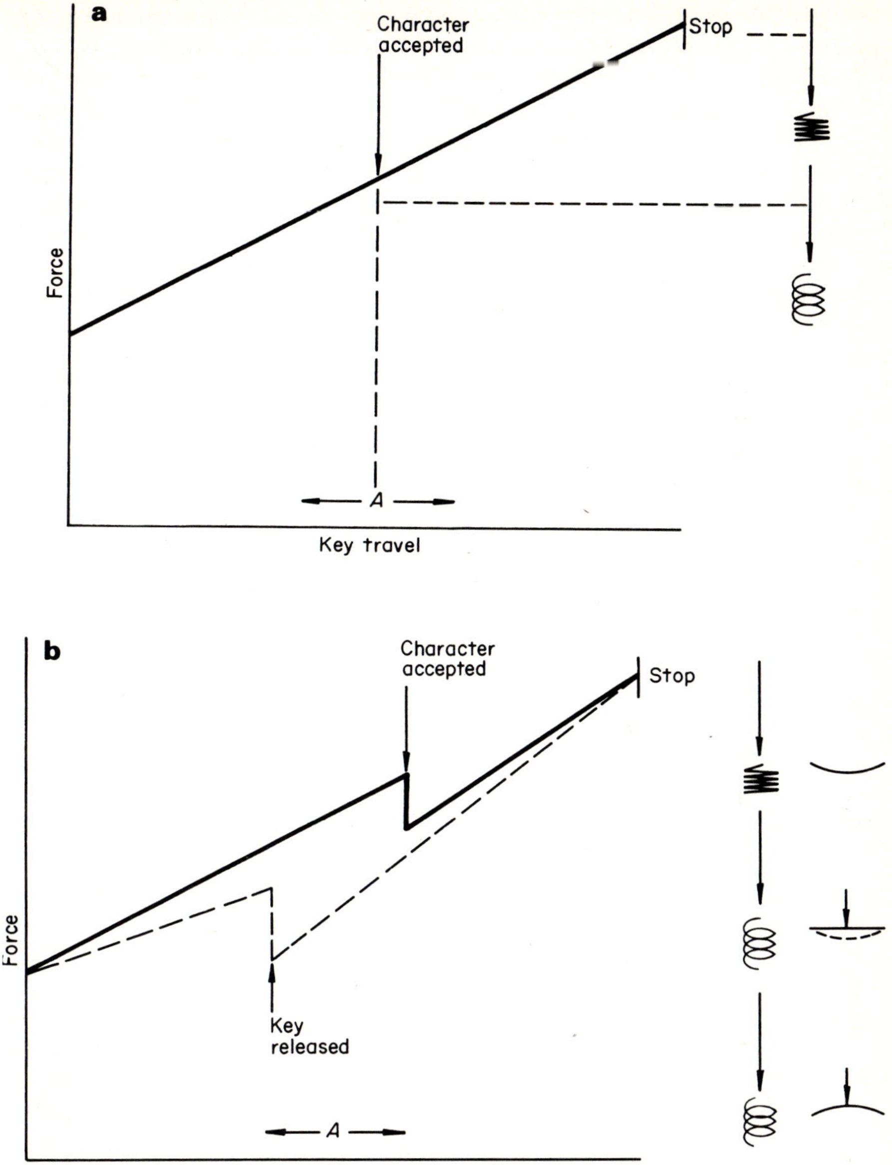

Figure 6.2. Keyboard systems without (a) and with (b) tactile feedback.

personnel. An overall productivity increase of 6.2% was realised by all operators, and in addition the percentage of keyboard errors (mainly omitted or duplicated keystrokes) was reduced by 23%.

Another important parameter is *key roll*, which defines when keystrokes hit in rapid succession are accepted; it is illustrated in Figure 6.3. With two-key roll this happens irregularly, when the first key is depressed and, for the second character, when the first key is released. This leads to irregular audible feedback. With *n*-key roll each key is accepted by the system when it is depressed.

Another phenomenon which can occur is called *shadow roll* (Figure 6.4). It occurs when the operator presses the first and then the second character but

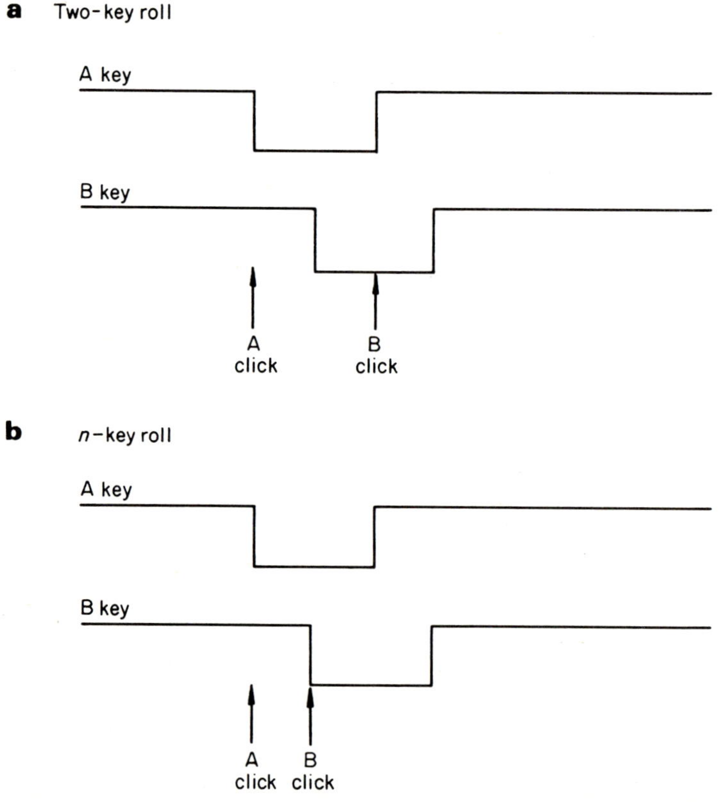

Figure 6.3. Key roll: (a) two-key roll, giving uneven feedback; (b) n*-key roll, giving even feedback.*

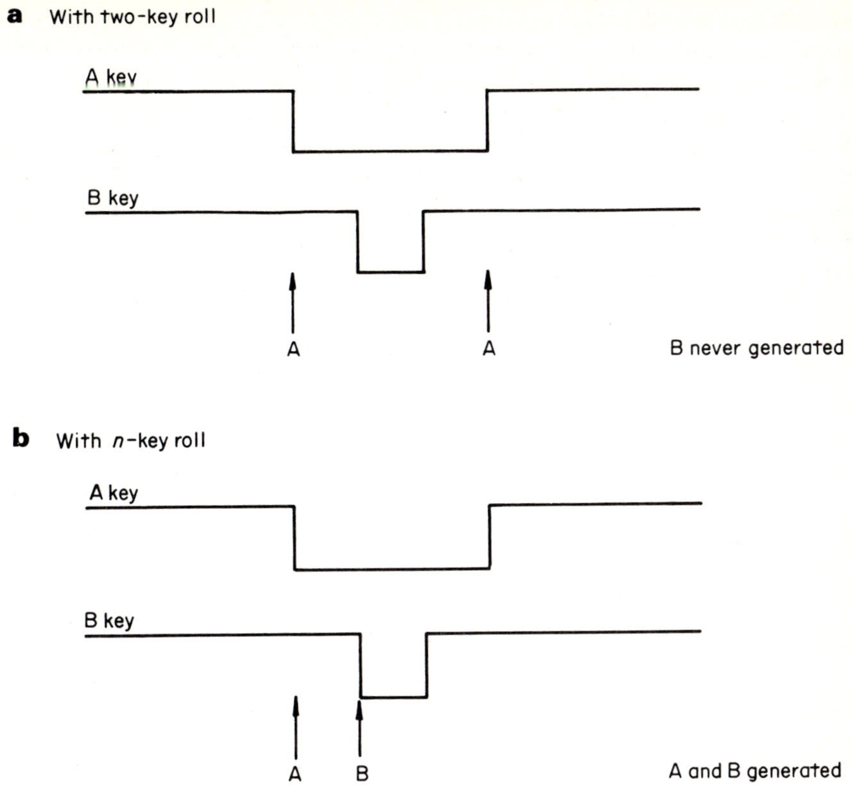

Figure 6.4. Shadow roll: (a) with two-key roll — the character 'B' is never generated; (b) with n*-key roll — both 'A' and 'B' are generated.*

releases the second before the first. On two-key roll the second character is lost and the first is generated twice; on *n*-key roll the second character is accepted when pressed.

Special keys are also worthy of consideration, the main ones being typamatic, repeat and insert/delete keys.

There are certain functions which an operator legitimately might wish to perform repetitively and rapidly. For example, the period and dash might be used for delineation and the cursor movement keys might also be used in this way. An operator could perform these functions by holding down a repeat key with one hand and the functional key with the other. In fact, many keyboards are designed this way. However, this would require the operator to remove his or her hand from data entry documents and place it on the keyboard.

Many users prefer a *typamatic key*. The operator simply keeps the desired key depressed and the keyboard performs the action for the first time. After a pause sufficiently long to ensure that the operator could remove his finger when only a single action is required (usually about half a second) the keyboard repeats the function rapidly at around 10 times a second. However, a word of caution: this may be a disadvantage if implemented on data keys. Alphabetic and numeric characters are seldom repeated in an application environment. Where they are repeated, it is faster for the operator to key the data twice so as not to break rhythm.

Another example is the insertion/deletion of characters. In some devices this function is implemented by requiring the operator to depress an insert key as many times as there are characters to be inserted. This moves the previously entered data one position to the right for each depression of the insert key, leaving the affected character positions blank. The operator then keys in each of the data characters to be inserted. Obviously, he must be aware of the number of positions to be inserted prior to beginning this operation. In other displays the operator, in contrast, places the device in the insert mode with a single key depression and then directly keys the data whilst simultaneously the system moves the previous data a position to the right for each character keyed. This removes the requirement for duplicate keystrokes and the associated requirement to count the positions before starting the insert operation.

Looking at the keyboard layout as a whole, one should ensure that all frequently used keys are within easy reach of the home row. Infrequently used keys, or keys which should not be used inadvertently, should be out of touch-typing reach of the operator. This is made possible by the use of the electronic keyboard. Mechanical keyboards with their underlying arrangement of levers require an offset arrangement of keys. Electronic keyboards do not have this requirement and so allow keys to be placed in a rectilinear layout. The advantage of this arrangement is the ability to arrange the keyboard by functional types of keys and maintain a compact arrangement, thereby reducing the hand motion required to perform keyboard operations.

An aspect of keyboard human factors which is frequently overlooked is that of the physical characteristics of the keys themselves. The shape of the surface of the keys, as well as the slant of the keyboard, can affect the confidence of the operator, and hence the keying rate achieved. Typewriter keys are traditionally stepped whilst data entry keyboards are traditionally sloped. One recent keyboard combines these characteristics into a concave or dish-shaped

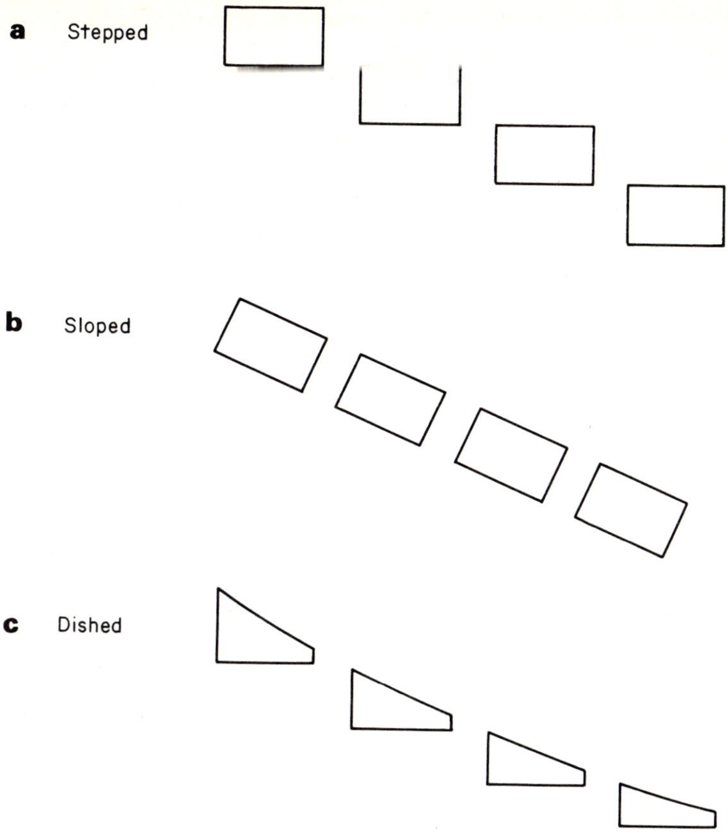

Figure 6.5. Key types.

keyboard (*see* Figure 6.5) with a dish-shaped key. The keytops are mounted at a 12° slant. The result is shorter finger travel from the home row to adjacent rows.

The disked keys have a rounded depression to fit the finger, and there are slightly differently shaped keys for each row. These, in combination with the deeper-than-normal depression of the four (4), five (5), and six (6) keys on the data entry keyboard and the F and J keys on the typewriter keyboard (commonly referred to as the 'home row'), instil a sense of confidence in the operator that he or she can reliably locate the 'home row' keys without having to glance from the source document. These characteristics all help build better confidence, rhythm, speed and accuracy, whatever the keying spead of the operator.

Lastly, the keyboard should be movable to accommodate the differing operating environments, but of sufficient weight (about 20 pounds — 9 kilos) to give the operator a feeling of stability and minimum risk of inadvertent movement. For example, in a data entry environment, an operator keys significant amounts of data from a source document. However, the document is seldom marked or altered during entry. Visual attention is centred on the document while the keyboard is operated by touch. The operator occasionally looks at the screen, usually to verify or check indicators. Therefore, the document and screen should be in line to minimise head movement. In contrast, interactive applications primarily involve the operator, the display and the keyboard. Keying rates are relatively low and often visually guided. Therefore, the operator's position, the display and the keyboard should line up to minimise head movements by the operator.

The display work station

Work station layout and environmental conditions have an effect on efficiency, particularly when the operator is required to operate the terminal for periods longer than half an hour.

A first essential for all seated work stations is to make sure that when the display is placed on its work table the centre of the display is at eye-level height for the average size of operator. Adjustments for individual operators could be made by raising or lowering the chair.

As explained earlier, for data entry stations the source document and screen need to be in line and so the keyboard needs to be shifted to the right to accommodate this. This type of station needs a greater minimum working width (36 inches or 0.91 metre) than the interactive or enquiry station (28 inches or 0.71 metre), where the display operator and keyboard should be in line. Both require a depth of 28–30 inches (0.71–0.76 metre). For tasks of over half an hour's duration, enough space should be provided to permit the operator to change position while operating the equipment.

The following specifications should be considered if custom work stations are to be built.

Keyboard height (distance from home row of keyboard to floor):
28 to 29 inches (0.71–0.74 metre) for sustained (professional) keying
28 to 32 inches (0.71–0.81 metre) for other (hunt-and-peck, casual)

Operator spacing (centre-to-centre distances between work stations):
- 28 inches (0.71 metre) minimum
- 48 to 60 inches (1.2–1.5 metre) preferred

Leg room, width:
- 18 inches (0.46 metre) minimum at knee height
- 24 inches (0.61 metre) minimum at foot level

Leg room, depth:
- 12 inches (0.3 metre) minimum at knee height
- 18 inches (0.46 metre) or more preferred at knee height
- 18 inches (0.46 metre) minimum at foot level
- 24 inches (0.61 metre) or more preferred at foot level

See-over height (if operators are required to look over work stations):
- Seated work stations:
  - 42 inches (1.1 metre) or less for women
  - 54 inches (1.4 metre) or less for men
- Standing work station:
  - 54 inches (1.4 metre) or less for women
  - 58 inches (1.5 metre) or less for men

Writing shelf:
- 12 inches (0.3 metre) minimum depth
- Minimum width dependent upon number of documents. Allow 1 inch (250 millimetres) spacing between documents

Source document position:
- To left of keyboard for data entry tasks
- To right of keyboard for tasks that require notations or written entries on the source document

Telephone equipment position:
- Usually left of keyboard

Summary

There is more to be considered in the selection of a VDU for use in a particular application than simply cost and reliability. Whatever the amount of money the user is investing in machine rental, maintenance or purchase, he will be investing at least twice as much and probably three times as much in operator wages, overheads and training. Therefore the machine and the operator should never be considered in isolation.

The quality of data presented on the display should be considered, for example in relation to the amount to be viewed each working day and the conditions under which this will be done. The emphasis must be on the scanning of data rather than the reading of each individual character and many factors which contribute towards this have been described. The amount of data to be keyed should be considered in relation to factors such as the quality of the source document, the likelihood of errors, the ease of detecting them and the cost of correcting them. Keyboard layout, operator feedback and key roll are some of the many factors to be considered.

The emphasis must be on a comfortable and confident operator. The comfortable operator will get through more work and the one who is confident in the operation of the machine will make fewer mistakes. In this way the computer and the operator will both become more productive.

7 Human factors in the use of visual display units

Tom Stewart

The man–computer partnership

The successful return of the crippled Apollo 13 spaceship provided a convincing demonstration that man–machine partnerships can be designed so as to extend considerably the capabilities of both man and machine. The flexibility and ingenuity of the astronauts in, for example, improvising air conditioning from spacesuit parts seems a peculiarly human skill whereas the sophisticated and complex computations performed routinely and accurately by the on-board computers would be impossible by purely manual means, particularly in the time available.

The message which comes most strikingly from this and the other space missions, and which is applicable even to more humble earthbound computer systems, is that truly successful man–machine systems require not just good machines and trained, skilled men but also well-designed interfaces between men and machines. It can be argued that a good interface will obviate the need for training and user support personnel, but developing and maintaining a successful man–computer partnership requires a degree of flexibility unlikely to be achieved effectively or indeed economically without human support staff. Conversely it is often pointed out that with sufficient training and practice the user will eventually cope with even the poorest interface. Indeed some current systems may depend on this assumption for their existence. It should be emphasised, however, that this degree of human adaptation frequently results in errors and delays, not to mention user dissatisfaction, which can have catastrophic consequences for overall system performance. Since we are currently in an era when waste of all types is deprecated, it is hoped that a consideration of the following issues will enable designers to create a better interface between man and computer. The training of users and the design of the computer system are different though closely related issues, and in this chapter they will be discussed only where they have a direct bearing on interface characteristics.

Most machines for human use must interface with man's physical capabilities through his eyes, hands, arms or legs and therefore require controls he can reach and has the strength or dexterity to use and displays which he can see and read. This also applies to computer systems but since they are information processing machines they must also interface with man's information processing capability or mind (*see* Figure 7.1).

Increasingly, VDUs are being employed as the prime interface between user and computer system and the next section of this chapter discusses how human factors can help the designer to achieve a satisfactory software interface through creating a dialogue between man and computer. In a later section, recommendations are made about how the VDU may be introduced into the office and a checklist is proposed to help the designer and user jointly to create a satisfactory working environment. The hardware aspects of VDUs have already been discussed in the previous chapter.

Man–computer dialogues

There are two main requirements for a successful software interface (*see* Figure 7.2). First, it should fit the *function* it serves in the overall systems design. This depends on the nature and *purpose* of the system, say stock control or order

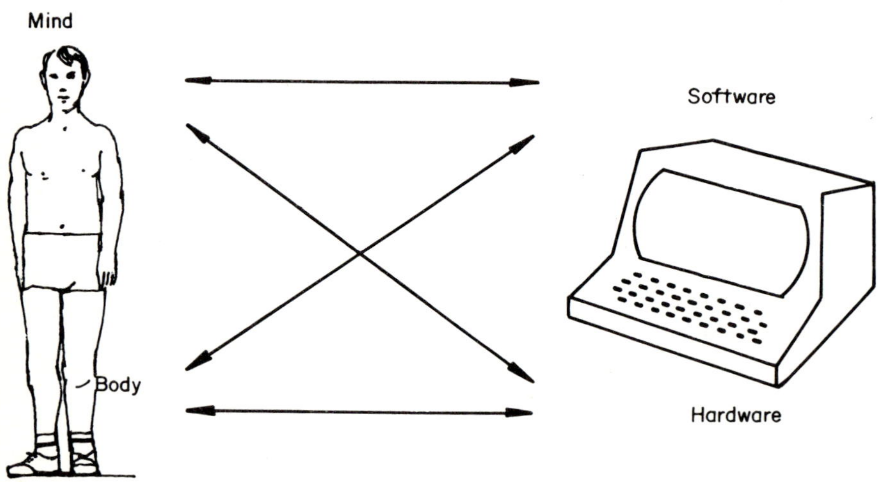

Figure 7.1. The man–computer interface.

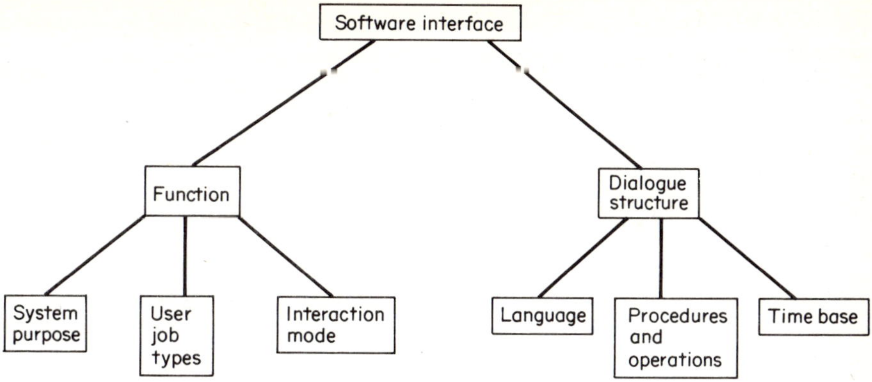

Figure 7.2. The software interface.

entry. It also depends on the type of *job* the user is performing. A general-purpose software interface seldom suits all users, and the interface must therefore be geared to the specific needs of the various tasks which comprise the user's job. Finally, the function depends on the interaction *mode*, the range of facilities available to the user. These may range from a mode which involves the user primarily in data entry, through menu selection of available displays to a direct programming mode.

Secondly, the *structure* of the dialogue should be such that it can fulfil its function, as defined above. The language through which man and computer communicate can range from a powerful programming language to a simple command language and must be matched to the function. The way in which the language is organised into *procedures and operations* through which the user interacts with the system must again match the function. Finally, it is important that the *time base* of the interaction is appropriate.

What the function of the interface should be depends on the specific system being designed. For a discussion of relevant human factors issues the reader is recommended to read the report by Eason, Damodaran and Stewart (1974), as cited in the section on 'Further Reading', p.176. The rest of this section is concerned with some general issues concerning the design of appropriate dialogue structures in VDU-based systems.

The language of the dialogue

In most situations, the user is already familiar with the language or vocabulary associated with the task being performed and it is important that the computer system should correspond to or be consistent with existing usage. The design and selection of terms, names and labels for the system should be regarded as an important part of the dialogue design.

Once the existing task language or vocabulary is determined it is highly likely that ambiguities, inaccuracies and repetitions may be found. These should be examined further and resolved in close consultation with the users. It may be that the task did not exist previously or that new terms will be needed for facilities or processes which will be introduced with the computer system. In this case, new terms which are internally consistent and appropriate to the task need to be added to the vocabulary.

Languages associated with computer systems, particularly VDU-based systems, are often of necessity terse, coded and abbreviated. This can cause problems for users who are accustomed to a task vocabulary which is powerful and rich in expression. Human languages contain considerable redundancy, and missing items can often be accurately inferred from the context of the communication. Thus -ost p-ople -ould -ave l-ttle -iffi-ulty -uess-ng th- miss-ng le-ters whereas it is more difficult to guess an incomplete code such as 294-322-6 correctly. Although such coding is usually for the computer's benefit it can, if properly constructed, facilitate data entry or even the assimilation of output.

There are two main principles by which codes may be derived or extracted from a full description. One type of code is derived by a process of transformation, e.g. *l*eft-*h*and *b*racket may be encoded as LHB. Alternatively, there may be a code, often numeric, which bears no apparent logical relationship to the full description but which, by virtue of prolonged exposure to the codes, the user comes to associate with the item (e.g. left-hand bracket may in this system be encoded as 0952). Combinations of these two principles are of course also possible but may be confusing. Where users are likely to become extremely familiar with the codes, associative numeric codes can be used most effectively. However, there may be a problem with new or infrequent users, and so look-up tables should be provided, either within the system, printed in manuals or on a separate card to be kept near the VDU.

Table 7.1 shows some of the abbreviations which were proposed for use in an order entry system and how they were revised using more obvious principles. It should be noted that in some of the examples a satisfactory solution was achieved by simply re-naming the command rather than modifying the code.

For relatively experienced operators, the greatest single source of errors in a typical data entry task is the substitution of one character for another and so a very brief error message is often sufficient (type (a), Table 7.2). The greatest single source of errors for the inexperienced user or operator is forgetting codes or procedures and he may not be able to identify the error, let alone take

Table 7.1. Some order entry system abbreviations

Proposed			*Suggested improvement*	
Command/procedure	*Code*		*Command/procedure*	*Code*
Stock receipt	STR	✓	*	*
Stock enquiry	STQ	X	Stock query	*
Compile load sheet	CLS	✓	*	*
Print delivery note	PRD	X	*	PDN
Additional delivery instructions	ADD	X	Extra delivery instructions	EDI
Alternative delivery instructions	ALT	X	*	ADI
Page back	PRP	X	Previous page	*
Page forward	NXP	X	Next page	*

* = keep as proposed

Table 7.2. Types of error message

Type (a)	**Coded error message only**
Example	MAGIC 32 0 DEBUG 0 678 543 0 1 70321 TERMINATED
Action	
either	Recognise and check why program Magic 32 requested a non-existent output device
or	Consult colleague or manual (incidentally most of the numbers represent register states which are only likely to be used by highly experienced programmers to trace the approximate area of rare errors).
Type (b)	**Short error messages plus more details on request**
Example	EXCESSIVE VARIABLES
Action	
either	Recognise and correct error
or	Press '?' key for further details and get for example ATTEMPT TO DECLARE MORE THAN 286 VARIABLES. Pressing the '?' key again might lead to more explanation and a reference to the appropriate section in the manual.
Type (c)	**Long error message which can be interrupted**
Example	NON-EXISTENT OUTPUT DEVICE HAS BEEN SPECIFIED IN PROGRAM: MAGIC NUMBER: 32. PROGRAM HAS BEEN TERMINATED AT LOCATION: 70321 OTHER REGISTERS: 0 678 543 0 1 FURTHER INFORMATION: PP239-342 OPS MANUAL.

corrective action, when the simple message 'error' is presented. Most systems have to cope with both types of operator at various times and there may be a conflict between the inexperienced operator's need for explanation with guidance as to the appropriate corrective action and the experienced operator's need for brevity.

There are several possible solutions to this problem and the circumstances of the particular systems design, the users' tasks and the user population will determine which is more appropriate. One solution is to provide short coded error messages backed up by a facility whereby the user can press a 'help' or '?' key and obtain a longer, more informative and detailed error message (type (b), Table 7.2). An advantage of this solution is that experienced operators also have the back-up facility available for infrequently used codes or to refresh their memories after an absence.

A second solution is basically similar but automatically follows up the short coded version with help or explanation until the user interrupts by pressing another key (type (c), Table 7.2). If the error messages can be written so as to become progressively more detailed and helpful, rather like programmed learning material, then the users can effectively choose their own level of detail by interrupting at the appropriate time. In this way the system can offer more different 'levels' of error message without complicated switching from one level to another.

In the third solution, the system determines an appropriate level of help for a given user and given type of error. This may be done either by monitoring the user's performance or by identifying each user by his logging-in code. Provided that this facility can be at least partially overridden by the user then it could provide the most flexible type of error message system.

In practice it may be more appropriate to combine various features of these three different types of system. While it is true that some of these solutions may place a considerable load on the system designer, probably at a stage in the design where he is under considerable time pressure, it must be stressed that an unsatisfactory error detection, identification and message system wastes a considerable amount of both system and user time and can blight the entire system.

Dialogue procedures and operations

The second important aspect of the dialogue is the way in which the language is organised into the procedure and operations through which the user interacts with the system.

One of the most striking features of all but the most boring and routine user tasks is that they can and often need to be handled in slightly different ways by different users, or by the same user at different times or in other circumstances. This flexibility is one of the main reasons why man has an important role to play in ensuring adequate system performance. It is therefore important that the computer system should not inhibit essential human flexibility in performing various tasks.

When a system has to serve inexperienced or naïve users, the displaying of 'menus' of available options and structuring these into 'trees' can greatly simplify the interface. However, this sometimes results in inflexibility when experienced users are forced to work through well-known tree structures and decision points. However, bypass codes can be introduced so that, provided the user knows both the sequence of decision points and the response options, he can enter a string of responses simply separated by a bypass character, such as '/'.

In an order entry system studied by the author it was intended that the user should enter a complete order in one episode and that a VDU left unattended for some time would revert to a waiting mode and be available for other transactions. However, an examination of the future users and their tasks made it clear that they might frequently be interrupted during a transaction, for example to answer the telephone. While it was desirable that this should not cause the terminal to be totally inaccessible to other users for the duration of the interruption, it had not been fully worked out whether the original user would be able to recall a partially complete transaction or even if he could find out where he was in the interaction. The system therefore had to be able not only to store partial transactions but also to indicate clearly to the user at what point the transaction had been interrupted.

Inevitably, systems design focuses on the operational characteristics of a normally functioning system but equally inevitably a system will sometimes malfunction. These situations are particularly worrying for users who are unfamiliar with computer technology, and it is therefore important that there are well-established procedures for non-routine start-ups and recovery from crashes.

If the central computer of a remote system goes down, users may lose data in buffer store, and the provision of system 'heartbeats' or some other indication that a system is live can prevent the problems caused by failures in mid-transaction. Procedures for helping users to identify the nature of particular types of failure, and to select the appropriate action, should also help them to re-establish contact with the system with the minimum disruption to the work flow.

The *sequence* or order in which instructions or data have to be entered into the system should form a logical and consistent progression corresponding to any order implied by the user's task. Thus, for example, if the user has to obtain data from a series of documents or from a telephone conversation and enter them into a terminal, it should be possible to follow the sequence of the source (human, documentary or whatever) and neither overload the short term memory of the user nor disorganise the source.

Where the user has to enter data obtained from customers, the sense and the logic behind the sequence should derive from the user's task rather than from convenience for the computer. Thus in the U.K. the Post Office has been able to reduce the mean transaction time in telephone directory enquiries by ensuring that enquiries are first greeted with the question, 'Which town, please?', which allows the operator to start the search process by selecting the appropriate directory while the customer completes his enquiry. Even the first time it is encountered it seems to the user to be a relevant and appropriate question. This would not be the case if, for some perhaps sound computer reason, a customer was first greeted by 'How do you intend to pay?' when enquiring about the availability of theatre tickets. In many situations it is neither possible nor desirable for the designer to control the sequence of the dialogue in this manner, particularly if, for example, different users handle the task differently or if different tasks demand flexibility in the way they are handled by the user.

There are two main reasons why it is difficult to achieve consistent sequences of operations at all times. First, the system will almost certainly be designed in stages, modules or some other components. Frequently it is not until implementation that the interaction which will be experienced by users is seen in total as one sequence. At this point, it may well be too late to change certain features of the design and so all too often the user interface is compromised and errors, delays and frustrations result.

Secondly however, it is difficult for designers intimately involved in developing a system to put themselves realistically in the user's place. Similarly it is difficult for future users who are not at all familiar with any computer, let alone the proposed system, to assess realistically how they will react in the future. Therefore, one of the functions of involving users in the design process is to provide a pool of informed comment at various stages.

An alternative solution is to use human factors specialists who are familiar with man–computer problems in general. These specialists have the techniques, and the training, to examine users and their tasks and relate these meaningfully to systems design proposals, specifications or partial solutions. An excerpt from a case study may illustrate how this can work in practice.

The author's experience of a particular order entry system was as follows. On the VDU proposed for the system there was one key at the top left of the keyboard which brought the cursor to the *home* position in lower shift and which *cleared* the screen in upper shift. These are hardly ideal functions to share a key under any circumstances, but following through various sequences proposed in the system, several possibly disastrous combinations were revealed. For example, the operator entering a customer's order may need to continue a list of quantities onto the next page. To do this he would home the cursor in order to write the command into the control area. At this point it will be obvious that if the keyboard was in upper shift (for various reasons a most likely situation) the user could easily clear the screen by mistake. In fact it emerged that this possibility had not been considered fully and the operator would be unable to recall the screen. Unfortunately the system would be unaware that the screen had been cleared since this was a local function. At the very least therefore there was considerable scope for confusion and many opportunities for double entering of orders.

The main requirement for good *formats* is that the communication or language from the computer should be organised and structured within the display in a form appropriate to the task and frame of reference of the user. Where several different types of user need to perform different tasks with essentially the same information, it may seem necessary to compromise individual user and task requirements in the interest of economy or standardisation. However, in the long term it may be better to provide different displays with virtually identical information content, since the way in which information is used or the conclusions that may be drawn from it are influenced by the way it is presented and organised.

The following general principles (Table 7.3) contribute to good format design, although in practice it may be necessary to compromise in order to achieve satisfactory displays.

Logical sequencing. The sequence or order in which information is presented should where possible be logical both to the system and in relation to the user's task or other information sources.

When it is not possible to achieve both these objectives, it is the sequence in which the user requires the information which should be used, even if this is not obviously logical to the computer or to the system designer. If this is not possible and it is necessary to design the displays according to some other logical framework, then at least the user should be informed of that logical basis to help him to make sense of what may otherwise be a meaningless format.

Grouping. Grouping similar items together in a display improves their readability, and can also highlight relationships between different items of data.

Table 7.3. Examples of good and bad format design

(a) Bad format

```
PART NUMBER FILE SUB-FILE MISC BKTS
SUPPLIER J. BLOGGS & SON, ROTHERHAM
PART 0926431X DESCRIPTION LH BRONZE STUD BRACKET
GROUP B CLASS R STATUS NOT YET ALLOCATED
SUB-ACCOUNT 92 BUDGET GROUP 2413
QUANTITY UNIT DOZENS DEPRECIATION PERIOD 15 ACTION
DATE OF ADDITION 1/12/75 ADDED BY F. BRIGGS DES 9
DATE LAST AMENDED 14/5/75 AMENDED BY PROC 11 R. SMITH
DATE OF DELETION
COMPONENTS NONE
SUB ASSEMBLIES NONE
```

(b) Better format

PART NUMBER FILE:		MISCELLANEOUS BRACKETS		
PART:	0926431X	LH BRONZE STUD BRACKET		
GROUP:	B	BUDGET GROUP:		2413
CLASS:	R	SUB-ACCOUNT		92
UNITS:	DOZENS	DEPRECIATION PERIOD:		15
ACTION	----	PRODUCT STATUS:		NOT YET ALLOCATED
ADDITION DATE:		1 DEC 75	F. BRIGGS DES 9	
LAST AMENDED:		14 MAY 75	R. SMITH PROC 11	
DELETION DATE:		NONE		
MAIN SUPPLIER:		J. BLOGGS & SON, ROTHERHAM		

Thus, grouping of many similar items like lists of numbers into manageable 'chunks' allows them to be searched and identified more accurately and more quickly. Grouping can also be used to provide structure in the display and to highlight interrelationships between various items of data.

Spaciousness. Spacing and blanks on a VDU screen are necessary to aid in the identification and recognition of items of information and also to emphasise and maintain the structure of the display. Clutter on a display greatly reduces the legibility and increases both search times and errors. Where a large amount of information must be available, it is often more satisfactory to provide a series of displays rather than to try to cram all the information onto one screen.

Relevance. Only information that is directly relevant to the user should be displayed. It is often the inclusion of material only potentially relevant that gives rise to clutter and reduces the legibility of the truly relevant information. When users received printouts from batch processing systems it was often necessary to include all the information which the user might conceivably need since computer runs were slow and could take days. With VDU systems it is possible for the user to 'dig' for progressively more detailed and complex displays. The basic displays can therefore be made easy to read and assimilate to an extent that few printouts can achieve.

Consistency. The screen formats should be consistent both internally and between different displays. The overall need for consistency in the language and the organisation of the language of man–computer communication has already been emphasised. The prime value of consistency, particularly in screen formats, is that an unfamiliar or new format can be more readily and accurately interpreted if it conforms to existing practices in its use of language and structure.

Simplicity. Formats should be as simple as possible. This does not mean that highly detailed, complex displays have no place, but if they are necessary they can still be structured and organised to avoid inessential complexity.

Assuming that the designer takes these principles into account, there are still two further stages in producing optimum formats.

First, it is absolutely essential to try out all the proposed formats on the type of VDU screen which will be used. There are considerable differences between different VDUs in terms of character geometry, spacing and the other factors discussed in the previous chapter, and these can have a radical effect on the legibility and acceptability of different formats.

Secondly, the users can well be involved in this process, particularly since they are the ones who will need to live with the formats. Also, if possible, it is worth getting professional help from graphic designers and other specialists in obtaining the best formats. The rawest recruit to the design team working in isolation with a stubby pencil and a pile of coding sheets is unlikely to be in a position to produce ideal displays.

Finally, even the best-designed displays may need to be changed once the system is operational in order to suit the users, or owing to changes in the company's circumstances, markets or products. It is therefore desirable to write the display software in such a way that display formats can be changed, developed or refined without re-writing the entire system.

Time-base

The third main aspect of the dialogue is the time-base which pervades the other aspects of the interface and in many ways determines the relative significance of the other components. The dialogue therefore consists of words or language which are organised in various ways into different procedures and operations and it is the timing underlying this organisation which is the subject of this section.

The time taken by a system to respond to a query or instruction from a user (*system response time*) has been regarded by many as the only important time-base issue in man–computer dialogue design. While it is not the only issue, it is the one which has received most attention since it can have some fairly obvious consequences for the user. It has been suggested that if the response time is more than 1 minute, then this disrupts human decision-making and problem-solving. Various sources suggest different critical response times and there is little unequivocal evidence about what is an acceptable delay for real-world tasks. There is growing evidence that 'instantaneous' or zero response delays are ideal, but that users will probably tolerate a few seconds' delay without any difficulty. It is the predictability of the likely delay which is critical to the user and this can make longer response delays acceptable.

In determining or predicting the likely response delay in a given design or system it is important that the designer consider the situation which is likely to be experienced by an individual user. While involved in a system evaluation exercise, the author was puzzled to find that users complained about delays of several minutes which they experienced fairly regularly, whereas the system designers and system maintenance personnel were adamant that the system never produced delays of more than 5 seconds. On closer investigation it emerged that indeed the 'system' never produced long delays but the network onto which the users' terminals were connected frequently suffered long delays at peak times and often 'crashed' for periods of minutes.

One of the time-base aspects most critical to the user is the likely time it will take from approaching or switching on the terminal to walking away or switching it off with the task successfully performed (*task completion time*). A whole range of factors influence this total time including many of the ease of use issues discussed earlier.

Hardware reliability and system reliability are also highly important in determining this task completion time. These may not seem to be human factors issues but they do considerably affect the quality of the computer service received by the user. The effect for the system may be different depending on whether a failure is due to terminal malfunction or a software 'crash', but what is important to the user is how quickly he or she can find out what has happened, whether any action by him is necessary and, of course, how long he is likely to have to wait for the system to be functioning correctly again. It is particularly important for users to have some idea of whether it is worth waiting for the system to recover or to switch to manual standby procedures.

The final aspect of the role of time in the dialogue which will be discussed in this chapter concerns the organisation of system processing. Many articles and even books have been written about the relative merits of batch processing versus time sharing for aiding human problem solving. In order to create some kind of order in this attempt to compare 'chalk' (batch processing) and 'cheese' (time sharing), it has apparently proved necessary to erode the obvious, everyday, practical differences. Distinctions between 'instant' batch processing and 'time sharing' become increasingly meaningless and more a matter of definition. More important, however, are the consequences for different users of organising a computer's processing in particular ways and this is much more difficult to untangle.

This processing can be organised in three identifiably different ways. First, a number of operators can apparently simultaneously and independently use the computer for different tasks. The normal commercial time sharing services usually operate in this way. A second way involves all operators using the one system and the computer processing each transaction as it occurs (*real-time transaction processing*). Thus, for example, in an airline seat reservation system all users can access the same flights and if one user books a number of seats then simultaneously the seats are booked as far as all users are concerned. A third way is basically identical to the second except that the processing does not occur in real time (*delayed transaction processing*). Thus, for example, in a banking system, balances may be computed overnight when the day's business is complete.

Some current systems involve combinations of these three ways. As yet, little is known about the degree to which computer systems can be used as additional communication channels, but there is some evidence that computer conferencing can be a useful means of carrying out particular kinds of decision-making and problem-solving.

There is also some evidence that in large, geographically distributed

Table 7.4. VDU work station checklist

User and task factors: who will use the work station and what tasks will they perform?

Range and limits of users' characteristics? e.g. age
sex
body size
experience
training

Tasks to be performed? e.g. activities
functions

Man–machine factors: will the work station suit the size, shape and other characteristics of the actual or potential users?

Can the users reach and operate the controls? e.g. alphanumeric keyboard
special function keys
power and other VDU controls
other computer equipment
other office equipment

Can the user see and read the displays? e.g. VDU screen
VDU control and indicator lights
other equipment displays
source or other necessary documents
look-up lists, operating details
other office lists or directories

Can the user work in a comfortable position and get in and out easily? e.g. posture
leg and knee room
table and desk height
seat height
stretching or bending

Workspace factors: will the work station suit the tasks the user needs to perform and the job aids required?

Work surfaces? e.g. size, number
accessibility

Storage? e.g. for printout and manuals
other work documents
job aids (such as calculators, pencils, etc.)
personal belongings
'buffer' for batching

Seating? (if any) e.g. adjustable
swivel or fixed
arms
stable

Interaction with other equipment? e.g. telephone
calculator, etc.

Sharing the VDU? e.g. queues
access
privacy
security
audience effects

Clutter? e.g. bins for rubbish
trailing wires

Maintenance access? e.g. regular
non-routine

Environment factors: is the physical environment conducive to effective use of the VDU and will the VDU create an environmental problem for users or others?

Acoustic environment? e.g. noise caused by VDU
noise caused by ancillary equipment
noisy environment for user

Thermal environment? e.g. VDU sensitive to heat
VDU generating heat

Visual environment? e.g. adequate light for source documents
adequate ambient illumination
reflections from screen or other surfaces
glare from screen or other surfaces

Safety environment? e.g. electrical hazards
vibrations/knocks
chemical hazards

The checklist may be used to compare or evaluate proposed work stations. The answers or responses to the various checks and questions can be simply yes/no or more complex ratings. The relative importance of these and any other factors will depend on the specific combination of user, task and system.

organisations with computer links a facility for sending messages to other users or operators can, for example, improve co-operation and communications between otherwise isolated depots.

There may be far-reaching consequences both for individuals and the organisation in choosing particular ways of organising computer system processing. For example, it may influence task interdependencies among different users, it may considerably influence the dissemination and security of confidential information or it may create or modify communication channels within an organisation.

Introducing the VDU into the office environment

Introducing any computer system into an office environment raises a number of organisational and work design issues which must be considered and resolved if the system is to be successfully implemented. The behavioural aspects of implementing major organisational changes are beyond the scope of this chapter but it cannot be stressed too strongly that the involvement of future users at every stage of the design process is an important feature of successful system implementation. This section of the chapter will focus on the more general practical considerations in simply locating a VDU in an office.

There cannot, of course, be one single solution which will suit all situations, and it is strongly recommended that work station and location decisions should be taken with full collaboration and involvement of the potential users. If the users have been involved fully from an early stage in the design, then by the time work stations and locations are being considered they should have developed a sufficiently detailed appreciation of what using the system will involve to enable them to participate in a realistic and informed manner.

A checklist (Table 7.4) is proposed as an aid to users and designers. Its purpose is to point out some of the factors (including some of the ones which are most likely to be forgotten) which should be used in assessing a prospective solution for their own situation.

User and task factors

The first step in the process is to identify the range of likely users and establish both the range and the limits of such characteristics as age, body size and experience, in addition to examining the various tasks they will perform in using the computer and in other associated parts of their jobs.

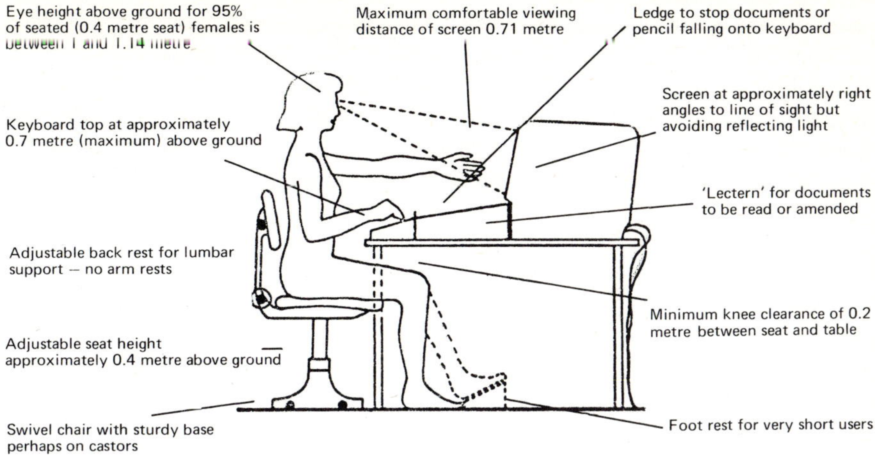

*Figure 7.3. Typical dimensions for a VDU work station. For further details, consult Van Cott and Kinkade (*see *'Further Reading' section, p.176).*

Man–machine factors

There are a number of dimensions or clearances which may need to be adjusted in a given work station to suit the size and shapes of the potential users (Figure 7.3). There are three main areas in which to check the fit between the user and the VDU work station.

Can the user reach and operate the controls? The different controls which a user may need to operate at various points in an interaction should all be easily accessible. The major controls which may need to be operated are keyboard, special function keys; power or other VDU controls (e.g. brightness), modems, etc. There are also likely to be a number of controls on other office equipment which the user may have to operate in conjunction with computer equipment, e.g. lighting, telephones, calculators, photocopiers, heating, etc.

Can the user see and read the displays? The different displays which the user may need to read or use during the interaction should be at a suitable distance and not, for example, concealed by other objects if the user sits down.

Can the user work in a comfortable position and get in and out easily? There are a number of basic clearances which are necessary to prevent the user having to adopt an uncomfortable or damaging posture either when using the work station or when getting in or out. Thus, for example, short operators may need a footrest, but adequate knee clearance is required between table or desk and seat top. The screen should be at a comfortable viewing distance.

Suitably sized equipment and seating is necessary not just for comfort, essential though this is for efficient work, it is also a matter of health and safety. Back problems account for a substantial proportion of industrial ill health, and bad work station design is a major contribution to poor posture and backstrain.

Workspace factors

Work surfaces or desk space may be needed to lay out, read and write on documents and printouts. The work surfaces should be appropriate for such needs both in terms of size and in position and accessibility (Figure 7.4). A lectern between a detachable keyboard and the VDU screen can be useful for supporting source documents at an appropriate reading distance. While working at the VDU, the user may wish to *store* computer printouts, other work material or even personal belongings, such as a handbag (Figure 7.5). Another storage need which is often neglected is for a short-term 'buffer area' where incoming or outgoing documents or work can be 'batched' or sorted. Items such as calculators, pencils, etc. also need to be stored.

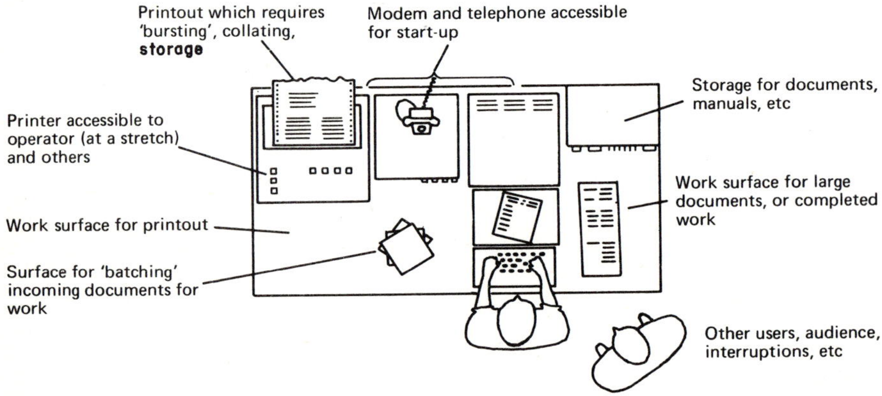

Figure 7.4. VDU-printer work station with work surfaces and storage facilities. This layout was designed to meet specific requirements for large documents, independent printer operation and using existing furniture. Within these constraints, the accessibility of printer, modem and manual storage could not be optimised.

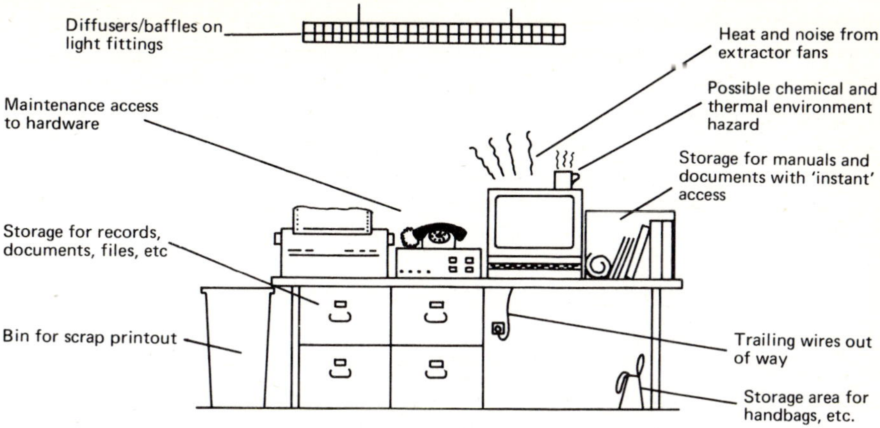

Figure 7.5. Other points to note in a VDU-printer work station.

The type of *seating* required depends on the length of time the user is likely to spend at the VDU and how frequently he or she will need to move away from it during interaction. A swivel chair (with a stable base but without arms) can be used to provide mobility if a fixed chair is not appropriate.

Some tasks, such as referring to indexes or telephoning, require frequent movements away from the terminal, and a 'sit–stand' arrangement may be preferable; that is, the work station is placed at a height suitable for standing operation but for seated operation a high chair or stool (with a stable base) is provided.

If more than one user or group of users is to *share* the VDU then there may be difficulties in locating the terminal in a mutually convenient place. If it is located in one user's office, there may be interference to the normal work of the office caused by other users either interacting with the system or queuing up for their turn. To overcome these difficulties it may be appropriate to place the VDU in a separate room altogether. If this room is open to a wide range of people then various security devices may be necessary to prevent unauthorised use or to limit access to specific facilities. Such devices may include *badge readers, passwords* or a *locking power supply*; they can all be effective in limiting or preventing unauthorised access but are inconvenient to authorised users.

Terminal work stations require a considerable quantity of equipment and materials to be accessible to the user and unless adequate provision is made for rubbish, such as scrap printouts from Teletypes or associated printers, wires from VDUs, modems, telephone, etc., the result is *clutter*, which is not only aesthetically unpleasant but can also present a real hazard.

Access will be required to even the best equipment (or perhaps *especially* the best equipment) for routine servicing and maintenance. It is worthwhile also considering when designing the work station what access might be needed for non-routine repairs and servicing. Maintenance access should not be regarded as the main consideration as it should be only infrequent or at least less frequent than normal usage.

Environment factors

There are a number of different physical environments to consider, in each of which the VDU can create a problem or be threatened. Its location should take account of these and should result in a suitable environment being created.

One of the main advantages of VDUs compared with their Teletype forerunners is the greatly reduced *noise* level while operating. They are seldom completely silent, however, since many have cooling fans or transformers which can whirr, roar or hum. The level of these noises may be low but their frequency or other characteristics can make them distracting in an office environment. The likelihood of the VDU forming a focus for other activities should also be considered when its location is being selected. The user at the VDU may be involved in activities which demand considerable attention and concentration and so it is also important that its location should reflect this need and avoid sources of excessive noise.

There are two aspects of the *thermal environment* to be considered. VDUs may be sensitive to extremes of heat and cold and although these should not be found in an office there are many working environments in which such extremes do occur. VDUs also generate heat and although it may only be at the height of summer that such a quantity of heat would be objectionable it is worth ensuring that vents or grills for cooling air will not create draughts or hot air blasts for other staff.

One of the most difficult compromises which must be made is to provide sufficient *lighting* adequately to illuminate source documents or other printed or written materials, without lighting up the VDU screen and reducing its contrast. Indeed it is not even entirely satisfactory to provide individual directional lighting (like that of the Anglepoise type) for the reading of documents and have a more diffuse, lower level of illumination for viewing the screen and other activities. The human eye then continually has to adjust from light to dark when moving from screen to paper and the greater the difference, the greater the amount of adjustment.

The VDU screen therefore should not be completely black or completely shaded since this increases the difference between screen and source papers or documents. By the use of baffles and diffusers fitted to overhead lighting and by appropriate positioning of the lighting a satisfactory compromise can usually be achieved. It is usually possible to tilt the screen a few degrees away from the vertical to provide a suitable viewing angle and degree of illumination while also preventing unnecessary reflections from distracting the user. Reflections and glare in a VDU are possible from a variety of sources ranging from the screen and stainless steel trim to dished keytops and light-coloured keyboard surrounds. If the trim round the terminal is unsatisfactory in this respect the manufacturer should be approached and asked to change it or at least treat it with a non-reflective coating or paint.

There are a number of features of VDUs which lead to potential *safety* problems for users. In addition to the electrical hazards common to other office equipment, VDUs have high voltages at various places within them and although these should be well protected under normal circumstances, it is important that objects such as hairpins should not be able to fall into sensitive areas through grilles or slots.

The VDU itself is vulnerable to a number of hazards ranging from vibrations or knocks to fluctuations in the power supply which can cause screens to clear and data to be corrupted. Even if these effects are temporary they can be extremely disruptive to users. Hot coffee split down the back of a VDU can be considered a chemical hazard, but more typical chemical hazards are that plastic components may be attacked by cleaning solvents and inflammable liquids may be ignited by sparking contacts.

Using the checklist

One of the best ways of using the checklist is for users and designers to work together through some of the possible work station arrangements using either paper and pencil or full-size mock-ups and rate them all on each point. Such mock-ups do not need to involve the real computer equipment and in fact large cardboard boxes of the appropriate dimensions (from the local supermarket) can more easily be moved and experimented with.

Once satisfactory arrangements have been produced it is a simple matter to photograph or draw the layout and any structural or other alterations can be completed before the proper equipment is installed. Properly conducted, these mock-up trials can be useful in involving junior levels of personnel who might not have been around to be involved at earlier stages of the design.

Possible pitfalls

Finally, there are two major pitfalls open to the designer who tries to create a man–computer interface which really meets the needs of human users.

Link or barrier

First, it is not enough to create a totally 'transparent' link because this would overload the user. Free and apparently unconstrained interaction between man and computer requires an interface which acts both as a link and as a barrier between man and computer. The ideal interface protects the user from unnecessary information such as the exact state of particular parts of computer core or the current flowing in certain wires. The most effective interaction occurs when the user is protected by the interface from aspects of the computer which are either too complex for him to understand or which are not required in his current task. However, in order to be protected from unnecessary complexity, for example of machine code programming, the user must accept that he is prevented from realising the full potential of the system. Many users (e.g. managers) are so concerned that using computers should involve little effort that they find this a necessary compromise. However, some users, particularly engineers, designers and other specialists, would rather learn complex routines and tackle a complex interface in order to exploit the computer's full potential than be protected from useful but perhaps infrequently used facilities. In designing systems for different types of user, designers need to examine closely the users' tasks and the way in which they are performed, in order to design an appropriate interface for each type of user.

Average man

There are many situations in which it makes sense to design to suit an 'average' man. Unfortunately there are also situations where the result is that neither one end of the range nor the other receives satisfactory attention. Thus when we select the best height for a chair or the best format for a screen or the best layout for a workplace we mean the best compromise for a large proportion, usually 95%, of the users. This may be quite different from the height, format or layout that best suits the average user. The reason for this is that the effects of a mis-match may not be balanced at both ends of the scale; for example, it might be disastrous if an emergency stop button was too high for short users whereas a low button would merely be inconvenient for tall users. Unfortunately, even designing for 95% of the population will still mean that 1 person in 20 finds it impossible or difficult to use. This may be too great a proportion to ignore, particularly for systems which are to be used by the general public. The alternative solution is to provide some kind of range so that users can select or have selected for them an interface which best suits their needs.

Conclusions

The aim of this chapter has been to discuss a number of the important human factors and ergonomic considerations in the creation of man–computer dialogues and in the design of VDU work stations. The language, procedures and operations, and time-base of the dialogue have been discussed at some length (pp. 154–168), as have user, task, location and environment factors (pp. 168–173). However, there are a number of other important human issues which have barely been mentioned. These include job and organisation design, the implications of changes in work flow and payment systems due to the introduction of a computer system and the need for user support and training. Although these are important areas worthy of detailed attention in their own right, there is one theme that has run through the entire chapter which could help the designer to appreciate and overcome many of the problems commonly experienced in all these areas. That theme is *user involvement*. Involving the actual or potential users at all stages in the design process helps to provide the system designer with detailed knowledge of the users' requirements, helps to train the users to appreciate, understand and use the system and helps to ensure that the final system will be both useful and used.

It is hoped therefore that the recommendations and discussion in this chapter will help users and designers jointly to create suitable man–computer dialogues and satisfactory working environments for using VDUs.

Acknowledgements

The author wishes to acknowledge the help of the many computer users and computer professionals whose experiences (bitter and otherwise) have contributed to this chapter. The advice and encouragement of his colleagues in the Department of Human Sciences at Loughborough University has also been greatly appreciated.

Further reading

The following further reading is recommended to those who wish to pursue points raised in the text in more detail.

Displays, *IEE Conference Proceedings No. 80*, 1971.

K.D. Eason, L. Damodaran and T.F.M. Stewart, MICA survey: report of a survey of man–computer interaction in commercial applications. *SSRC Grant Report HR 1844/1*. London, 1974.

Man–computer interaction, *IEE Conference Proceedings No. 68*, 1970.

J. Martin, *Design of man–computer dialogues*. Prentice–Hall, New York, 1973.

B. Shackel, General framework and workstation analysis. *Appl. Ergon.*, (1969), 33–41.

H.P. Van Cott and R.G. Kinkade, *Human engineering guide to equipment design*. U.S. Government Publication, Washington, 1972.

Glossary

Aberrations
Non-linear effects which degrade the fidelity of scanning systems.

Acceleration potential
The voltage between electron source and tube face which attracts the stream of focused electrons, causing them to impinge on the phosphor. Approximately 1 kilovolt per inch (250 millimetres) diameter is normally required, and potentials below about 15 kilovolts have insufficient energy to radiate substantially outside the glass envelope of the cathode ray tube.

ACK
Affirmative acknowledgement which indicates that the transmission block was accepted by the receiver and that it is now ready to receive the next transmission block.

Address
The unique identification of a particular terminal from the many sharing the same facility — usually set up manually for each terminal.

The line and character position on the screen at which a message is positioned.

Alphanumerics
Both alphabetic characters and numerals.

Anisochronous data channel
A communication channel capable of transmitting data but not timing information. Sometimes called an 'asynchronous' data channel.

Anisotropic
Relating to material which affects the passage of light differently in different directions.

ARQ
Automatic repeat request. A method of error correction whereby a transmitting

terminal is commanded to re-transmit any data block(s) found by the receiving terminal to contain errors.

Artificial click
An audio feedback device useful to the operator in which he hears an artificial click that replaces the real click from a typewriter keyboard mechanism.

ASCII
Pronounced 'asky'. Strictly, USASCII, the U.S.A. standard code for information interchange, the United States version of the ISO (*q.v.*) 7-bit data code.

Associative code
A code associated with a label or message, probably with no obvious derivation.

Astigmatism
The failure of a cathode ray tube spot to focus sharply in vertical and horizontal co-ordinates simultaneously.

Asynchronous data channel
See Anisochronous data channel.

Asynchronous modem
A modem (*q.v.*) which cannot transmit timing information in addition to data.

A modem which does not require synchronization with the associated terminal equipment. Sometimes called an 'anisochronous' modem.

Asynchronous terminal
A terminal using the start–stop data transmission method.

Automatic dialling
A method of establishing a communications connection whereby the computer dials the connection over the telephone network.

Badge reader
A card, usually of plastic, containing a code of notches or magnetic stripes for identifying the operator.

Bandwidth
The range of signal frequencies that can be transmitted by a communication channel with defined maximum loss or distortion.

Barrel distortion
The tendency for the corners of a rectangular raster to be both narrower and less deep

than the width and height of the scan at its vertical and horizontal centre lines.

Batch processing
A technique of data processing in which jobs are collected together for processing. The batch is then processed.

Baud
A measure of the speed capability of a communications line or system; the reciprocal of the shortest bit time. Thus 1 bit in 1 millisecond is a rate of 1000 baud.

Bit
A binary digit represented by '1' or '0'.

Block
A sequence of contiguous data characters or bytes.

Block check character
A character occurring at the end of a message block and incorporating check bits.

Bps
Bits per second; a measure of the rate of transfer of information.

Byte
A collection of 8 bits.

Buffer
A storage device used to compensate for a difference in the rate of data flow in the transmission of data from one device to another.

Buffered terminal
A terminal which has a buffer built into it.

Capacitive sensors
Sensors in which the presence of a human finger is sensed by the change in local capacitance.

Cathode ray tube (CRT)
A display tube which generates an electron beam that is controlled to energise a phosphor screen and emit visible light.

Central processor
The computer at the centre of an on-line system which performs the processing.

Character generator
An encoding device which converts the ASÇII stored code into appropriate information in the correct order for writing on the cathode ray tube face so that the appropriate character is formed and becomes visible to the operator.

Checkpointing
The method by which a task is interrupted because the main storage resources are required by a higher-priority task. The task is temporarily swapped out to backing store.

Cigar distortion
The tendency for the height of written characters to be greater in the centre of a line than at either end.

Clock
Shorthand term for the source(s) of timing signals used in isochronous data channels.

Cluster
A data network in which two or more terminals are connected to a line or data channel at a single point.

CMOS
Complementary MOS — a technology requiring a very low power consumption.

Concentrator
A device used to divide a data channel into two or more channels of lower average speed, dynamically allocating channel space according to demand in order to maximise data throughput at all times.

Connectivity
A measure of a terminal controller's ability to drive simultaneously a number of peripheral devices.

Contention
A condition on a communication line when two or more terminals attempt to transmit at the same time.

Control character
A character whose occurrence in a particular context initiates, modifies or stops a function. There are 32 such characters in ASCII.

CRC
Cyclic redundancy check. An error detection scheme in which the check character is

generated by taking the remainder after dividing all the serialised bits in a block of data by a predetermined binary number.

CRT
Cathode ray tube (*q.v.*).

Cursive characters
Characters which have the appearance of free-flowing, connected handwriting.

Cursor
A symbol or sign which acts as a flag to identify one, and only one, of the visible characters that will be affected by a command or action.

Cursor control keys
Those keys which specifically control movement of the cursor, necessary for editing operations and for rapid access to any part of the screen.

Cursor register
An alternative method of keeping track of the cursor position, the older technique being to identify an extra bit in the appropriate character. The cursor 'count position' can be logically operated on.

Data
Here regarded as a collection of facts, letters, symbols and numbers that refer to or describe an object, idea, situation, condition or other factor.

Datadial
A user service provided by Datran, giving fast (less than 1 second) dial-up connections.

Data link
A communication circuit established in order that the data may be transmitted in coded form.

Data reduction
The removal of superfluous data from a message.

Data store
A method of storing data. The most economic method for this is the use of binary coding. A standard coding system using combinations of up to 8 bits has been formalised by ASCII.

The part of a terminal in which received data is held during operation.

Data transmission
The automatic transfer of data between two points, usually a computer and a data terminal. The data are transferred via a telegraph, telephone or radio circuit.

DDS
A network service provided in the U.S.A. especially designed for serial digital data transmission.

Decoding
Translating coded data back to an original format.

Determining the meaning of a coded instruction or command.

Deflection defocusing
Occurs when the beam is deflected away from the centre of the tube face, where it is already in sharp focus. This happens because the tube face deviates from a section of a sphere.

Deflection sensitivity
The surface movement of the cathode ray tube spot related to the driving power. It would be constant for a truly spherical display surface, but is affected by non-conformity, i.e. surface 'flatness'.

Delay line
A circular data store which continually reconstitutes delayed data for re-circulating in an acoustic line.

A form of transmission circuit in which signals are deliberately delayed.

Delete
The ability to remove surplus material from text, simultaneously eliminating the gaps which would otherwise be formed.

Device control cell
An area of store which describes the various parameters which relate to the state, etc. of a device.

Dialogue generator
A computer program to aid the programmer to format the screen.

'Diddle'
A jargon name for a technique of minor scan which permits characters to be written sequentially during a left to right progression of the 'stripe'.

Digital data network
A network specifically designed for transmission of digital data as distinct from networks such as the telephone system which are designed primarily for other purposes.

Direct parallel connection
The keyboard is connected to the computer using the normal serial interface and the display is connected via a high-speed parallel interface.

Dot matrix memories
Commercially available integrated circuits which produce defined dot sequences when driven by the code and timing of a character.

DSU
Data service unit. A short-distance modem, for connecting terminals to some digital data networks.

Dynamic allocation
The allocation of peripheral units or core storage to a program or subprogram as and when it is required.

Dynamic store
A regenerative store from which information can be retrieved at fixed intervals in a cycle.

EBCDIC
Extended binary coded decimal interchange code. An 8-bit character code used primarily in IBM equipment.

Echo mode
Each key depression is consigned to line as it occurs and a character is placed in the screen slot designated by the processor, using the cursor. Commonly used in interactive Teletype operation.

Echoplex
A method of checking the accuracy of transmission of data in which the received data are returned to the sender for checking. It is commonly used with Teletype terminals for error checking and uses a full duplex communications line.

ECMA
European Computer Manufacturers' Association. A valuable source of computer standards. Address: rue du Rhône 114, 1204 Geneva, Switzerland.

Editing
The ability to replace, delete or add to information already on the screen without otherwise losing data already there.

Edit module
The software module responsible for the control of a display unit connected to a soft-centred terminal controller. This module is responsible for the interpretation of keyboard data and mainframe commands.

EHT
Extra-high tension — usually measured in kilovolts.

EIA
Electronics Industries Association.

Eidophor
A projection television system in which light is reflected from an oil film modulated by an electron beam.

Electrochromics
A display cell in which electrodes are plated with material of contrasting colour by application of a voltage to the electrodes.

Electroluminescence
A means of exciting a phosphor material to emit light by applying a voltage to two electrodes.

Electrophoresis
A display cell in which particles are suspended in a liquid of a contrasting colour. The particles migrate to the front or back of the cell depending on the electric field.

Emulator, emulation
In this context, a soft-centred implementation of a hard-wired display system. Some emulators are exact copies, others give enhanced or reduced facilities.

ENCDIC code
Extended binary coded decimal interchange code (an extension of the 4-bit binary coded decimal representation); an 8-bit code giving 256 combinations.

Encode
To represent data in coded form according to a set of rules such that subsequent decoding is possible.

Enhancement
The technique of improving the shape of a character within its basic limitations by stretching or moving certain dots with respect to others.

Envelope
The part of a total message which is concerned with the control and command of transmission to and from defined destinations of the data (message) included within it.

EPSS
The U.K. Post Office experimental packet switching network. The channels are shared by all users, with the data transmitted in short interleaved blocks each accompanied by a destination code.

Equalisation
Compensation for signal loss at higher frequencies in a transmission circuit.

ESC
A control character which indicates that a special function is to follow. The characters that follow define the function.

ETB
Indicates the end of a transmission block.

ETX
Indicates the end of transmission of text, which may include one or more transmission blocks.

Executive or **organiser**
The control program within a soft-centred terminal controller which is responsible for the allocation of resources, control of dynamic working store allocation, etc.

Facsimile
The technique of writing characters on a tube face by copying those already written in the master.

Feedback
The return of part of the output of a machine or system as part of another phase of the same system.

Fixed data
Data, written on a display screen by the computer, that cannot be altered by the operator.

Flag
A character used to signal the occurrence of a condition or event.

An item of information used as an indicator.

Flat-faced display
One in which the tube face is substantially flat for viewing purposes. To preserve focus and scan linearity the cathode ray tube face should be a section of a sphere with its centre of rotation at the gun, but this gives an unacceptable viewing area.

Formatting
The process of transposing data on transfer from one peripheral device to another so that the resultant data is presented to the recipient peripheral device in a more suitable form.

Structuring the display screen into protected and accessible areas within which various actions can be performed on fields.

Form filling
The user enters predefined fields into predefined areas on the screen. Appropriate for buffered terminals only.

Free-wheeling terminals
Teletypes or Teletype-compatible terminals.

Fringe-area vision
A characteristic of the human eye, which is more sensitive to flicker and movement at the edge of its normal field of vision than at the centre. One of the animal defence qualities with which nature has endowed us.

Full duplex channel
A channel capable of transmitting data in both directions at once.

Function
A program or piece of code that performs a given operation.

In communications, a machine action such as carriage return.

Functionally dedicated task
A task which is dedicated to a specific function.

Function keyboard
A collection of keys, each of which is associated with a special command.

General poll
Where a cluster controller is polled to see if any of the terminals attached to it has a message to transmit.

Greyscales
Refers to a display technique where the brightness of the display mechanism can be varied to give many levels, thus permitting pictorial information.

Half-duplex channel
A channel capable of transmitting data in either direction but only in one direction at any one time.

Half-shift
A technique for enhancing the basically sparse dot matrix character. The effect is to move selectively some of the horizontally disposed dots half of the dot separation to the right or left as required.

Hall effect
The effect of generating a potential difference across certain materials by the influence of a magnetic field.

Hard copy or **permanent copy unit**
An associated printer which can print out the information on a terminal screen on demand.

Hardware interface
Those aspects of the hardware which are directly experienced by a user ('human factors'). The matching of two or more hardware devices.

HDLC
High level data link control. An ISO draft standard.

Header
A series of characters preceding a message providing addressing and other information on the message to follow.

The front part of a message envelope; it contains the information necessary to allow the system to carry the data to and from its proper destinations.

Highways
Busbars which carry common information from module to module within a terminal. Usually parallel printed circuits on the module-carrying mother board.

Host computer
The computer on which the applications program runs. Often used to mean the central computer in a centralised computer network (*see* Mainframe and Central processor).

Intelligent terminal
A terminal incorporating a mini- or microprocessor capable of performing simple processing functions.

Interlace
A technique used in commercial television in which alternate frames are displayed so that their rasters interleave. The basic picture rate of 25 frames per second is thereby made to appear refreshed at 50 times per second. Acceptable for random picture content, but has an irritating strobing characteristic when used for alphanumeric writing.

I/O handlers
The software programs which perform the physical input–output to the data transmission devices.

ISO
International Standards Organization.

Isochronous data channel
A communication channel capable of transmitting timing information in addition to data. Sometimes called a 'synchronous' data channel.

Leased line
A telephone or telegraph line leased from the Post Office/PTT or their 'carrier' and dedicated to use by the lessee.

Leased network
A data network of telephone or telegraph lines or channels leased from the Post Office/PTT or their 'carrier' and dedicated to use by the lessee.

Lens system
An assembly of magnetic and/or electrostatic components which modifies the path of the electron beam emitted from the cathode of a cathode ray tube. Typically, the system is used to achieve a sharp focus of the beam at the tube surface.

Light-emitting diode
A diode which produces light in one of three colours (red, yellow, green) when driven by a low voltage.

Limited-distance modem
A simplified modem designed for operation over distances up to about 35 miles, usually over privately owned wires, where the bandwidth (*q.v.*) limitations of the telephone system do not apply. Sometimes called a 'baseband' or 'short-haul' modem.

Line control module
The software module responsible for the interpretation and control of the communication link to a mainframe.

Line switching
A method of establishing communication in a switched network (*q.v.*), for example by dialling, whereby the channel so established remains dedicated to the user for the duration of his 'call'.

Line time
The time that the transmission line is occupied in transmitting a block or message.

Liquid crystal
A display material with a rod-like molecular structure. The molecular orientations are caused by an electric field either to pass or to inhibit light.

Local
Refers to the proximity of a terminal to the computer. In practice it means that transmission is not over PTT-leased or switched lines.

Local terminal
A VDU linked directly to a computer or control unit.

Magnetic relay
A ferrous device in which closure of contacts is induced by the presence of an external magnetic field.

Mainframe
The central processing unit of a large computer system.

Man–computer dialogue
Two-way communication between user and computer.

Menu
A collection of items from which the operator selects a choice.

Menu selector
A device connected with or to a display unit (but not a keyboard) which allows an operator quickly to choose an item from a selection presented on the display screen.

Message switching
Similar to packet switching (*q.v.*), except that complete messages rather than data blocks are interleaved and the transit time through the network is very much greater. Not much used for computer data transmission, but rather for administrative messages.

Microcomputer
An integrated circuit performing basic program instructions.

Modem
A contraction of the term 'modulator–demodulator'. A device used to convert serial digital data from a transmitting terminal to a signal suitable for transmission over a telephone channel and to reconvert the signal to serial digital data for acceptance by a receiving terminal.

Monoscope
A facsimile character generator, in which characters are deposited on the surface of the final anode of a special-purpose cathode ray tube, which when systematically searched by an interrogating electron beam yields information in the correct order for its reproduction.

MOS
Metal oxide silicon technology.

Multi-dropped line
A single communication line to which terminals are attached at more than one point.

Multiplexer
A device used to divide a data channel into two or more independent fixed data channels of lower speed (cf. Concentrator).

Multi-point
A line or data channel connecting terminals at more than one point. Sometimes called 'multi-drop' (cf. Cluster).

Multi-tasking
The apparent ability of a computer to perform more than one task at the same time.

Multi-threading
The apparent ability of the computer to handle more than one terminal user simultaneously. There are various ways in which this can be achieved. The term is more specifically used in the context of multi-threading through a piece of code.

Nematic
Relating to a thread-like molecular structure.

New line
A special control/display character which terminates the given line, re-sets the remainder to space, and positions the cursor at the start of the next line. NEW LINE may or may not be transmitted with data.

Operating system
The software that controls the execution of the computer programs which make up the computer system. It will provide scheduling, input, output and other services.

Organiser
An executive (*q.v.*).

Overlay
A detachable plastic sheet carrying information for identifying function keys or position on a surface.

Packet switching
A method of establishing communication in a switched network in which individual data blocks or 'packets' are routed to their destination by address information contained within the packet. All parts of the network can be shared by all users at all times and are never dedicated to one user, the packets from different users being interleaved.

PACX
Private automatic computer exchange. A device for controlling private switched networks.

Pad character
With some terminals it is necessary to insert pad characters into the transmission screen after certain characters. This need is related to the transmission speed, the buffer size if any, and the time taken to action the character by the terminal.

Parallel data transmission
A transmission method where data is transmitted one character or byte at a time, each bit making up the byte being transmitted over a separate path.

Parity
The addition of extra check bits to data according to a predetermined formula.

Password
A word to be typed in at a terminal to identify the operator and permit access to the system.

Penetron tube
A colour cathode ray tube with two layers of phosphor. The colour depends on the energy of the electron beam, which penetrates either one or both phosphor layers.

Persistence
The ability of a phosphor to emit light after the original stimulus has gone. Some phosphors can do this for appreciable times — a second or more. There are combination phosphors which provide a bright, short, flash of light, followed by a long persisting glow, often of another colour.

Perspex screen
A secondary protective plate interposed between operator and cathode ray tube to limit the movement of small airborne particles in the event of tube failure. It can also be decorative and utilitarian — improving viewing contrast, for example.

Phosphor
A coating of luminescent material which emits visible light when struck by a beam of electrons within an evacuated glass envelope.

Pincushion distortion
The tendency for the corners of a rectangular scan raster to be both higher and wider than the height and width of the scan at its vertical and horizontal centre lines.

Plasma panel
A collection of neon tubes assembled in matrix form to provide a display screen.

Point to point
Refers to a line or data channel connecting two, and only two, terminals.

Polling
A method of controlling terminals on a multi-point or clustered data network where each terminal is interrogated in turn by the computer to determine whether it is ready to receive or transmit and where data transmission is only initiated by the computer.

Polling overhead
The 'lost' time due to the processor having to make routine polling interrogations of all terminals in order to remain in control of the system.

Processor utilisation
The amount of time, usually expressed as a percentage, during which the processor is occupied in performing necessary and useful functions.

Programmable ROM
A read-only memory which can be set to any desired pattern by a development machine, and which thereafter retains the characteristics of a commercial read-only memory, i.e. it is indestructible in normal use.

Protected data
See Fixed data.

Protected field
A designated field within which no keyboard-initiated action can make any amendment whatever.

Protocol
A set of rules governing information flow in a communication system.

Raster scan
A method of scanning a display in horizontal lines. The technique is used for television and many VDUs.

Redundancy checking
A technique of error detection involving the transmission of additional data related to the basic data in such a way that the receiving terminal, by comparing the two sets of data, can determine to a certain degree of probability whether an error has occurred in transmission.

Re-entrant
Refers to code that is pure, which means that it can be simultaneously executed for more than one thread.

Refresh
Since the light emitted by phosphors is transient, characters have to be re-written regularly if they are to appear to endure. This is called 'refresh' and usually occurs at about 50 times a second.

Remote
A 'remote' connection refers to the situation when a terminal, or device, is located remote from the computer system. In general this means over a switched or leased telephone line.

Remote terminal
A VDU with its own refresh store, editing capability and a modem interface.

Rim-guard CRT
The technique of clamping a tension band around the edges of a cathode ray tube face plate so that it will compress the fragments during shattering and prevent them from flying out. In practice, the shrink band effectively guards against the gun bursting through the face plate.

Screen buffer
The buffer from which a VDU refreshes the display.

Screen format
The structuring of a VDU screen into protected and unprotected areas. Data may be input only to the unprotected areas.

Secondary radiation
Unwanted radiations within the X band or gamma-ray bands can occur from EHT electron beams, but are not usually significant for glass-enveloped systems with EHT potentials below 15 kilovolts.

Select
The process of inviting a terminal to receive data.

Semaphore
A flag (*q.v.*).

Serial data transmission
A transmission method where data characters or bytes are transmitted one bit (binary digit) at a time over a single path.

Serially reusable
Refers to code that may be executed sequentially by more than one thread but not simultaneously.

Single-line buffer
A necessary part of a television raster generator, in which a whole line of information must be available sequentially up to ten times for horizontal slicing.

Site polling
A technique in which all terminals at a given site are polled as a community, the local controller assuming the role of supervisor for this purpose. It reduces the polling overhead.

Specific poll
The process by which a specific terminal is invited to transmit.

Spooling and despooling
Spooling is the writing to a backing store of data normally sent directly to the host mainframe or other peripheral device. The data is usually stored temporarily on the backing store until it can be despooled, i.e. read from the backing stores and sent to its eventual destination.

Stand-alone display
A display unit which is capable of being connected to a modem directly (i.e. not a cluster).

Stand-alone processing system
A processing system which for normal operation does not depend upon a host mainframe.

Start–stop method
A serial data transmission method in which each character or byte is transmitted as a self-contained piece of information needing no additional synchronising or timing information to be transmitted (*see also* Asynchronous).

Static store
One which does not circulate information for the purpose of refreshing it. A static store preserves information consigned to it indefinitely without loss or degradation.

Status poll
A computer-initiated request for information about the present status of a terminal.

Storage tube
A special-purpose cathode ray tube with a wire mesh on which is stored alphanumeric or diagrammatic information. The information is displayed on the screen without refreshing from a dynamic store.

Stored program VDU
A VDU whose principal external and internal characteristics are contained within a stored program control section. The program may be re-written with greater or lesser facility depending on the design and techniques employed.

STX
Control character which precedes a sequence of characters and indicates the start of text.

Supervisory code
A code within the ASCII range which has functional meaning, used to command and control the systems handling data.

Supervisory control module
A terminal controller resident software module which gives supervisory facilities to a designated display operator, e.g. control of the cluster's peripheral resources (printers, etc.).

Switched network
A network which is shared among many users, any one of whom can establish communication between desired points when required.

Symbolray
Another facsimile source. Unlike the monoscope, which had a solid final anode, the Symbolray resembled a stencil, the beam being permitted to pass through the holes to a final collector.

SYN
Character used to establish synchronisation on a synchronous communications line.

Synchronising characters
Necessary to achieve synchronisation between data bits and some system clock — that provided by, and necessary to the proper operation of, data modems, for example.

Synchronous data channel
See Isochronous data channel.

Synchronous modem
A modem (*q.v.*) which can transmit timing information in addition to data.

A modem which must be synchronised with the associated terminal equipment by timing signals. Sometimes called an 'isochronous' modem.

Synchronous terminal
A terminal requiring the transmission of timing information for the data source for proper reception of data. Usually more efficient than a start–stop terminal (*q.v.*).

System response time
The time from last entry into system by user to first output by computer.

Tabulation markers
Used to delineate protected fields, but may also be used as tabulation settings similar to the use of 'tabs' on a typewriter.

Tail
The last part of a message envelope (*see* Header).

Task
The unit of program scheduled or run by the operating system.

Task completion time
Total time taken for user to complete computer task (in the human factors context).

Task per terminal
In this case there is a task for each thread or terminal in the system.

Teleloading
The process by which a terminal controller's programs are loaded via a communication link from the host mainframe.

Teletext
An information system employing a standard television set incorporating back-up store and data formatting facilities.

Teletype
Refers to the keyboard printers manufactured by Teletype Corporation.

Teletype-compatible
Refers to terminals which are compatible with Teletypes, either at the functional or software level. Terminals may be hard copy or VDUs.

Television scan system
An orderly progression of horizontal lines from top to bottom of the tube face in the manner familiar to domestic television viewers. Both line scan rate and frame scan (top to bottom) are defined by international standard (for a 625-line system, for example).

Terminal
A device for sending and/or receiving data on a communication channel.

Thread
The sequence of operations carried out on behalf of a terminal.

Threshold
The voltage or electric field at which a response is caused in a material or system.

Touch wire
A short wire placed on a VDU screen. A command written on the screen adjacent to the wire is activated by touching the wire.

Transformation code
A code produced by applying a given rule or transformation to the full label or message.

Tree structure
A sequence of multi-choice decision points arranged so that specific decisions made form one path through the sequence.

A datastructure where the choices branch out from a previous choice.

Turn-round time
The time taken to reverse the direction of data flow in a half-duplex channel (*q.v.*).

Two-key lockout
A technique which inhibits all action when more than one key is held down. Correctly ordered release may permit rollover.

Two-key rollover
A technique which permits the key sequence A then B with overlap to be interpreted correctly as though the overlap did not occur.

Two-shot moulding
A technique in which two-stage moulding is carried out. Keys have durable and deep legends moulded heavily into the surface.

Ultrafiche
A form of photographic plate which permits 2000–7000 pages of information on one plate.

Unit-buffer terminals
Terminals which do not have a communications buffer, e.g. Teletypes.

Unprotected data
See Variable data.

Unprotected field
An area on a display screen which may be altered by the operator.

Variable data
Data on a VDU screen which can be altered by the operator.

Vector drawing
A technique of steering, magnetically or electrostatically, the electron beam so that it

writes the required character on the cathode ray tube face. The beam brightness is also controlled so that only the required strokes are made visible.

Visual display terminal
A terminal which comprises a keyboard for input and a display for output.

Visual flicker
The apparent unsteadiness of a refreshed image in which the refresh rate is below the flicker threshold. This threshold, for very bright short-persistence phosphors, is about 50 times per second.

Index

Index

Addressing of display store, 16
Air traffic control, 121
Airline seat reservation systems, 8, 106, 165
Anisochronous channel, 66, 79
ASCII code, 43, 44, 67–69, 76, 84, 113, 125
Asynchronous channel, *see* Anisochronous channel
Asynchronous data transmission, 110, 115
Automatic repeat request systems, 84, 85

Badge reader, use in security, 20, 171
Baseband modems, 79
Batch processing, 127, 135, 165
Block check character, 20
Broadcast teletext, 26
BS 4421 interface, 64
Buffer, 55, 115
  single-line, 51

CAMAC interface, 64
Cathode ray tube (CRT), 23, 40, 138
  distortion of image, 41
  focusing, 42
  future of, 25, 26
  inability to write two characters simultaneously, 52
  phosphor coating, 14, 15, 33, 34, 43, 139
  power supply to, 61
  rear port type, 25, 29
  replacements for, 31, 33
  safety of, 42
  surface glare from, 142
  technology of, 40, 42
CCITT recommendations, 79, 81–83, 86, 87
CEEFAX broadcast teletext system, 26
Characters on screen,
  cursive, 52
  dots forming, 36, 50, 51, 139, 140
  generation of, 47, 48
  height, 141
  number per row, 139
  width, 139
Charactron tube, 15
Checking for errors, 85, 93, 105, 106, 127
Clock, 66, 79, 81
Cluster controller, 94, 118
Clustering, 72, 90, 94, 97
Codes, 10, 14, 67, 116
  ASCII, 20, 43, 44, 67, 76, 84, 113, 125
  conversion from one to another, 113
  EBCDIC, 67, 113
  ISO, 67
Colour displays, 25
Communication interface, 55

standards for, 81
Communication lines, 76, 77
Communications, 16, 64–87
Concentration, 75
Connectivity, 97
Contention, 76, 117
Control units, 19
Core store, 96
Cursor, 11, 13, 15, 46, 47, 94
types of, 141
spatial, 17
store position, 17

Data,
fields, 43–47
fixed, 13, 16, 124
variable, 13, 16, 124
formats, *see* Formatting
inputting sequence, 159–162
reduction, 16
storage, 43–47
transmission, *see* Transmission of data
validation, 95
Data validation software, 22
Debugging of computer programs, 10
Delayed transaction processing, 165
Design,
characters, of, 139, 141
format, of, 161–163
work station, of, 169–172
VDU systems, of, human factors aspects, 137–175
Despooling of data, 103
Dialogues, man-computer, 123, 154–168
control, 120, 126, 128
structure of, 120, 121
Digital data networks, 87
Digital data transmission, 77–79
serial, 63, 64
Display station, supervisory, 103
Displays, 23
colour, 25
electrochromic, 25, 37, 38
electrophoretic, 25, 37
legibility of, 138
liquid crystal, 35, 36
optical, 7
optically aided, 29
storage tube, 17, 30
Distortion of image on cathode ray tube face, 41
Dot matrix,
of liquid crystal display, 36, 50
memory, 51
Drift, 30

EBCDIC code, 67, 113
Editing facilities, 27, 93, 102, 115
debugging computer programs, for, 10
insertion/deletion of characters, 46, 148
microcomputer used to give, 14
performed by terminal handler, 113
Eidophor light controller, 25
Electrochromic displays, 25, 37, 38
Electroluminescence, 23
Electrophoretic displays, 25, 37
Enhancement, 51, 52
Errors,
checks for, 85, 93, 105, 106, 116, 127
correction of, 113, 115, 123, 127
data entry, in,
rates of, 144
sources of, 156
undetected, 143
Equalisation, 77
Executive, 93, 107

Facsimile reproduction, 49
Monoscope tube, 50
Symbolray tube, 50
Feedback from keyboard to operator, 54, 143, 144, 152
Fixed data fields, 13, 16, 105, 124
Flicker, 31, 140

Formatting, 102, 104, 124
  aids to, 120
  principles of good design, 161–163
Full duplex operation, 69, 79, 83, 86, 110
Function key, 13, 17
Functionally dedicated task, 129

Glare from screen, 173
Graphics, 30, 31, 119
Half-duplex operation, 69, 83, 86, 110, 113
Hard copy unit, 57
Hardwired VDUs, 88, 95, 96, 100
Hazards to VDUs, 173
Highways, 60
Human factors, 52, 54, 137–175

Information retrieval, 10
Information transducer, VDU as, 8
Inherent memory, 31, 37, 38
Input/output handler, 111, 119
Inputting, sequence of data entry, 159–162
Integration of components, 89
Intelligence, 88–107
  cost of, 107
  dispersal of, 98
  reasons for use, 89, 101
Intelligent multiplexers, 87
Intelligent terminals, 14, 89, 90, 95, 103
Interactive methods, 10, 17
Interlacing, 140
Interrupt line, 19
ISO standards, 67, 87
Isochronous channel, 66, 67, 75, 79, 86

Key roll, 53, 143, 144, 146
Keyboard, 52–54, 113, 119, 147
  electronic, 143, 148
  key design, 54
  layout, 52, 148
  mechanical, 143
Keys,
  shape of, 54, 148, 149
  typamatic, 148

Language of man-computer dialogue, 155, 156
Large-scale integration, 89
  effect on cost of VDUs, 38
Leased communication lines, 76, 82
Light controllers, 23, 25, 35–38
Light emitters, 23, 25, 32–35
Light-emitting diodes, 35
Light-emitting films, 35
Light pen, 19, 31
Lighting, ambient, 142
Limited-distance modems, 79
Line adaptors, 79
Line control module, 93
Line sharing, 57
Liquid crystal displays, 35, 36
Local terminal, 14
Long-line driver, 79

Mainframe, 95, 98, 106
  failure of, 103
Man-computer dialogues, 154–168
  language, 155, 156
  structure, 155, 158
  time-base, 155, 164
Man-computer partnership, effectiveness of, 153
'Master', definition of, 19
Memories,
  dot matrix, 51
  programmable read-only, 51, 60, 95, 96
  read-only, 95, 96
'Menu' of choices, 10, 103, 120
Message switching systems, 76
Microcomputer, in intelligent terminals, 14

Microfiche, 7, 27
Microfilm, 7, 27
Microprocessor, 23
Modem, 38, 78, 79, 82, 91
  simulator, 81
Modular construction, 59
Module,
  line control, 83
  edit, 93, 94
  supervisory control, 95
  table control, 95
Monoscope, 15
Multi-dropping, 72, 117
Multiplexed networks, 73, 74
Multiplexers, 73
  intelligent, 75, 87
Multi-point operation, 83, 117
Multi-tasking, 127
Multi-threaded task, 130

Network configurations,
  control of, 108, 118
  point-to-point, 71
  polled, 72
  multiplex, 73
Network processor, 75, 87
Noise level of VDUs, effect on environment, 172

Off-line operations, 103
On-line system, 127
Operator, feedback to,
  audible, 54, 143
  tactile, 143, 144
Optic fibres, 38
Optical displays, 7
Optically aided displays, 29
ORACLE broadcast teletext system, 26
Organiser, *see* Executive
Overlay, 14

Packet switching networks, 77, 86
Parallax problems, 18
Parallel connection, as way of linking VDU to computer, 63, 64
Parity check, 20
Password, use in security, 20, 171
Penetron tube, 25
Phosphor coating of cathode ray tube, 14, 29, 33, 34
  soft phosphors, 15
  hard phosphors, 15
  response time, 139
Plasma panels, 23, 32
Plug-compatible terminals, 64
Point-to-point network, 71
Point-to-point transmission, 83
Polling, 19, 56, 72, 84, 117
  overhead involved, 57
  status, 57
Power supply for VDUs, 61
Processor unit, 90
  centralised, 10, 101
  utilisation of, 100
Programmable read-only memories, 51, 60, 95, 96
Protocols, 22, 83, 84, 86, 108, 117, 126
  standardisation of, 86, 87, 98

Random access memory chips, 96
Read-only memories, 95, 96
Real-time transaction processing, 165
Redundancy checking, 85, 115
Refresh store, 15
Refreshing of screen information, 14, 31
  rate of, 15, 42, 140
Remote job entry, 97
Remote terminal, 14, 97
Rollover, *see* Key roll

Safety aspects of VDUs, 42, 61, 173
Security, 19, 20, 38, 123, 171
Serial data transmission, 63, 64, 77, 119
Serial store, 15

Shadow roll, 146
Skipping, 140
'Slave', definition of, 19
Soft-centred terminal controllers, 88, 99, 100, 106
Solid state displays, 31–38
Spatial addressing, 30
Standardisation, 119
Start–stop data transmission, 66, 67, 78, 113
Stock control, 9
Storage tube displays, 17, 30
Stores, 15, 43–47, 95
Supervisory display station, 103
Synchronous channel, *see* Isochronous channel
Synchronous data transmission, 66, 110, 115

Tablet, as sensing device, 38
Tabulation markers, 47
Teleloading, 97
Telephone lines and networks, 77, 78
Teletext systems, 26, 27, 38
Teletype-compatible VDUs, 56, 66, 67, 69, 73, 113–115, 126
  protocol used by, 83
Teletypewriters, 7, 83, 110, 114, 126
Television techniques, 15, 26
  scan system, 48
Terminal controllers, 88, 97, 98, 109
  intelligent, 89, 90, 103
  soft-centred, 88, 95
  power of, 96
Terminal handling, 108, 110, 111, 113
  software for, 132, 135
Terminals, intelligent, 126
Thermal environment, effect on VDUs, 172
Threshold, 36
Toggling, 57
Touch wire, 18
Transaction processing, 165
Transmission of data, 110, 113
  asynchronous, 110, 115
  digital, 63, 64, 77–79
  prices of facilities, 80
  rates of, 55
  synchronous, 66, 67, 110, 115
  using telephone network, 77
Tree data structure, 10
Trends in VDU technology and usage, 23–38, 62, 87, 106, 107

Ultrafiche, 7, 28
Unbuffered communication interfaces, 55, 113
Unprotected fields, *see* Variable data fields
Updating of information, 10–12
USASCII code, *see* ASCII code
User interactions with VDUs, 106; *see also* Operator, feedback to
User interface, with VDU, 104, 126
User involvement, desirability of, 160, 168, 175

Validation of data entry, 95, 101, 104; *see also* Checking for errors
Variable data fields, 13, 16, 105, 124
Vector drawing method of character generation, 47
Video format, 8

Wired teletext, 26
  Viewdata system, 27
Work station design, 150, 151, 169–172

DATE	ISSUED TO